The ANIME Companion 2

# MORE . . .

# WHAT'S
# JAPANESE
# IN JAPANESE
# ANIMATION?

# The ANIME Companion 2

## GILLES POITRAS

**Stone Bridge Press** • *Berkeley, California*

**PUBLISHED BY**

Stone Bridge Press, P. O. Box 8208, Berkeley, CA 94707

tel 510-524-8732 • sbp@stonebridge.com • www.stonebridge.com

Text © 2005 Gilles Poitras.

Front-cover image © GAINAX/ProjectEVA.TX.

Line drawings by Cynthia E. Olen.

Front-cover lettering, display capitals, icons, "Companion" face designs, and original book design by L.J.C. Shimoda (www.shimodaworks.com).

*FLCL* images used with permission from Broccoli International USA, Inc. and Production I.G LLC. All rights reserved.

Credits and copyright notices accompany their respective images throughout the text. The publisher thanks all rightsholders who generously permitted reproduction of their works and wishes all studios and distributors were so easy to work with!

Printed in the United States of America.

10  9  8  7  6  5  4  3  2  1
2011  2010  2009  2008  2007  2006  2005

LIBRARY OF CONGRESS CATALOGING-IN-PUBLICATION DATA
Poitras, Gilles.
    The anime companion: what's Japanese in Japanese animation? / Gilles Poitras.
    p.  cm.
  Includes bibliographical references.
  ISBN 1-880656-96-5
  1. Animated films—Japan—Themes, motives. I. Title.
  NC1766.J3 P65 1998
  791.43'3—ddc21

                                                              98-44487
                                                              CIP

# CONTENTS

# THE ANIME
# COMPANION 2

## GOT ZEN?

Yes, there are entries on two different things called "zen" in this volume of *The Anime Companion*. Several people have asked me why there was no entry for Zen Buddhism in Volume 1. The fact is, up to the time I wrote that book I hadn't seen Zen featured in anime or manga released in the United States. Given the large number of books in English on Zen, it comes as a surprise to many Westerners that Zen is not all that important to many Japanese. This is reflected in the lack of references to Zen in anime and manga. Sure, there are plenty to Buddhism, but few to Zen Buddhism.

## WHAT'S JAPANESE IN ANIME AND MANGA?

For those unfamiliar with Volume 1 of *The Anime Companion*, that book and this are not so much about anime as about things Japanese found in anime and manga. It may seem odd to learn about Japan by consuming popular media like anime or manga. But think about it: Is it any odder to learn about Japan this way than by studying Zen, temple gardens, kabuki theater, poetry, ancient literature, or any other topic that has been available to Westerners in the past?

If you were to only study these subjects and then visit Japan, you would be shocked to discover how modern, even Western, Japan appears, at least on the surface. You might even ask yourself, as have many others, "Where is the *real* Japan?" This is a silly question; the real Japan is right in front of your eyes! Japan is both a modern society and a culture with a long and rich history. But all of it is the real Japan. I think that someone who has watched lots of anime and read lots of manga is better equipped to deal with the culture shock of visiting Japan than a person with a romantic expectation of finding temples, gardens, Zen meditation, poetry, samurai culture, and all the other things that are common subjects in many books about Japan.

Both views are imperfect, but the view presented in anime and manga is more in tune with contemporary Japan than is the high culture of the other. Hence, the purpose of this book is to explain and illuminate many of the details that native Japanese people take for granted but might go right past us *gaijin*.

## WHAT'S NEW IN VOLUME 2

I had hoped to have this second volume
done some time ago, but several factors
delayed its release, not least of which is
the dramatic increase in the number
of anime and manga released in recent
years and demanding to be watched
and read. One of the best aspects of this
growth is the significant broadening of
genres available for consumption.

**DEDICATION**

To Fred Patten, a pioneer of anime and manga fandom,
who for decades has led the way for so many of us.

One major change is the increasing number of titles set in Japan's past. When I
wrote Volume 1, there were only a handful of titles set before 1940. Today, you can
build an impressive anime and manga collection with such works exclusively. This
means that Volume 2 of *The Anime Companion* has a dramatically larger collection of
historical and geographical entries than Volume 1.

Another effect of the growth of the industry is the popularity of anime and manga
among girls and women. The U.S. animation and comics industries have largely ig-
nored this market, and that gap is a major factor in the rapid growth in sales of manga
for girls in the United States. This also means that more fans are now being exposed to
aspects of Japanese society that had been largely the realm of scholars.

The number of anime and manga set in contemporary Japan is also much larger.
Again, the new geographical entries reflect this, as do the various modern landmarks
I have included. I have also tried to add more entries on the small details of Japanese
day-to-day life. It has been surprisingly difficult to locate information in this area. The
Selected References section includes several books by anthropologists who have been
very helpful in locating such tidbits.

Another thing to note is that certain works have a higher density of cultural references. This is why Volume 1 had so many references to the works of Takahashi
Rumiko. Readers of this volume will notice a large number of citations to *Rurouni Kenshin* and a few other works. This is not because I have gone out of my way to explore
a particular show; it's just that some works have more material to work with.

## USING THIS BOOK

This book can be used just like an encyclopedia. All entries are arranged alphabetically, and there is a cross-referenced index at the back. Entries are arranged by the Japanese words most likely to be encountered in anime, since the English translations of those words in subtitled or dubbed versions are often inconsistent. For convenience, a brief translation or explanation of the term in English appears next to the entry. Where the translation is complicated or unnecessary (as in the case of a place name, for example), no English appears.

A word in **boldface** type at first mention in an entry indicates a cross-reference to another entry, either to an entry in this Volume 2 or, if followed by a reference in the form "AC vol. 1, p. #," to an entry in Volume 1. The Reverse Lookup Glossary will help you find Japanese entries if you only know the English word or concept (some entries are cross-referenced by more than one English word). The Reverse Lookup Glossary and the section Entries Arranged by Category both contain link-references to Volume 1, on the assumption that many readers of this Volume 2 already own Volume 1 and will benefit from being able to search the contents of both comprehensively. Entries in Volume 1 are distinguished from those in Volume 2, so there should not be any confusion if you don't (yet!) own Volume 1. With regard to categories, these are useful if you are interested in finding particular types of examples in anime and manga; a list of category icons appears on page 2, just before the main entries begin.

The romanization system for transliterating character-based Japanese words into letters of the English alphabet is based on the standard Hepburn system, except that the letter $n$ is used before consonants $b$, $m$, and $p$ (other English texts often use an $m$ here instead). Macrons, or "long signs" ($\bar{o}$, $\bar{u}$, etc.), indicate extended vowels on Japanese words. However, the usage here is inconsistent when it comes to anime or manga titles and character names. This is because I've tried to follow the spellings seen in the Japanese export versions, and their various publishers and production companies do not consistently apply macrons to words that need them (in fact, they generally leave them out). Macrons are also not used in familiar Japanese place names (Tokyo, Osaka, Honshu, etc.) unless the names appear in a Japanese-language context (e.g., "Tokyo Bay," but "Tōkyō Wan"). Personal names follow Japanese usage, that is, the family name is given first, as in "Takahashi Rumiko."

Examples from anime and manga are included at the end of each entry with as much identifying information as is needed to enable readers to find the actual source if they are so inclined.

### Titles Cited in This Volume

Some of the titles cited in this book will be out of print by the time you read it. Some titles actually went out of and came back into print while I was writing. The U.S. market is dynamic, with a high growth rate and a staggering amount of material available for purchase. For this reason, many worthy

**FOR THE LATEST ANIME COMPANION NEWS . . .**

No book like this can ever be complete. For this reason, I will maintain a supplement on the World Wide Web with corrections to entries in this book, as well as new entries. The Web pages contain notes for each of the entries detailing the secondary reference sources I used to track down information on aspects of Japanese culture. They also contain useful links to sites on the Internet relating to many entries.

The Anime Companion Web Supplement can be accessed at: **www.koyagi.com**.

titles are simply not included in the examples given. Another thing to be aware of is the phenomenon of licenses expiring and another company releasing the work with a new translation. Also, some companies have been revising their older VHS translations for DVD release. The change from VHS to DVD has largely eliminated the problem of unnumbered series. This means that I no longer have to spell out the episode titles for some series, as I did in the first volume. Instead, I have simply used the episode number. For a comparison chart of titles originally released without episode numbers, see the supplement to this book on my Web site at www.koyagi.com.

### Kanji and Kana

This Volume 2 includes kanji or kana for almost every entry. In the case of food, I have attempted to include both forms, as some menus in Japan may have either. For the kanji and kana for entries in Volume 1, see the supplement on my Web site.

While writing this volume, a friend pointed out that I was using both the old and the new forms of kanji for various entries. In 1946 while still under the U.S. Occupation, the Japanese government reformed the system of kanji then in use. Some characters were simplified, and the use of obscure variants was discouraged. This was to make it easier for children to learn kanji and to make it easier for adults to read books and newspapers. These kanji are still encountered in older books and in scholarly works. For this reason, both the current commonly used kanji and the old form are included in this book. As far as I know this is the first time such a dual listing of the old and new forms has been used in an English-language work intended for the general public, although not every example of old-form equivalents is included.

For clarity, the characters 市 (*shi*, "city") , 町 (*machi* or *chō*, "village"), and 区 (*ku*, "ward") appear in brackets in the entry titles for some cities. The kanji 市 is used, for example, on some maps to clarify that the name is that of a city, as some prefectures have capital cities with the same name.

## ACKNOWLEDGMENTS

I would like to thank:

Studio Gainax for allowing us to use the gorgeous image of Rei from *Neon Genesis Evangelion* on the cover, as well as several images from their works.

Aniplex, Broccoli International USA, Central Park Media, Fuji Creative Corporation, Geneon, Sunrise Inc., Viz, LLC, and Voyager Entertainment for generously granting image permissions. Also AnimEigo and Bandai Entertainment for their generosity in sending me copies of specific titles I requested for research even though I was not using them to write reviews.

Peter Goodman and Barry Harris of Stone Bridge Press for their assistance and patience in the production of this volume.

Special thanks to Cindy for her work on the line drawings, and to L.J.C. Shimoda for her lettering, drawings, and icons, which also appeared in Volume 1.

Anime V and Comic Relief in Berkeley, as well as Kinokuniya and Japan Video in San Francisco, all stores that have seen my credit card on a regular basis.

Peets Coffee on Mission Street in downtown San Francisco for fixing my espresso each morning before work. Some of the manuscript was revised there.

Special thanks also to Ono Masahiro who sent me extensive notes on Volume 1 and the previous edition of the supplement. He generously provided a very large percentage of the kanji in this volume. He is the person who pointed out the old and new kanji styles. Our correspondence over the past few years has been a great help in my learning more about Japan.

## ICONS AND ABBREVIATIONS

The following icons are used to indicate subject categories:

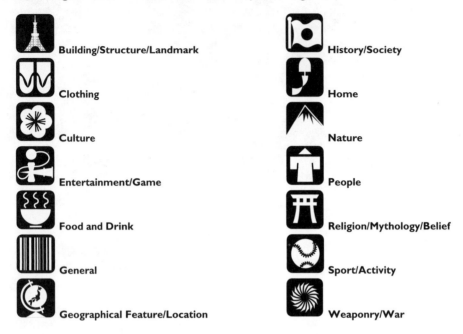

Building/Structure/Landmark

Clothing

Culture

Entertainment/Game

Food and Drink

General

Geographical Feature/Location

History/Society

Home

Nature

People

Religion/Mythology/Belief

Sport/Activity

Weaponry/War

The following icons are used to indicate anime/manga reference categories:

**A**      examples seen in anime

**M**      examples seen in manga

**AM**      examples seen in both anime and manga

## Abbreviations:

| | |
|---|---|
| **AC, vol. I** | *The Anime Companion*, volume I |
| **anim. seq.** | animation sequence |
| **chapt.** | chapter |
| **ep.** | episode |
| **OVA** | **Original Video Animation (sometimes seen as OAV)** |
| **p., pp.** | page, pages |
| **pt.** | part |
| **vol.** | volume |

# A

## 足立区 OLD FORM 足立區
## ADACHI-KU

A ward in northeast **Tokyo** bordered by Kita Ward to the west, **Arakawa-ku** to the south, Katsushika Ward to the east, and Saitama Prefecture to the north. The Arakawa river runs through the southern part of this ward and the southern border is marked by the **Sumidagawa** river, while part of the eastern border is marked by the Nakagawa river. Expressway 6 runs through Adachi Ward. Adachi Ward dates from 1932 when administrative reforms united the prefecture and city of Tokyo. Adachi was a factory district in WWII but today it is mainly residential. In the **Edo period** (AC vol. 1, p. 25) the Adachi area had been a **shukuba machi** on the Ōshū Kaidō. This is not the same Adachi featured in the story *Demoness of Adachi;* that one is **Adachigahara**.

🅰 Natsumi and Miyuki head to the Ayase animal hospital in Adachi Ward in *You're Under Arrest* (ep. 2).

## 安達ヶ原
## ADACHIGAHARA

A place in **Fukushima Ken**. This is the location of a famous story of a group of **yamabushi** (AC vol. 1, p. 146) who discover that the old woman whose hut they are staying in is an **oni** (AC vol. 1, p. 101) who eats passersby. This story has been made into a **Nō** drama also called Adachigahara.

🅜 Cherry warns Ataru about the demoness of Adachi in *Lum Urusei Yatsura Perfect Collection* (p. 384).

## 合気道 OLD FORM 合氣道
## AIKIDŌ

A martial art based on techniques from **jūjutsu** (AC vol. 1, p. 56; specifically the daitō aiki system of aiki-jūjutsu), **kenjutsu**, and **naginata** (AC vol. 1, p. 91) techniques. Created by Ueshiba Morihei, who wanted to develop a **ryū** that did not contain foreign (i.e., Chinese) elements. Aikidō focuses on mental self-training and unarmed self-defense techniques and does sometimes include weapon training.

🅰 In *Patlabor the TV Series* (ep. 14) we find out that Kanuka knows **jūdō** (AC vol. 1, p. 56) and aikidō.

## 会津盆地 OLD FORM 會津盆地
## AIZU BONCHI (AIZU BASIN)

Located in northern **Honshu** (AC vol. 1, p. 47), originally in Mutsu Province, today in **Fukushima Ken**. The basin is primarily an agricultural area that produces rice and vegetables, but it is also known for its lacquerware.

🅰 That Hotta is from Aizu is mentioned in *Botchan* (pt. 2).

## 会津藩 OLD FORM 會津藩
## AIZU HAN

A domain ruled by the Gamō family in 1590–98 and 1601–27, and then by the Katō family until 1643 when it was granted to Hoshina Masayuki, the son of Tokugawa Hidetada, the second **Tokugawa** (AC vol. 1, p. 137) **shōgun** (AC vol. 1, p. 123). The family name was changed to Matsudaira in 1696 and the last **daimyō**, Matsudaira Katamori, fought against the imperial forces during the **Boshin Sensō**. This area now forms a part of **Fukushima Ken**.

Ⓜ Megumi is from Aizu domain in *Rurouni Kenshin* (TV ep. 8 and manga vol. 3, p. 76).

## 赤べこ
## AKABEKO (BOBBING OX TOY)

Red cow toy. Originating in the vicinity of **Fukushima Ken**. These toys are made with the head suspended in a cavity at the front of the body allowing the head to bob when it is moved. Legend has it that when a temple was being built only one red cow was able to last for the entire time the construction was happening.

Ⓐ This toy is seen in *Rurouni Kenshin* (TV ep. 2) at a restaurant, which is also called Akabeko.

© NOBUHIRO WATSUKI/SHUEISHA · FUJI-TV · ANIPLEX INC.

*This **akabeko** in* RUROUNI KENSHIN *is a bit close to the edge. Quick, duck!*

## あかがい OR 赤貝
## AKAGAI

A type of clam with reddish meat. Also known in English as cockle, ark shell, and blood clam. Spring is the best time of year to eat it. It can be served as **sushi** (AC vol. 1, p. 128) or raw with a dipping sauce. It is also used in a variety of cooked dishes.

Ⓐ Salmon roe (**ikura**), ark shell, and sweet shrimp are some of the items Onizuka orders at an expensive sushi place in *GTO* (ep. 18).

## 赤坂
## AKASAKA

A district located in northern **Minato-ku** of **Tokyo**. In the **Edo period** (AC vol. 1, p. 25) this locality had many **daimyō** residences. Today the area is a well-off residential area, with entertainment and shopping districts. The Geihinkan, the official state guesthouse; Hotel New Ōtani; the TBS Studios; and the U.S. Embassy are in this area.

Ⓐ Okubo Toshimichi visits the cabinet in Akasaka in *Rurouni Kenshin* (TV ep. 31). • A meeting takes place in a ryōtei, traditional restaurant, in Akasaka, Minato District Tokyo in *Otaku no Video* (pt. 2, 2nd anim. seq.).

Ⓜ In *Club 9* (vol. 1, ch. 5) we find that Aki lives in Akasaka when Haruo stays with her. • At the beginning of *Samurai Legend* government officials come to visit **Katsu Kaishū** in his Akasaka residence.

## 秋葉原駅 OLD FORM 秋葉原驛
## AKIHABARA EKI (AKIHABARA STATION)

Akihabara Station. A train station at the junction of the Yamanote, Keihin Tōhoku, and Sōbu train lines in **Tokyo**, specifically in **Chiyoda-ku**. A black-market in this area after WWII eventually became the famous **Akihabara** (AC vol. 1, p. 5) shopping district.

Ⓐ Akihabara Station is mentioned in *City Hunter: The Motion Picture*.

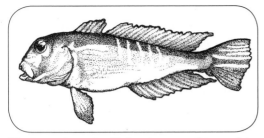

*Sliced raw, steamed, grilled, or in a soup, this **amadai** has several possibilities.*

## あまだい OR 甘鯛
## AMADAI

Tile fish, a type of **tai**, also known as guji, blanquillo, and ocean whitefish. *Branchiostegus japonicus*. This fish from western Japan is best eaten between October and March. The red or white varieties are best; the yellow isn't quite as tasty.

Ⓐ Tile fish is mentioned by Yaegashi in *Blue Seed* (ep. 16).

Ⓜ Jan choses to use tile fish in a cooking contest in *Iron Wok Jan* (vol. 6, p. 112).

## 天草四郎
## AMAKUSA SHIRŌ

?–1638. Amakusa Shirō was a charismatic young man whose father had been a vassal of **Konishi Yukinaga**. In 1637 he led the Christian **ikki** known as the **Shimabara no Ran**. He is also known by the names Amakusa Shirō Tokisada and Masuda Shirō Tokisada.

Ⓜ A legend of treasure carried from Shimabara to **Okinawa** (AC vol. 1, p. 99) by Amakusa Shiro results in some interesting adventures in *GTO* (ep. 38 and vol. 13).

Ⓐ He is a major character in *Ninja Resurrection* (ep. 1).

## あんこう OR 鮟鱇
## ANKŌ

Anger fish. A homely looking deep-sea fish, the best tasting of which are caught in the winter months. Everything but the head and bones is eaten; the skin and liver are often used in recipes.

Ⓐ Ankō is mentioned in *Kimagure Orange Road* (TV ep. 23).

## あんパン OR あんぱん OR 餡麭包
## ANPAN

Bread filled with *an*, a sweet bean paste. These are similar in shape and size to hamburger buns, and since they are baked often confuse non-Japanese who bite or cut into them to find the filling.

Ⓐ Shinohara eats anpan in *Patlabor the TV Series* (ep. 4).

## 安政の大獄
## ANSEI NO TAIGOKU (ANSEI PURGE)

The Ansei crackdown. A political purge lasting from 1858 to 1860 when opponents of the Tokugawa **bakufu**'s policy of opening up Japan to the outside world were suppressed. Led by **Ii Naosuke**, more than 100

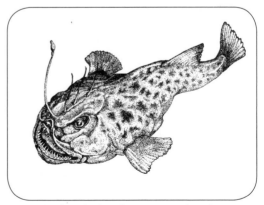

*Can such a homely thing be tasty? Yep, don't let its looks deceive you; this **ankō** makes for really good eatin'.*

© 1990 HEADGEAR / EMOTION / TFC / NTV

*Shinohara in* PATLABOR *does not look very happy, even with* **anpan** *to snack on.*

**daimyō**, nobles, and others were forced to retire, placed under arrest, or exiled. Some such as **Yoshida Shōin** were executed. The Ansei no Taigoku ended after Ii was assassinated by opponents.

Ⓐ The Great Ansei Crackdown is mentioned as Madoka and Kyosuke study in the *Kimagure Orange Road Movie: I Want to Return to That Day.*

## 新居町
## ARAI-CHŌ

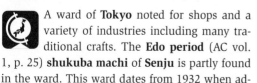 In the **Edo period** (AC vol. 1, p. 25) this was a **shukuba machi** and location of a barrier station on the **Tōkaidō**. Located in **Shizuoka Ken**, this town lies near where Lake Hamana meets the Pacific Ocean. Today the economy centers mainly around fishing and the commercial raising of **unagi** (AC vol. 1, p. 144).

Ⓜ Arai is mentioned as being on the Tōkaidō in *Lone Wolf and Cub* (vol. 14, p. 96).

## 荒川区 OLD FORM 荒川區
## ARAKAWA-KU

A ward of **Tokyo** noted for shops and a variety of industries including many traditional crafts. The **Edo period** (AC vol. 1, p. 25) **shukuba machi** of **Senju** is partly found in the ward. This ward dates from 1932 when ad-

ministrative reforms united the prefecture and city of Tokyo merging the villages of Minami-Senju, Mikawashima, Ogu, and Nippori into Arakawa Ward. Arakawa Ward is bordered by **Adachi-ku** on the north, Sumida Ward on the east, **Taitō-ku** on the south, and Kita Ward to the west. The **Sumidagawa** flows along the north and east sides of the borders.

Ⓜ Arakawa Ward is mentioned in *Mobile Police Patlabor* (vol. 1, p. 112) and *Patlabor New Files* (ep. 3).

## 嵐山
## ARASHIYAMA

The name of both a hill in western **Kyoto** (AC vol. 1, p. 77) and that part of the city at the base of the hill located near the Hozugawa river. This hill is known for its **sakura** (AC vol. 1, p. 110) in the spring and colorful foliage in the autumn. At those times of year the area can be filled with sightseers. Arashiyama is also known as Ranzan.

Ⓐ Anzai Jurobei claims he saw the Battousai in the Arashiyama area during the **Ikedaya Jiken** incident in the *Rurouni Kenshin* TV series (ep. 77).

## 有馬喜兵衛 OLD FORM 有馬喜兵衞
## ARIMA KIHEI

d. late-1590s. A swordsman of the **Shintō Ryū** who died on a **musha shugyō** in a **taryū-jiai** against a thirteen-year-old opponent, an opponent who would later become known as **Miyamoto Musashi** (AC vol. 1, p. 86).

Ⓜ In *Vagabond* (vol. 2, ch. 15) we see the combat between the young Takezō and Arima Kihei.

## 足軽
## ASHIGARU (FOOT SOLDIERS)

Originally, farmers and mercenaries were recruited to fight in wars as low class soldiers, many eventually becoming fulltime soldiers. During the **Sengoku jidai**

(AC vol. 1, p. 113) they became more important in warfare with specialized units playing significant roles in battle, often in the highly honorable vanguard. Perhaps the most famous *ashigaru* of this period was **Toyotomi Hideyoshi** (AC vol. 1, p. 140) who rose to a very high rank. Usually they were armed with a lance or bow and arrow; some carried firearms (**teppō**, AC vol. 1, p. 135). Their battle dress usually included armor and a simple helmet, provided by their **daimyō** often with his **mon** (AC vol. 1, p. 89) on the front. Such armor was called *okashi gusoku* or "honorable loan armor." During the Sengoku jidai ashigaru carried a single short sword. Ashigaru are seen in almost all anime and manga that depict battles from this time. Not only are they seen in battle scenes during wartime, they continued to exist as low-ranking **samurai** (AC vol. 1, p. 110) during the **Edo period** (AC vol. 1, p. 25). When firm lines between farmers and samurai were drawn by Toyotomi Hideyoshi and **Tokugawa Ieyasu** the ashigaru were placed on the samurai side and were allowed to wear the two swords distinctive of a samurai.

🅰 *Ashigaru* are seen in almost any early or pre-Edo period anime with battle scenes, for example *The Legend of the Dog Warriors The Hakkenden.*

🅼 There is a mention of a wife running off with an *ashigaru* in *Lone Wolf and Cub* (vol. 1, p. 12).

## 淡路島
## AWAJISHIMA

Awaji Island in the **Seto Naikai**. This large island is located west of Osaka Bay, east of the Harima Sea, north of the Kii Channel, and south of the mainland part of **Hyōgo Ken**. It is also part of that prefecture. It also lies directly between **Shikoku** and **Osaka** (AC vol. 1, p. 102). Agriculture is mainly flowers, fruit, onions, dairy products, and beef cattle. Tourism is popular, and major sights include the Naruto whirlpools and ruins of the Awaji Kokubunji.

🅰 The Awaji police are mentioned in *Ghost in the Shell: Stand Alone Complex* (ep. 2).

*The **ayame** like these in* Samurai X Trust and Betrayal *are beautiful in the rain, as water seems to bring out the color.*

🅼 Awaji Island is mentioned in *Lone Wolf and Cub* (vol. 3, p. 21). • American bombers fly over Awajishima island on their way to Kobe in *Adolf: 1945 and All That Remains* (p. 100).

## 菖蒲
## AYAME (IRIS)

A type of iris. The ayame, with its purple blossom, is probably the best known iris species in Japan. The blooming season is late spring through summer. Parts of the plant are used for dyes. There are other species that are also grown as ornamentals, as well as several wild species.

🅰 In *Samurai X: Trust and Betrayal* ayame are seen and are the object of a conversation at the inn.

## 麻布
## AZABU

Originally the name of a low hill. In the **Edo period** (AC vol. 1, p. 25) this area was the location of many **samurai** (AC vol. 1, p. 110) homes. Today the Azabu area is located in **Minato-ku**, **Tokyo** and is where many embassies and expensive homes are found.

🅼 Hira suggests going to Azabu in *Bringing Home*

the Sushi (p. 85) • Takeuchi Naoko, author of the *Sailor Moon* manga, lives in Azabu (*Sailor Moon* vol. 1, p. 57). • Freddy drops by to visit Suekichi after having lunch with his producer in Azabu in *Dance Till Tomorrow* (vol. 7, p. 181).

幕府
## BAKUFU (SHOGUNATE)

Military government, literally "tent government," usually translated as shogunate. In Japan this term was originally used to refer to the Headquarters of the Inner Palace Guards (the Konoefu) and also to the commander's residence or to the commander himself. When Minamoto no Yoritomo became the head of the guards the term was applied to his household and later, when he became shōgun, the two terms were associated. In any story taking place during the **Edo period** (AC vol. 1, p. 25) it refers to the **Tokugawa** (AC vol. 1, p. 137) government in **Edo**.

**A** The bakufu is referred to in *Samurai X: Trust and Betrayal.*

**M** Lord Habaki speaks of the weakness of the **samurai** (AC vol. 1, p. 110) under the peaceful rule of the Tokugawa bakufu in *Blade of the Immortal: Dark Shadows.*

幕末
## BAKUMATSU

The years at the end of the rule of the **Tokugawa** (AC vol. 1, p. 137) **bakufu**. Usually considered to be 1853–68.

**A** *Dagger of Kamui* and *Samurai X: Trust and Betrayal* take place in this period. References to it are often made in the *Rurouni Kenshin* TV series.

坂東玉三郎
## BANDŌ TAMASABURŌ V

The name Bandō Tamasaburō belongs to a lineage of **kabuki** actors going back to the early 19th century. Many of the actors who are in this lineage were *onnagata*, that is, male kabuki actors who specialize in playing women on stage. Bandō Tamasaburō V is the most famous *onnagata* presently on the stage, a true superstar in Japan. His performances have brought many young people back to the kabuki audience. More than just a kabuki actor, he performs other dance styles, has acted in Shakespearean plays, portrayed both genders in movies, and even directed films. There are several region-free DVD discs available from Japan containing some of his more dance-oriented kabuki performances.

**A** Soichiro is compared to Tamasaburō the kabuki actor by Yotsuya in *Maison Ikkoku* (ep. 7).

芭蕉
## BASHŌ

1644–94. Full name Matsuo Bashō. Famous haiku poet who helped establish the style. He traveled around **Kyoto** (AC vol. 1, p. 77) for several years before moving to **Edo** in 1672. He became a popular teacher of poetry and in 1680 settled in **Fukagawa** where he took the literary name of Bashō. Starting in 1684 he began a series of trips during which he would visit places and write poetry. It was on one of these that he left Edo in 1689 at the age of forty-five via the **shukuba machi** of **Senju** for his famous 1,500-mile trip by foot through the north of

Japan. It was on such a trip that he died in **Osaka** (AC vol. 1, p. 102) of food poisoning.

Ⓜ In *The Return of Lum Feudal Furor* (p. 143) we see Bashō greeting **Kobayashi Issa.**

## 抜刀術 OLD FORM 拔刀術
## BATTŌ-JUTSU

A sword technique based on drawing the sword with great speed, force, and skill to cut one's opponent. Also known as iai-jutsu 居合術. There are many **ryū** whose origins date as far back as the 15th century that systematically teach battō-jutsu techniques from several postures. After the lifting of the ban on martial arts in 1947 some styles of battō-jutsu became iai-dō, and sword drawing techniques were incorporated into **kendō** (AC vol. 1, p. 66), which by now had become more of a sport than a martial art for many of its practitioners.

Ⓜ The most famous practitioner of battō-jutsu in anime and manga is Himura Kenshin in *Rurouni Kenshin.*

## ベルサイユのばら
## BERUSAIYU NO BARA (THE ROSE OF VERSAILLES)

A famous eighty-two-installment manga by Ikeda Riyoko that was first published in 1972. The story is set in the royal court of France just before and during the French Revolution. The main character is Oscar François de Jarjayes, a young woman raised as a boy who becomes a guard at the Versailles palace. Given its exotic European location and the cross-dressing of the main character, this work was a strong candidate for a **Takarazuka Kagekidan** (AC vol. 1, p. 131) stage show, which began in 1974 and became an incredible success with millions of tickets sold. This was the first manga adaptation the troupe had ever done. There was even a live-action movie made in English in 1978, entitled *Lady Oscar*, directed by Jacques Demy. In 1980 an anime version began broadcasting on TV.

### FIRE AS A WEAPON

Selectively applied arson has long been used in Japan as a weapon in surprise attacks often to force the enemy to retreat in chosen directions for easier destruction or to trap them in a simple flaming death. **Oda Nobunaga** once surrounded a garrison filled with his opponents, including women and children, built a large wooden wall to lock them in, ordered brush piled against it, then, when the strong winds that blow in the area began, lit the brush. The resulting conflagration burned everything and resulted in something like 20,000 deaths.

Ⓐ In *Samurai X: Trust and Betrayal* we see the fire that took place during the **Hamaguri Gomon no Hen.** • In *Gasaraki* (ep. 16, "Karma") we see the capital set fire as a strategic maneuver.

Ⓜ A *Rose of Versailles* poster is among the items tossed down by an angry grandson at a funeral in *Rumic Theater: One or Double* (p. 143). • Part of the story is translated in Frederik Schodt's book *Manga! Manga!*

## 一式陸上攻撃機 ISSHIKIRIKUJŌKŌGEKIKI
## BETTY (AIRCRAFT)

"Betty" is the U.S. military code name assigned to a twin-engine bomber widely used throughout the Pacific in WWII by the Japanese Navy. There were several different models made by **Mitsubishi** starting early in the war. The use of these planes from islands enabled aircraft carriers to be used elsewhere. Near the end of the war they carried **Ōka** in a desperate effort to defend Japan from the Allied fleets. The code name is said to come from the name of a nurse in Bridgewater, Pennsylvania, who was endowed with twin protrusions similar to those of the two large engines the plane sported.

## JUST LOOK IT UP ON THE WEB

I don't know how many times I have heard the sentence "Just look it up on the Web." More than enough to get me a bit POed at times. It is amazing how people believe the Web is a reliable source of information about Japan. The Web can be a good source of information or it can be a source of the most stupid drivel you could ever have the misfortune to find. Usually it is somewhere in between. After all, anyone with a little time can set up a Web page about anything. I recall trying to get some information about the **Shinsengumi**. I found a nice site that looked like it had some good information. I was not going to rely on it exclusively, of course. I was just planning to see if it cited any good sources for information or gave me new information that I then could use to track down other sources. I was about half-way through the site when I realized that there were references to the *Rurouni Kenshin* TV series, and nowhere on the page did it mention the show or state that it was using a fictional work as a source. The entire page looked like it was totally serious and historical. This is bad, and an example of why the Web is more like a pile of zines reproduced at the local copy shop than a scholarly library.

Sure, there are good sites, usually set up by an organization, government agency, or company, where you can track down specific information. Me, I'll use the Web as a general tool, but when I write, I want my sources to be reliable. I'll stick with print or online databases of material from reputable journals.

Ⓐ In *The Cockpit* story 2, "Mach Thunder Force," the pilot of a U.S. scout plane identifies a Betty with Zero (**Zerosen**) escorts. In the interview that accompanies this episode, the director identifies it specifically as a Mitsubishi Type 24 bomber, a type used late in the war.

## 琵琶湖
## BIWAKO (LAKE BIWA)

The largest freshwater lake in Japan is located in Shiga Prefecture. It has long been used for transportation and fishing. The lake is commonly divided into the larger North Lake and smaller South Lake. The town of **Ōtsu** is on the edge of the South Lake.

Ⓐ In *Samurai X: Trust and Betrayal* Kenshin and Tomoe pause and look at Biwako when they go into town.

Ⓜ In the town of Natta on the shores of Lake Biwa, Ōgami meditates in *Lone Wolf and Cub* (vol. 16, p. 134).

## 戊辰戦争 OLD FORM 戊辰戰爭
## BOSHIN SENSŌ (BOSHIN CIVIL WAR)

A series of battles that took place between the forces of the **bakufu** and pro-imperial troops led by the **Satsuma Han** and the **Chōshū Han** at the end of the **Edo period** (AC vol. 1, p. 25), which led to the **Meiji period** (AC vol. 1, p. 81). The civil war began on January 27, 1868, with the **Toba-Fushimi no Tatakai**, and ended with the **Goryōkaku no Tatakai** in June 20–27, 1869.

Ⓐ The battle of Goryōkaku is seen in *Dagger of Kamui.* • The ending of *Samurai X: Trust and Betrayal* is a series of scenes set during the Boshin Sensō.

## 舞楽 OLD FORM 舞樂
## BUGAKU

An ancient style of dance and music. The word literally means "dance music" or "dance entertainment." Bugaku was introduced into Japan in the 8th century from China. It became an aristocratic art form and has remained largely unchanged, even to the degree that new masks are copies of old ones, not original designs. One unusual type of bugaku mask is the **zōmen**. The characters represented in bugaku are usually foreign gods or **kami** (AC vol. 1, p.

59). Interestingly, bugaku of Japanese origin do not use masks. During the **Sengoku jidai** (AC vol. 1, p. 113) bugaku almost died out as a result of the social turmoil of the time. In the early **Meiji period** (AC vol. 1, p. 81), bugaku artists were gathered together in **Tokyo** to become the official musicians for the imperial household.

🄰 Early in *Spirited Away* we see several red-robed figures leave a ferry wearing bugaku zōmen.

## 武士
## BUSHI (WARRIOR)

 There are many terms used to describe warriors in early Japanese history. Bushi is only one of them. The early bushi were specialists in warfare, usually mounted archers. The term came to mean any professional warrior rather than a farmer drafted as an occasional foot soldier. In the **Edo period** (AC vol. 1, p. 25) the word was used interchangeably with **samurai** (AC vol. 1, p. 110), as the two were legally identical. In fact most anime, manga, and Japanese movies do not use the word samurai much; instead bushi is used and is often "translated" into English as samurai.

🄰 Bushi is the word used in Aboshi's last speech but is translated as samurai in the *The Legend of the Dog Warriors The Hakkenden* (ep. 11).

🄼 Many bushi are seen in historical tales such as *Lone Wolf and Cub, Samurai Executioner,* and *Vagabond.*

## 武士道
## BUSHIDŌ (WAY OF THE WARRIOR)

A code of ethics that grew out of **bushi** tradition. Originally consisting of unwritten customs, it was codified mainly in the **Edo period** (AC vol. 1, p. 25) when several important works were written. The term also came into being in the Edo period, replacing earlier phrases. Great emphasis is placed on loyalty to one's lord as well as the importance of honing one's skill with weapons. Bushidō continued to be a signifi-cant part of military life until after WWII. Today it is mainly found in martial arts and depicted in entertainment, but widely rejected as incompatible with democratic society.

🄰 Any anime with bushi is likely to have expressions of bushidō. Strong examples of this are *The Legend of the Dog Warriors The Hakkenden* and *Rurouni Kenshin.*

🄼 *Lone Wolf and Cub, Blade of the Immortal,* and *Vagabond* are set in the past where bushidō plays a major part in the story.

## 白虎隊
## BYAKKOTAI (WHITE TIGER BRIGADE)

In March 1868, during the **Boshin Sensō**, a military unit composed of a few hundred young men was organized in the **Aizu Han**. Most died on October 8, 1868, in the battle of Tonokuchihara. Twenty survived to return to find Wakamatsu Castle in flames, whereupon they assumed the worst and committed **seppuku** (AC vol. 1, p. 115) on Iimoriyama, a nearby mountain.

🄰 Kenshin refers to the Byakkotai atrocity in *Samurai X: The Motion Picture.*

## びょうぶ OR 屏風
## BYŌBU (FOLDING SCREEN)

A series of hinged panels that can be unfolded to make a screen that stands on its own. This screen design came to Japan from China in the 7th century. Usually byōbu are decorated with **shōheiga**. When they are placed upside down it is a sign of mourning.

🄰 A byōbu is seen behind Oshita in *Suikoden Demon Century* and in the opening sequence of *Ai Yori Aoshi.*

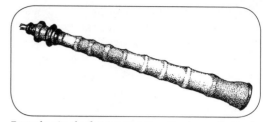

*From the simple **charumera** comes the strangest sound.*

## チャルメラ
## CHARUMERA

A small double-reed instrument played by **rāmen** (AC vol. 1, p. 105) vendors serving their food from **yatai** (AC vol. 1, p. 147) as they move through the neighborhoods at night looking for customers. The origin of this instrument is unknown but it is probably Chinese or Portuguese. The name is probably related to the Portuguese word *charamela*. The high-pitched whine is distinctive and easy to spot when you hear it.

🅰 As Mr. Yotsuya leaves to go to the Chachamaru at night, we hear the sound of a charumera in *Maison Ikkoku* (ep. 23) and before Ryo and Kaori eat rāmen at truck-driven *yatai* in *City Hunter 2* (ep. 24).

## 違棚 or 違い棚
## CHIGAI-DANA (CLOUD SHELVES)

Alternating shelves placed at different heights and not fully crossing the space they are in can look very much like stylized clouds in some Asian paintings. The horizontal portions of the shelves are connected by vertical pieces.

🅰 Cloud shelves are visible in the room when Okoto starts teaching Sasuke in the *Tale of Shunkin*. • Cloud shelves and a **kamidana** (AC vol. 1, p. 60) are behind Momiji as she speaks to her sister in *Blue Seed* (ep. 21). • We also see them in *Ghost Story* and in Aboshi's flashback in the *The Legend of the Dog Warriors The Hakkenden* (ep. 11).

## 茅ヶ崎 [市]
## CHIGASAKI

A city located at the mouth of the Sagamigawa river in **Kanagawa Ken** (AC vol. 1, p. 60) in southern **Honshu** (AC vol. 1, p. 47). In 1898 a station on the **Tōkaidō** rail line opened at Chigasaki City and many villas were built here.

🅰 Chigasaki is mentioned in *Shonan Bakusozoku*.

## ちくわ or 竹輪
## CHIKUWA (FISH SAUSAGE)

Chikuwa is a long, hollow fish sausage. The name literally means "bamboo wheels." They are made by grinding fish into a paste, mixing it with egg white, salt, sugar, seasonings, and starch, forming it around a bamboo or stainless steel rod, then steaming or grilling it. Chikuwa is often used in dishes such as **oden** (AC vol. 1, p. 98) and **chanpon** (AC vol. 1, p. 18).

🅰 Chikuwa is used in martial arts training with very bad results in *Ranma 1/2: Anything Goes Martial Arts* (ep. 5). • Oji orders chikuwa at a **yatai** (AC vol. 1, p. 147) in *The Legend of Black Heaven* (ep. 6 and 12) and Shinshi orders it in *Patlabor the TV Series* (ep. 14).

## ちりなべ or ちり鍋
## CHIRINABE (HOT POT DISH)

A **nabemono** in which vegetables, fish, and **tōfu** are simmered together, usually in a **donabe**. Each item is dipped in a

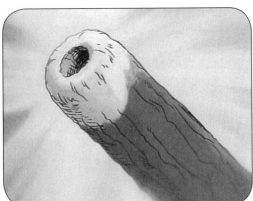

*Nope, this isn't a cigarette butt. It's a close-up of* **chikuwa** *in* RANMA 1/2.

sauce of **shōyu** (AC vol. 1, p. 124) and vinegar or citric juice before it is eaten. This is considered a winter dish. A popular chirinabe of **Shimonoseki** is **fugu-chiri.**

**A** In Shimonoseki many of the major cast in the *Urusei Yatsura* TV series (ep. 55, st. 78) have unfortunate symptoms after enjoying fugu-chiri served in a donabe.

**M** Chirinabe is served in *Cannon God Exaxxion* (vol. 3, p. 144). Note the bowl with sliced citrus fruit on the table, which is a clue that what is being served is not the similar-looking food dish called *dotenabe.*

### 千代田区 OLD FORM 千代田區
### CHIYODA-KU

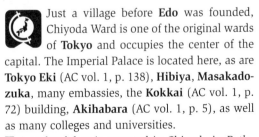 Just a village before **Edo** was founded, Chiyoda Ward is one of the original wards of **Tokyo** and occupies the center of the capital. The Imperial Palace is located here, as are **Tokyo Eki** (AC vol. 1, p. 138), **Hibiya**, **Masakado-zuka,** many embassies, the **Kokkai** (AC vol. 1, p. 72) building, **Akihabara** (AC vol. 1, p. 5), as well as many colleges and universities.

**A** A stolen labor is reported in Chiyoda in *Patlabor the TV Series* (ep. 22). • Nenene meets Mr. Lee in the Kanda neighborhood of Chiyoda Ward in *R.O.D TV* (ep. 3).

### チョコフレーク
### CHOCO FLAKE

A snack manufactured by the Morinaga company. Choco Flake is simply corn flakes covered with chocolate. The taste is slightly sweet and quite yummy.

**A** Spike picks up a package of Choco Flake after knocking it out of a woman's grocery bag in *Cowboy Bebop* (ep. 1).

**M** We see Choco bags next to the phone while Kunio uses it to talk to Fujiyoshi in chapter 20 of *GTO* (vol. 3).

### 銚子 [市]
### CHŌSHI

A town in **Chiba Ken** (AC vol. 1, p. 18) located where the Tonegawa river runs into the Pacific Ocean. This coastal town makes **shōyu** (soy sauce) (AC vol. 1, p. 124) and has a sizable fishing and seafood processing industry.

**A** Chōshi is mentioned in the *Patlabor Original Series* (ep. 6).

### 長州藩
### CHŌSHŪ HAN

An **Edo period** (AC vol. 1, p. 25) **han** consisting of the provinces of Suō and Nagato, what is now **Yamaguchi Ken.** It was first granted to Mōri Terumoto for having sided with **Tokugawa Ieyasu** after the **Sekigahara no Tatakai.** Because the Mori had fought against the Tokugawa during the battle itself, they were simultaneously rewarded and punished by having their lands greatly reduced from the vast area they had controlled before instead of having them completely taken away. This led to a grudge against the **bakufu,** and the Chōshū domain under the leadership of **Takasugi Shinsaku** and **Kido Takayoshi** was central to the overthrow of the bakufu and the establishment of the **Meiji period** (AC vol. 1, p. 81).

**A** We see the **Kiheitai** training in Chōshū domain

## IS IT CLAN OR IS IT HAN?

One thing that always upsets me is how often **han** is translated as "clan." *Han* and clan are two very different things. For example, one of the most famous *han* that you see mentioned in anime and manga is the **Chōshū han**. However, when you translate this as Chōshū clan the term takes on an incorrect meaning. A clan is composed of people related by blood even if those ties are distant. A *han*, on the other hand, is a geographically defined political unit. Obviously, these are very different things. The Chōshū *han* was not ruled by a clan called the Chōshū, but by the Mōri clan. Also, a clan can have more than one *han*, as did the **Tokugawa** (AC vol. 1, p. 137), the major branch families of which controlled several separate *han*. Call me picky.

early in *Samurai X: Trust and Betrayal,* and several major characters in that story are from there.
Ⓜ The resentment of the Mori for the reduction of their vast lands is mentioned in *Samurai Legend* (ch. 3).

## 中華料理屋
## CHŪKA RYŌRI-YA (CHINESE RESTAURANT)

Chinese restaurants can be divided into two broad categories: the more expensive authentic restaurants and the cheaper places that serve food modified for the Japanese palate, much like cheap Chinese places in the United States.
Ⓜ The Cat Cafe in *Ranma 1/2* is an example of a good quality place to enjoy Chinese food. • In *GTO* (ep. 10, vol. 3, ch. 33) Tomoko's family runs a chūka ryōri-ya, as we can tell from the food served and the **kanji** (AC vol. 1, p. 61) on the **noren** (AC vol. 1, p. 96).

Ⓐ In the *Patlabor* stories a local cheap chūka ryōri-ya, the Shanghai, is a major source of food for the isolated heroes. In ep. 29 of *Patlabor the TV Series,* "The Destruction of the Special Vehicles, Second Section," the entire story revolves around troubled relations between SV2 and the Shanghai.
• In *Macross* Minmay's relatives run an upscale chūka ryōri-ya.

## 大日本帝国陸軍 OLD FORM 大日本帝國陸軍
## DAI NIPPON TEIKOKU RIKUGUN (IMPERIAL JAPANESE ARMY)

The army of Japan that officially was under the command of the emperor from 1868, during the **Meiji period** (AC vol. 1, p. 81) and until the disbanding of the Japanese military in 1945. Originally modeled after the French army, it was later reorganized along the lines of the Prussian military, including autonomy from civilian control. At the time of its greatest strength in WWII, there were around 6.4 million troops in the army.
Ⓐ In the *Rurouni Kenshin* TV series (ep. 3), we see **Yamagata Aritomo,** a high-ranking officer of the Dai Nippon Teikoku Rikugun. • Of course, many WWII anime include the army, such as *The Cockpit* story "Iron Dragon."

## 代官
## DAIKAN

An administrative representative or intendant. Originally these were assigned positions by the **bakufu** or estate owners. By the early **Edo period** (AC vol. 1, p. 25) the term meant the civil administrator of a **daimyō**. In the Edo period it became mainly used for administrators of a division of the land held by the **shōgun** (AC vol. 1, p. 123) or a daimyō. Most of the Shōgun's daikan were **hatamoto**; their duties included agricultural development, police supervision, judging cases, and tax collection. The position was abolished early in the **Meiji period** (AC vol. 1, p. 81).

Ⓜ A daikan chooses to ignore the existence of a gold mine in a neighboring **han** in *Lone Wolf and Cub* (vol. 1, p. 75).

## 大名
## DAIMYŌ (HAN LORD)

The leader of a **han**. Sometimes translated as lord, but the word lord is also used to translate other Japanese titles. The term daimyō literally means "great name" or "big name" and comes from two words: *dai*, or large, and *myō*, which is short for *myōden*, or "name land." The earlier use of the term referred to both military and civilian landholders. By the **Sengoku jidai** (AC vol. 1, p. 113) all daimyō were military rulers. During the **Edo period** (AC vol. 1, p. 25) daimyō were required to state allegiance to the **Tokugawa** (AC vol. 1, p. 137) **shōgun** (AC vol. 1, p. 123). During the reforms of the **Meiji period** (AC vol. 1, p. 81) the daimyō had their domains taken away and were relocated to **Tokyo** and given pensions.

Ⓜ An unfortunate incident involving a daimyō is recounted in *Blade of the Immortal: Cry of the Worm*. • In the *Lone Wolf and Cub* series followers of daimyō more than once hire Ōgami to assist in removing problems for their han.

## だんご OR 団子 OLD FORM 團子
## DANGO (DUMPLING)

Dumpling or ball of food. Rice flour, buckwheat flour, or wheat flour can be used to make dango. If they are steamed or boiled, they are served with a sweet sauce. Grilled dango on skewers are called **kushi-dango**. Dango can also be made with meat. These are deep -ried and often served in **oden** (AC vol. 1, p. 98).

Ⓐ A plate of dango sits on the counter next to a platter with sauce as everyone talks in the restaurant in *Saber Marionette J Again* (ep. 4).

Ⓜ Hyakurin brings Manji some dango in *Blade of the Immortal: Secrets* while he is recovering at Sori's place.

## だし OR 出し
## DASHI (SOUP STOCK)

A soup stock usually made from **konbu** or **katsuobushi** that has been freshly shaved into **kezuribushi** or both. Dashi is used not only for soups such as **misoshiru** (AC vol. 1, p. 85) but also for cooking many other dishes, such as noodles (**men rui**) and vegetables. This is why strict vegetarian cooking is actually quite uncommon in Japan. Dashi is also used as a base for dipping sauces and to cook *nimono* (simmered dishes) and **nabemono** (hotpot dishes). It is also possible to make dashi with small dried anchovies, *niboshi*. One way to do this is to simply soak the dried fish overnight in water (just be sure to discard the heads first). If you are traveling to Japan and have a seafood allergy, be aware that dashi is commonly used in cooking. For vegetarian cooking, dashi can be made with **shiitake**. Dashi is also known as *dashijiru* (出し汁).

Ⓐ Dried fish-flavor soup stock is used by Shinji to make the soup in *Neon Genesis Evangelion* (ep. 15).

*Demae: one hand to steer, the other to balance the box. Don't mess with Shampoo in RANMA 1/2 when she's making a delivery.*

## 出前
### DEMAE (DELIVERY OF PREPARED FOOD)

Delivery of food from restaurants to the home or office is usually done by scooter or bicycle. Soup delivery scooters may have a special carrier to prevent spilling. Bicycle deliverers typically balance the containers of food in one hand while steering with the other. There is no extra charge for this service. Dirty dishes are picked up by the restaurant either shortly after you are finished or the following day.

Ⓜ The most famous bicycle-riding food delivery person is probably Shampoo from the *Ranma 1/2* series (TV ep. 24).

Ⓐ Sakura in *Key the Metal Idol* delivers pizza by scooter. • In the *City Hunter 1* TV series (ep. 3) we see a delivery motorbike with the special carrier for soups.

## 泥鰌掬い OR 泥鰌掬
### DOJŌSUKUI

A funny dance in which the performer pretends to use a basket to scoop up *dojō* (loach), a type of small fish. The traditional garb for this dance includes a cloth wrapped around the head and clothing tucked up as if the dancer was in shallow water. Some-

times a coin is tied under the nose. This dance originated in the city of Yasugi in **Shimane Ken** (AC vol. 1, p. 118) and is performed to the folk tune "Yasugi-bushi."

Ⓐ A dance with a coin on the nose is one entertainment shown in *Urusei Yatsura* (TV ep. 11, st. 21–22). • The King does this dance while wearing a humorous mask on the side of his head in *Dragon Half* (pt. 1 ending credits). • The dance with a basket and **hashi** (AC vol. 1, p. 42) in the nose is done by Sasuke in *Ranma 1/2* (OVA 2).

Ⓜ The dance is seen in the upper panel in *Return of Lum Feudal Furor* (p. 70).

## 毒痛み OR 蕺草
### DOKUDAMI

This common flowering plant, known as Lizard's Tail, Pig Thigh, or Saruraceae, can be found as far north as **Honshu** (AC vol. 1, p. 47) and as far south as Taiwan. The botanical name is *Houttunia cordata*. At first glance its flowers seem simple, with four white petals. Actually, they consist of clusters of a very large number of small yellow flowers and four white bracts at the base of the cluster. The leaves are heart shaped and emit a strong odor when rubbed. There is a large body of writing on this plant's medical uses.

Ⓐ Megumi gives Akito a stamina drink made from dokudami, **sanshō, shiitake**, burdock (**gobō**), lo-

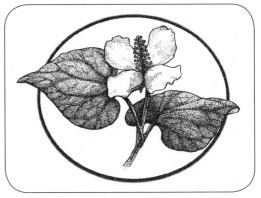

*Simple but easy to identify, the **dokudami** shows up in several anime.*

tus root (**renkon**), snapping turtle (**suppon**), and pit viper blood, plus a few other ingredients in *Martian Successor Nadesico* (ep. 10).

## どなべ OR 土鍋
## DONABE (CERAMIC POT)

 A ceramic **nabe** with a lid for cooking. One way to cook with these is to place them on a **shichirin** (AC vol. 1, p. 117), though a gas ring or stovetop will also work. While many dishes may be cooked in a donabe, they are often used for **nabemono.** The exterior of a donabe is usually unglazed.

🅐 In **Shimonoseki** many of the major cast in the *Urusei Yatsura* TV series (ep. 55, st. 78) have unfortunate symptoms after enjoying **fugu-chiri** served in a donabe. • Other dishes seen cooking in a donabe include **udon** in episode 27 of the *Kimagure Orange Road* TV series and **sukiyaki** (AC vol. 1, p. 126) in *Maison Ikkoku* ep. 31.

🅜 A donabe, containing **nabeyaki-udon,** is brought by Kyoko to Godai as he studies in *Maison Ikkoku* (vol. 7, p. 83). • In *Cannon God Exaxxion* (vol. 3, p. 144), we see **chirinabe** cooking in a donabe on a table top.

## 土蔵 OLD FORM 土藏
## DOZŌ (TRADITIONAL STOREHOUSE)

Storehouse with thick earthen walls, sometimes referred to as a kura. A general term for storehouse. This specific style of storehouse came into existence in the **Muromachi period** (AC vol. 1, p. 90). These tall buildings have few windows, walls 20–30 cm thick (8–12 inches), and a **kawara**-covered roof. Such buildings were highly fire and thief resistant and were used to store valuables and documents. There is a similar word, *dosō*, which also meant storehouse but came to be used for moneylenders who used such storehouses to safeguard valuables.

🅐 In *Samurai X: Trust and Betrayal*, we see part of the interior of a dozō (what is being hit is a prisoner) and the doorway with its thick fireproof

*Large, solid, and fire resistant, a dozō, such as this one in* RUROUNI KENSHIN, *is the place to store family treasures.*

doors. • In the first episode of the *Rurouni Kenshin* TV series, Kenshin gets locked up for perceived bad behavior.

🅜 In *Lone Wolf and Cub* (vol. 2, p. 151), it is Daigoro who is locked in a dozō. • And in *Futaba-kun Change* (vol. 8), Futaba is locked up in one to ensure his attendance at a wedding.

## E

## えだまめ OR 枝豆
## EDAMAME

 Soybeans in the pod. A summer snack, young soybean pods are boiled and salted, and the beans are eaten as an accompaniment to **bīru** (AC vol. 1, p. 10). They are commonly bought frozen in stores.

**A** Edamame is seen in a green in bowl on a bar in *Maison Ikkoku* (ep. 14).

## 江戸 OLD FORM 江戶
## EDO

Located on the coast of central **Honshu** (AC vol. 1, p. 47) at the mouth of several rivers on a large bay, the name means "rivergate." It had been just a village with a small castle built in the 15th century by Ota Dōkan, but in 1590 **Toyotomi Hideyoshi** (AC vol. 1, p. 140) placed the **daimyō Tokugawa Ieyasu** in charge of the Kantō Plain. Tokugawa Ieyasu chose Edo as the place to build his headquarters, rebuilding the castle into the massive **Edojō**. During the **Edo period** (AC vol. 1, p. 25) the city was the headquarters and home of the **shōgun** (AC vol. 1, p. 123). As such, it was the defacto capital of Japan while the official emperor's capital was **Kyoto** (AC vol. 1, p. 77). As the capital, it grew to be a major city of its time, with over a million inhabitants. The population was roughly divided between households of **samurai** (AC vol. 1, p. 110) and townspeople, the large samurai population created in part by the practice of **sankin kōtai**. During the early **Meiji period** (AC vol. 1, p. 81), in 1867, the city of Edo was renamed **Tokyo** (Eastern Capital) and became the official capital of Japan.

**M** Much of *Blade of the Immortal* takes place in Edo and *Lone Wolf and Cub* starts and ends in Edo.

## 江戸川乱歩 OLD FORM 江戶川亂步
## EDOGAWA RAMPO

1894–1965. Real name Hirai Tarō. Born in Nabari, **Mie Ken.** Edogawa Rampo was the first modern mystery writer in Japan. He published his first mystery story, "Nisen dōka," in 1923 in the magazine *Shin Seinen*. His pseudonym is based on the Japanese pronunciation of Edgar Allan Poe but also means "strolling by the Edogawa river." He quickly gained popularity and wrote many works in the prewar period. During WWII, detective stories were suppressed by the government, so he turned to scientific stories under the name of Komatsu Ryūnosuke. After the war he worked to promote mystery fiction and established the Detective Story Writers Club. In 1956 a collection of his short stories was published in English as *Japanese Tales of Mystery and Imagination*, which is still in print.

**A** Three of his stories are in anime form: A *Walker in the Attic, A Psychological Test,* and *A Red Room.*
• In the original Japanese version of the *Case Closed* (*Detective Conan*) series the main character takes his name, Edogawa Conan, from a combination of Edogawa Rampo and Conan Doyle.
**M** Lupin in *Lupin III* (vol. 12, p. 102) tells us to not be impressed with the technique he is using as he lifted it from an Edogawa Rampo novel.

## 江戸川区 OLD FORM 江戶川區
## EDOGAWA-KU

A ku of **Tokyo** bordered by **Tōkyō Wan** on the south, **Chiba Ken** (AC vol. 1, p. 18) to the east, **Kōtō-ku** and Sumida Ward on the west, and Katsushika Ward to the north. The Arakawa river marks the Western border, the Edogawa river the northeast border, and the Kyū-edogawa river the southeast and southern border. The Shin-nakagawa river cuts through the center and the **shuto kōsoku wangan sen** crosses the southern tip of this ward. Now mainly a residential and industrial area, this ward was once a farming district known for producing **kingyo** (AC vol. 1, p. 68).

**A** The Edogawa district of Tokyo of the future is featured in *Otaku no Video* (pt. 2, 6th anim. seq.).

## 江戸城
## EDOJŌ (EDO CASTLE)

The castle of **Edo,** sometimes called Chiyodajō. Built largely between 1603 and 1651 by order of **Tokugawa Ieyasu** and his heirs on the location of an older ruined castle. When completed this was the largest castle in the world, with an outer perimeter of 16 kilometers (10 miles) designed like a spiral. The defenses when the complex was completed included ninety-nine gates, twenty-one towers, and twenty-eight store-houses for weapons. In the center of this was the *honmaru* complex of buildings that was not only the administrative headquarters for the **bakufu** but also the residence of the **shōgun** (AC vol. 1, p. 123). During the 1860s much of the complex was burned, and when the Emperor Meiji moved to the new capital of **Tokyo** in 1868 the location of the *honmaru* became the new Imperial Palace with only the inner perimeter stonework and moats remaining of the castle. Today the remains of the castle occupy the center of **Chiyoda-ku**.

🅰 The castle is in *Dagger of Kamui* and *Samurai Deeper Kyo* (ep. 6 and 26).

Ⓜ Toward the end of *Lone Wolf and Cub* Ōgami visits the castle (vol. 26, p. 220–).

## 二式飛行艇 (NISHIKIHIKŌTEI)
## EMILY (AIRCRAFT)

 The U.S. military code name assigned to a four-engine flying boat. Built by Kawa-nishi, the Emily was used extensively throughout WWII. Its range was so great that it was used to supply distant bases and had to be heavily armed, since fighters could not fly support for such long distances. The Emily was was used in a nighttime bombing raid on the Honolulu area on March 4–5, 1942.

🅰 In the first *You're Under Arrest* episode, an Emily, identified specifically as a H8K2-type 2 flying boat, is part of a clue given by "The Fox." • In the *City Hunter 1* TV series (ep. 30) when Ryo breaks into a mansion he finds an interesting collection including one Emily.

**SOUNDS LIKE …**

O.K., let's talk Japanese homophones, words that sound the same but have different meanings. This is actually pretty important for anime and manga fans because not only is it easy to be confused about the meanings of certain words, but some writers love to pun.

Context will often tell us the intended meaning of a word, but not always. A better way to know which meaning is intended is to look at the kanji. For example, if someone says they would like some sake in a restaurant, we can assume they mean the drink, or can we? You see, the word pronounced "sake" also means salmon, which means that the customer may end up with a plate instead of a cup. Of course, one could be witty and order sake *to have with their sake.* Speaking of kanji, do we mean kanji 漢字 as in the written Chinese characters used by the Japanese, or do we mean an organizer of events, a kanji 幹事? Same pronunciation, different meanings, in other words, homophones.

Then there is the mistake made by many English-speaking writers for ages. Referring to the famous Mount Fuji by using the phrase Fuji-yama when the Japanese call it Fuji-san. Then there is the related error some non-Japanese make in thinking that the san 山 in Fuji-san is the same as the san さん used to refer to people, as in Takahashi-san. Actually, this latter san is the Japanese pronunciation of the Chinese word *shan*, which means mountain. Wait it gets better! The Japanese have two words that mean mountain, *yama* and *san*, and both words are written with the same kanji 山. So, instead of having two homophones with different kanji we have one kanji that can be pronounced in two different ways, with the same meaning!

How's that for cool?

## 蝦夷
## EMISHI

Also known as the Ezo and the Ebisu. The Emishi were the northern people not under the control of the emperor. Some scholars identify them with the **Ainu** (AC vol. 1, p. 3), while others hold that the term was used in ancient documents to refer to any group to the north not under the control of the **Yamato** emperors. The **Nihon Shoki** describes the Yamato conflicts with these people, who were not defeated until the 8th century. In fact, the term *seii tai* **shōgun** (AC vol. 1, p. 123) was first given to the generals in charge of subduing the Emishi.

 Emishi are mentioned by Jiko as he and Ashitaka leave the village in *Princess Mononoke,* Ashitaka's people are an unconquered group of Emishi.

### 円 OLD FORM 圓
### EN (YEN)

The current Japanese unit of currency. The Shinka Jōrei (New Currency Regulation) in the early **Meiji period** (AC vol. 1, p. 81), specifically 1871, was established to replace the rather complex currencies of the **Edo period** (AC vol. 1, p. 25). The en was divided into 100 *sen* and the *sen* into 10 *rin*. Due to an obsolete transliteration system that put a "y" in front of any word that began with an "e" sound the en is known in the West as the yen. The word en means round, a reference to the shape of the coins. Officially, at the time it was enacted the en was worth 1 Mexican dollar, a standard coin in Asian trade at the time. Early en were made of paper or in the form of coins. The coins varied in value with gold coins for 20, 10, and 5 en; then there were silver 50-sen coins, nickel 5-sen coins, and copper for smaller coins.

Today the yen is available both in coins worth 1, 5, 10, 50, 100, and 500 yen and in larger bills. The 5- and 50-yen coins have a hole in the middle. The 10,000- and 5,000-yen notes are made with brownish ink, and 1,000-yen notes are blue.

 In ep. 30 of the *Kimagure Orange Road* TV series, Umao and Ushiko give change for a 10,000-yen note using 1,000-yen notes and coins. In ep. 47, time-traveling Kyosuke gives a 500-yen coin to a waitress in 1982; this was before the coin's release date, so she thinks it is play money.

 In *Futaba-kun Change* (vol. 2, chapt.: "Futaba-kun Joins the Fight!!") an opponent tosses a 500-yen coin at Futaba as a taunt.

### 延喜
### ENGI ERA

The *nengō* or era of Japanese history from 901 to 923. Set during the **Heian period** (AC vol. 1, p. 44) this era is perhaps best known for the death in exile of **Sugawara no Michizane.**

 A story that takes place in the Engi era is told in *Zenki* (ep. 7).

### 譜代大名
### FUDAI DAIMYŌ

Fudai are hereditary servants or vassals, that is, families who were by tradition the vassals of another family. In the **Edo period** (AC vol. 1, p. 25) many powerful families that had been vassals of **Tokugawa Ieyasu** before the **Sekigahara no Tatakai** were recognized as **daimyō**; these are commonly referred to as fudai daimyō. The fudai daimyō were given the highest posts in the **bakufu.** Because their loyalty was beyond doubt, they often held less land than the **tozama daimyo,** as their loyalty did not have to be bought. They also grew in number from less than 80 to over 160 by the time of the **bakumatsu.**

🅜 In *Lone Wolf and Cub* (vol. 18, p. 11), the New Year's visit of the fudai daimyō to the **Edojō** is mentioned.

## ふぐチリ
## FUGU-CHIRI

A **chirinabe** made with **fugu** (AC vol. 1, p. 29).

🅐 In **Shimonoseki** many of the major cast in the *Urusei Yatsura* TV series (ep. 55, st. 78) have unfortunate symptoms after enjoying fugu-chiri served in a **donabe.**

## 富士五湖
## FUJI GOKO (FUJI FIVE LAKES)

A series of lakes located on the northern slope of **Fuji-san** (AC vol. 1, p. 30) created by valleys blocked by lava flows during eruptions. The lakes are named Yamanakako, Kawaguchiko, Saiko, Shōjiko, and Motosuko.

🅐 The lakes are mentioned in *Neon Genesis Evangelion* (ep. 12) and *Moldiver* (ep. 5).

## 深川
## FUKAGAWA

A district in the southeast (*tatsumi*) of **Edo.** During the **Edo period** (AC vol. 1, p. 25) this area was famous for its lumberyards, teahouses (that served more than tea), places to eat, and lively festivals. It also was a significant seaport for shipping products to and from other parts of Japan. This area was also known for its frequent floods due to its low elevation and the nearby Tonegawa river. In the **Meiji period** (AC vol. 1, p. 81) modern factories were built in much of the area. In the **Kantō Daishinsai** and the air raids of WWII, the area was heavily burned. Today many of the factories are gone and their location occupied by office buildings and apartments. There have been local attempts to preserve older

traditions at festivals and in the Fukugawa Edo Folk Museum. One of the most famous inhabitants of this part of Edo was the poet **Bashō.**

🅜 Fukagawa is mentioned in *Lone Wolf and Cub* (vol. 21, p. 182). • Manji mentions a *tatsumi* **geisha** (AC vol. 1, p. 33) house in Fukagawa as he lies wounded at the end of the Conquest section of *Blade of the Immortal: Blood of a Thousand.* • Fukagawa is again mentioned in *Blade of the Immortal: Dreamsong* Part 2, this time by a geisha who tells a customer that if he wants physical satisfaction he had better go to Fukagawa.

## 福島県 OLD FORM 福島縣
### FUKUSHIMA KEN

Fukushima Prefecture. Located in northern **Honshu** (AC vol. 1, p. 47) in the Tōhoku region on the Pacific coast. Fukushima is an agricultural area with many mountains, hot summers, and cold winters. It includes major routes between the northern prefectures and central Honshu.

🅐 Yamayoshi from the Fukushima Prefecture Association is seen in *Rurouni Kenshin* (TV ep. 31).

🅜 That **Aizu Han** is part of present-day Fukushima Ken is noted in *Rurouni Kenshin* (vol. 3, p. 76).

*Ikumatsu plays the distinctively shaped **gekkin** in* SAMURAI X TRUST AND BETRAYAL.

## 蝦蟇の油
### GAMA NO ABURA (TOAD OIL)

Toad oil. A medicine used for treating skin conditions. Sellers, with great exaggeration, would often claim it had been extracted from toad sweat in ridiculously complex ways, including placing a toad in a box lined with mirrors so it would sweat at the sight of its own reflection.

🅐 The character Ogawa Heizo was a seller of gama no abura in the *Rurouni Kenshin* TV series (ep. 77). • In *Tenchi Universe* (ep. 7), Ryoko tries to sell such a medicine produced from a very unusual creature.

🅜 In *GTO* vol. 8 (ch. 68) three girls make a magic potion to use on Onizuka. One of the ingredients is toad oil from a toad made to sweat by looking into a mirror.

## 月琴
### GEKKIN (MOON LUTE)

A round, stringed instrument, often translated as "moon lute." Used to play popular tunes. This instrument originated in China and variants of it are found in many parts of East Asia.

🅐 **Ikumatsu** holds one of these while Katsura Kogorō (that is, **Kido Takayoshi**) and Katagai talk in *Samurai X: Trust and Betrayal*.

## 元服
### GENPUKU (BOY'S COMING OF AGE CEREMONY)

A ceremony once performed among the higher classes to signify that a boy was permitted to assume adult dress and hairstyle. There was no set age for this. Originally it was performed when the boy reached a certain height—136 centimeters (4.5 feet)—usually between the ages of ten and sixteen. There was a similar ceremony for girls called *mayu-harai* in which their eyebrows were shaved or plucked.

Today there is the national holiday **Seijin no Hi** for all new adults.

◪ In the *The Legend of the Dog Warriors The Hakkenden* (ep. 2) Shino's father cut his hair and arranges it in an adult style while telling him a tale of the family obligation to guard a special sword.

## 岐阜県 OLD FORM 岐阜縣
## GIFU KEN

A prefecture in central **Honshu** (AC vol. 1, p. 47) in the **Tōkai chihō**. The terrain is mainly mountainous, with the capital, Gifu City, occupying the southern plain. Lumber is a major natural resource, and the industrial base includes textiles, clothing, paper, ceramics, and transportation equipment. Gifu is bordered by Toyama Ken, Nagano Ken, **Aichi Ken** (AC vol. 1, p. 3), **Mie Ken**, Shiga Ken, Fukui Ken, and Ishikawa Ken. In 1876 it was formed by the merger of Hida and Mino provinces. The famous **Sekigahara no Tatakai** took place in southern Gifu Ken. ◪ That the Lupin III anime *Rupan III Fuma Conspiracy* takes place in Gifu is indicated by the No Trespassing sign on the old bridge having been posted by the Gifu police. • A sequence in *Blue Seed* (ep. 26) takes place in Gifu Ken as does *Geobreeders: Breakthrough*.

## 祇園祭
## GION MATSURI (GION FESTIVAL)

There are several Gion **matsuri** (AC vol. 1, p. 81) in various parts of Japan. The best known is that of the Yasaka **Jinja** (AC vol. 1, p. 54) in **Kyoto** (AC vol. 1, p. 77). The Kyoto festival originated in 869 as a worship service to pray for the end to an epidemic. Tall spears (*hoko*), sixty-six of them, were erected to represent the provinces of Japan as part of this service. In the **Edo period** (AC vol. 1, p. 25), the festival took on its present form with large floats on wheels, also called *hoko*, with tall spires taking the place of the spears. The *hoko* are structures about two stories tall often with performers inside them. The ones used today weigh about twelve tons. There are also smaller floats called *yama* (mountain),

which weigh about 1.5 tons. The matsuri lasts for the entire month of July with the parade of *hoko* and *yama* taking place on the 17th, preceded by a lottery to determine the lead float. ◪ We see part of the Gion Matsuri, with several kinds of floats, in *Samurai X: Trust and Betrayal*.

## ごぼう OR 牛蒡
## GOBŌ (BURDOCK)

Burdock root. *Arctium lappa*. Japan is the only country where burdock is eaten. The Chinese use it as a medicine. The roots are around a meter long and three centimeters thick, giving gobō the appearance of a straight stick. The root is washed and usually not peeled, as the skin has much of the flavor. To prepare it for cooking, it is shaved or cut into strips that are placed in water, sometimes with some vinegar to reduce the bitterness. Boiling is a common way to cook it. A common use for gobō is in **kinpira-gobō**. ◪ Megumi gives Akito a stamina drink made from

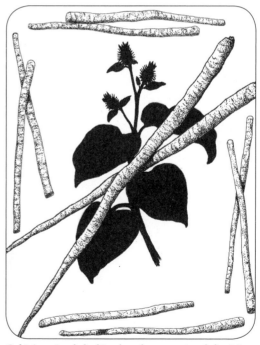

*Gobō is a simple-looking long brown root; ask for it in your local Asian market.*

23

dokudami, sanshō, shiitake, burdock, lotus root (renkon), snapping turtle (suppon), and pit viper blood, plus a few other ingredients in *Martian Successor Nadesico* (ep. 10). • At a yatai (AC vol. 1, p. 147), Goto orders burdock root and daikon (AC vol. 1, p. 21) in *Patlabor the TV Series* (ep. 14). • While translated simply as "burdock" in the beginning of episode 4 of *Rurouni Kenshin*, what Kenshin actually says is kinpira-gobō.

## 極楽 OLD FORM 極樂
## GOKURAKU (WESTERN PURE LAND)

The Western Pure Land of Amitābha Buddha, often simply translated as Paradise. Those desiring to be reborn there often practice nenbutsu (AC vol. 1, p. 92) chanting.

Ⓜ In *Video Girl Ai*, Gokuraku is the name of the video store where Yota rents Ai's tape.

Ⓐ In *Ranma 1/2 Anything Goes Martial Arts* (ep. 22), when Ranma and Happosai go to a very fancy sentō (AC vol. 1, p. 115) named Gokuraku, Happosai brings along some toys, including a floating model of the *Yamato* battleship.

## 五稜郭の戦い OLD FORM 五稜郭の戰い
## GORYŌKAKU NO TATAKAI (BATTLE OF GORYŌKAKU).

Fought at the fortress Goryōkaku located in Hakodate between June 20 and 27, 1869. This battle is considered to be the last of the Boshin Sensō.

Ⓐ The battle of Goryōkaku is seen in *Dagger of Kamui*.

## グリーンガム
## GREEN GUM

A brand of mint-flavored chewing gum made by Lotte Co, Ltd. It's pretty good; I'm chewing a stick of it as I type this.

Ⓐ In *Fushigi Yūgi* (eps. 3 and 4) we see Miaka chew Green Gum and later Tamahome attempts to auction some off as a rare item to a crowd.

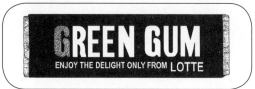

With such a simple design, **Green Gum** is easy to spot in Asian markets.

## 群馬県 OLD FORM 群馬縣
## GUNMA KEN

A prefecture in central Honshu (AC vol. 1, p. 47) bordered by Fukushima Ken, Tochigi Ken, and Saitama, Niigata, and Nagano prefectures. Gunma Prefecture is mainly mountainous except for where the Kantō Plain reaches into the southeast. Traditionally, it is an agricultural and textile area with a growing manufacturing industry, as well as a tourist industry for people drawn to the mountains and hot springs.

Ⓐ "Go North SV2" in *Patlabor Original Series* (ep. 7) takes place in Gunma Prefecture. • Asamayama (AC vol. 1, p. 7) in Gunma Prefecture erupts in *Blue Seed* (ep. 24). • Tomoko does a daikon (AC vol. 1, p. 21) commercial there in *GTO* (ep. 27).

Ⓜ Kusanami remembers going to Gunma Prefecture to recruit Don in *Wild 7* (vol. 5, p. 10). • Jan received his cooking instruction from his grandfather in their home in Gunma Prefecture in *Iron Wok Jan* (vol. 1, p. 102).

## 牛鍋
## GYŪNABE (BEEF HOT POT)

Often translated as beef hot pot or just hot pot. Gyūnabe is actually an old name for sukiyaki (AC vol. 1, p. 126). I am told that gyūnabe was the dish's old name in the area around Tokyo, while sukiyaki was used in the Kansai area and came to predominate.

Ⓜ In *Rurouni Kenshin* (TV ep. 2 and vol. 1, p. 128) Akabeko is the favorite beef hot pot (gyūnabe) restaurant of the Kenshin-gumi.

# H

of chores for her, including going all the way to Hachiōji for **rāmen** (AC vol. 1, p. 105) in *GTO* (vol. 8, ch. 61).

## 萩 [市]
### HAGI

Castle town for the **Chōshū Han** in the **Edo period** (AC vol. 1, p. 25) in present-day **Yamaguchi Ken** on the **Nihonkai** (Sea of Japan). Hagi was the birthplace of **Kido Takayoshi** and the location of the home and school of **Yoshida Shōin,** which still stands. Today Hagi is known for producing **mikan** (AC vol. 1, p. 82) and seafood.

**A** There is mention of a plot to take the emperor to Hagi in *Samurai X: Trust and Betrayal* and later there is a report on the political climate there.

## 廃刀令
### HAITŌREI

The Meiji government edict issued in March 1876 forbidding the wearing of swords. This was one of several edicts intended to do away with the old symbols of hereditary status that displeased many former **samurai** (AC vol. 1, p. 110).

**M** This edict is mentioned in *Rurouni Kenshin* (TV ep. 1 and vol. 1, p. 9), and of course Kenshin gets into trouble for carrying his reverse-bladed sword on more than one occasion.

## 函館 [市] OLD FORM 凾館 OR 箱館
### HAKODATE

A city located in southwest **Hokkaidō** (AC vol. 1, p. 46) and connected to the city of Aomori on the island of **Honshu** (AC vol. 1, p. 47) by a rail line through the Seikan tunnel. Originally a castle town dating from the 15th century, the name means "box castle." In 1855 it became a supply port for foreign ships and in 1859 was opened to foreign trade. In 1869 the Battle of Goryōkaku (**Goryōkaku no Tatakai**), also known as the Battle of Hakodate, was fought there.

## 八幡
### HACHIMAN

A very popular **kami** (AC vol. 1, p. 59) associated with archery, war, and the protection of the community. Popularly, he is considered to be the fifteenth emperor, Ōjin. Actually, the Iwashimizu Hachimangū in **Kyoto** (AC vol. 1, p. 77) enshrines Ōjin, his wife (often referred to as Himegami or Hime Ōkami), and mother, empress Jingū (deified as Okinagatarashi-hime no Mikoto), who became pregnant while leading an invasion of Korea in the 2nd century. The name Hachiman possibly means eight flags or eight fields, and the number eight is often associated with Hachiman. Hachiman is also seen as a protector of Buddhism.

**A** A Hachiman shrine is in the *Rurouni Kenshin* TV series (ep. 13). • Lupin has a meeting with some Fuma ninja at a Hachiman shrine in *Lupin the 3rd Royal Scramble* ("The Riddle of Tsukikage Castle").

## 八王子 [市]
### HACHIŌJI

A city located in the southwestern part of **Tokyo.** During the **Edo period** (AC vol. 1, p. 25), Hachiōji was a **shukuba machi** and silk market. Silk products are still part of the local industry, as is electronics. Several universities relocated to Hachiōji from central Tokyo, and today it has become a significant residential area.

**M** In the *Patlabor* stories, Hachiōji is the location of a major plant for Shinohara Heavy Industries and often is mentioned or seen.

**M** Urumi blackmails Onizuka into doing all sorts

The Hakodate administrative office and the Battle of Goryōkaku are seen in *Dagger of Kamui.*

## 蛤御門の変 OLD FORM 蛤御門の變
## HAMAGURI GOMON NO HEN

Also known as the Kinmon Incident or the Palace Gate Incident. In August 1864, just weeks after the **Ikedaya Jiken,** troops from the **Chōshū Han** attempted to force their way into **Kyoto** (AC vol. 1, p. 77), demanding pardons for exiled anti-**bakufu** nobles. The resulting battle resulted in a three-day-long fire that damaged a large part of Kyoto, including the Chōshū domain headquarters.

 The burning of Kyoto is seen in *Samurai X: Trust and Betrayal.*

## 藩
## HAN (DAIMYŌ DOMAIN)

The land and administrative system of a **daimyō.** In the **Edo period** (AC vol. 1, p. 25) domains were given by the **shōgun** (AC vol. 1, p. 123) to certain clans to administer. The term *han* was used in common speech from the 18th century and officially used in the early **Meiji period** (AC vol. 1, p. 81). The defining characteristic of a domain is that it produce at least 10,000 **koku** of rice per year. A domain did not have to be a single piece of territory but could be a series of areas with no direct connection. Domains were usually known by the name of their castle town rather than by that of the clan that held them.

 Domains that show up in some anime and manga include the **Chōshū Han, Mito Han,** and the **Satsuma Han.**

## はんぺん OR 半片 OR 半平
## HANPEN (FISH PASTE CAKE)

Hanpen is made by mixing white fish or shark meat with **yamanoimo** into a paste, placing it in molds, and boiling or steam-

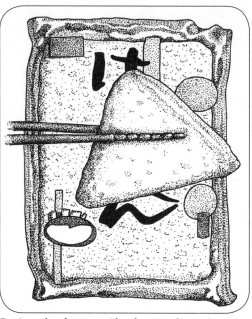

*Don't confuse **hanpen** with tofu, on a plate or in a package at the store, especially if you have a fish allergy.*

ing it until it hardens to a firm but soft texture. It is used in soup and is a common ingredient in **oden** (AC vol. 1, p. 98).

 Oji orders hanpen fish cake at a **yatai** (AC vol. 1, p. 147) in *The Legend of Black Heaven* (ep. 1).

 Babo orders another serving of hanpen at a yatai serving oden in *Caravan Kidd* (vol. 2, p. 142).

## はたはた OR 鰰
## HATAHATA (SANDFISH)

A fish found in the **Nihonkai,** especially near the prefectures of Akita and Yamagata. The meat is white and fatty and is often used in **sushi** (AC vol. 1, p. 128) and **tenpura.** It is also preserved by drying.

 Goto requests that Izumi and Shinohara bring him back hatahata as a **miyage** (AC vol. 1, p. 86) of their trip to **Sakata** in *Patlabor the TV Series* (ep. 9).

## 旗本
## HATAMOTO (BANNERMEN)

This term is often translated as "standard bearer" or "banner knight." Originally, a hatamoto was a **samurai** (AC vol. 1, p. 110) who was a personal guard of a military commander. During the **Edo period** (AC vol. 1, p. 25) hatamoto became a special title for high-ranking samurai who served the **bakufu.** In **Edo** they guarded the **Edojō** of the **shōgun** (AC vol. 1, p. 123) and performed many powerful administrative and investigative roles that could take them throughout Japan. **Tokugawa** (AC vol. 1, p. 137) hatamoto were granted estates or paid a salary directly from the shōgun's warehouses depending on their duties. They had a reputation for loyalty to the shōgun and great pride in their position, which at times led to arrogance and conflict. One of the reason for their loyalty was that a hatamoto could chose which one of his sons would inherit his title, which usually meant the most loyal and competent son. The position of hatamoto was not always hereditary; lower-ranking samurai could be promoted if their actions merited such a reward, and the rank could be revoked. Interestingly, there was once a non-Japanese hatamoto. William Adams, a shipwrecked navigator, so impressed **Tokugawa Ieyasu** that he was given this rank, and his half-Japanese son, Joseph, inherited the rank after William died.

Ⓜ In *Blade of the Immortal: Blood of a Thousand* someone refers to Manji as a hatamoto killer.

## 変態 FORMAL 變態
## HENTAI

 Usually translated as perverted or sexually explicit. The word has a much more complex meaning in Japanese, however. It can mean metamorphosis, weird, anomalous, or abnormal. Most of the time that you'll see or hear the term in anime or in fan circles, where it takes on its simplified meaning of perverted. Other ways of expressing this word include writing it with the capital letter H (pronounced by the Japanese as "etchi"). Etchi is occasionally used to mean mildly perverted or to refer to a sexual situation. English-speaking fans have taken to using the word as an adjective in ways the Japanese do not, as in refering to erotic anime as "hentai anime."

Ⓐ Hentai is listed as part of the research done under the umbrella of a Science Fiction Club by a person interviewed in *Otaku no Video* (pt. 1, 1st interview). • It is translated as fetish in *Kimagure Orange Road* (TV ep. 1). • Gradeschooler Naota is repeatedly called etchi by very hyper classmate after a girl spots a mark on his neck in *FLCL* (ep. 1). • Perhaps the best use of hentai is in the first episode of *Ranma 1/2* after Akane discovers Ranma's secret. Here there is wordplay on transformation and perverse situations.

## 日比谷
## HIBIYA

Originally an inlet of **Tōkyō Wan** in the **Edo period** (AC vol. 1, p.), it was near the southeast walls of the **Edojō**. After the **bakufu** fell, the buildings on the site were cleared and it became part of a huge parade ground for the military. In 1903, the first Western-style park in Japan opened on the site. It quickly became a popular place for political rallies, amorous couples, and **nozoki.** The **Masakado-zuka** is near this area.

Ⓐ In *Samurai Deeper Kyo* (ep. 6) Hibiya has yet to be filled in.

Ⓜ The Hibiya intersection is shown in *Adolf: 1945 and All That Remains* (p. 59). • A **Takarazuka Kagekidan** (AC vol. 1, p. 131) performance is seen at the "Hibiya musical theater" in *Rumic Theater: One or Double* (p. 167). • In the future world of *Astro Boy* (vol. 16, p. 18), the Ministry of Construction is located in Hibiya.

## 比叡山
## HIEIZAN (MOUNT HIEI)

A mountain northeast of **Kyoto** (AC vol. 1, p. 77), north of **Ōtsu,** and west of **Biwako.** Hieizan is famous for its **Buddhist** (AC vol. 1, p. 15) monasteries and temples. The Buddhist teacher Saichō left the capital of **Nara** and moved to the mountain in 785 to practice meditation and study sacred texts. Quickly his spiritual reputation grew and others joined him, resulting in a formal monastery being founded there in 788. The location of the mountain, to the northeast of the newer capital of Kyoto with its monasteries, makes it a barrier against the influences of the Kimon or Demon's Gate, a most inauspicious geomantic direction.

At its height, there were something like 3,000 buildings on the mountain. But Hieizan was also a source of problems; the monks became arrogant at times, even charging into Kyoto and intimidating the emperor, as described in the **Heike Monogatari** (AC vol. 1, p. 44), or attacking other monasteries. Eventually the monks sided against **Oda Nobunaga,** who in 1571 sent 25,000 troops against the mountain and destroyed everything, slaughtering everyone they could find. **Toyotomi Hideyoshi** (AC vol. 1, p. 140) and **Tokugawa Ieyasu** later allowed the monasteries to return to the mountain.

**A** In *Samurai X: Trust and Betrayal* Tomoe and Kenshin visit a small Buddhist shrine with a stone carving on a lower slope of Hieizan.

## 土方歳三
## HIJIKATA TOSHIZŌ

A master swordsman and, with **Kondō Isami,** originally from Musashi Province, one of the **Shinsengumi** leaders in **Kyoto** (AC vol. 1, p. 77). Even after the **Meiji period** (AC vol. 1, p. 81) began he continued to fight against the new government, eventually retreating to **Hokkaidō** (AC vol. 1, p. 46), until his death in battle.
**A** We see Hijikata in *Samurai X: Trust and Betrayal* and in *Peacemaker.*

## 姫路城 OLD FORM 姫路城
## HIMEJIJŌ (HIMEJI CASTLE)

A castle built in the 14th century by Akamatsu Sadanori in Himeji, a town in the province of Harima. Later, the Kodera family controlled it, and in 1580 **Oda Nobunaga** granted it to **Toyotomi Hideyoshi** (AC vol. 1, p. 140), who then expanded it. **Ikeda Terumasa** took control of the castle after the **Sekigahara no Tatakai** and rebuilt in it 1608. The tallest part is located on a 45-meter (148-foot) hill. After WWII it was restored with the walls painted white.
**A** Himeji Castle is seen in the *Urusei Yatsura* (TV ep. 55, st. 78).
**M** Himeji Castle is also seen in *Vagabond* (vol. 2, ch. 12).

## ヒレカツ
## HIREKATSU (FRIED PORK FILET)

A fried pork filet.
**A** A nervous Ota chooses the hirekatsu in his typically gentle manner in *Patlabor the TV Series* (ep. 27, "A Voice in the Darkness").

## 北辰一刀流
## HOKUSHIN ITTŌ RYŪ

A late **Edo period** (AC vol. 1, p. 25) **kenjutsu** school founded by Chiba Shūsaku Narimasa. While Hokushin Ittō Ryū emphasized the spiritual aspects of martial arts, it also maintained the importance of competition. This **ryū** became one of the most famous of its time. Students use long gloves, called *uchi-kote* or *oni-kode*, and a straight **bokken** (AC vol. 1, p. 12) during training. Competitions were held against opponents, at times women, using wooden bladed **naginata** (AC vol. 1, p. 91).
**A** Some practitioners of Hokushin Ittō Ryū fight Kenshin in *Samurai X: Trust and Betrayal.*
**M** That **Sakamoto Ryōma** is a master of the Hokushin school of fighting is mentioned in *Vanity Angel* (issue 6).

**28**

The **hōzuki**, a simple plant, here held by a Japanese beauty in SAMURAI X TRUST AND BETRAYAL.

## 酸漿
## HŌZUKI (CHINESE-LANTERN PLANT)

*Physalis alkekengi*. Also called ground cherry, Chinese-lantern plant, and winter cherry. This attractive perennial has a bright red berry inside the "lantern," which traditionally has been made into a girl's toy when emptied of seeds and placed in the mouth to make noises. Tea made from the hōzuki also has medicinal properties. Each July **Sensōji** (AC vol. 1, p. 114) in **Tokyo** holds the **hōzuki ichi.**

🅰 Tomoe holds hōzuki in Kiyosato's memory of her in *Samurai X: Trust and Betrayal.* • In the fourth episode of the original *Sakura Wars* OVA series. • In *Blue Seed* (ep. 1) we hear that Orochi-no-Orochi had eyes as red as ground cherries.

Ⓜ Hōzuki are seen during the **Bon** (AC vol. 1, p. 12) festivities in *Maison Ikkoku* (vol. 3, p. 122). • Hōzuki play a role in chapter 36 of *Lone Wolf and Cub* (vol. 7).

## 酸漿市
## HŌZUKI ICHI (CHINESE-LANTERN PLANT MARKET)

A fair held at **Sensōji** (AC vol. 1, p. 114) in **Tokyo** each July 9–10 with hundreds of stalls selling **hōzuki** in hanging pots. Other items such as **bonsai** (AC vol. 1, p. 13)

lanterns, small shrines, and cages are sold there. During the **Edo period** (AC vol. 1, p. 25) this fair was also a popular place to buy tea whisks, teethblackening cosmetics, and ears of corn as a charm against lightning.

🅰 In Kiyosato's memory of Tomoe in *Samurai X: Trust and Betrayal* we see the **Kaminarimon** (AC vol. 1, p. 60) at **Sensōji** (AC vol. 1, p. 114) and scenes from the hōzuki ichi.

## 兵庫県 OLD FORM 兵庫縣
## HYŌGO KEN

Hyōgo Prefecture, spanning central **Honshu** (AC vol. 1, p. 47) from the **Nihonkai** on the north to the **Seto Naikai** in the south. To the northeast and east is Kyoto Prefecture, to the east is Osaka Prefecture, and to the west are Tottori Ken and **Okayama Ken.** The capital of the prefecture is **Kōbe.**

Ⓜ Hyōgo Prefecture is the location of a significant murder in *Adolf: A Tale of the Twentieth Century* (p. 27). • The prefectural police have to deal with **yakuza** (AC vol. 1, p. 146) in *Sanctuary* vol. 6 (p. 8).

## 井伊直弼
## II NAOSUKE

1815–60. The **daimyō** of the Hikone Han. He held the title of great elder (Tairō) for the Tokugawa **bakufu,** he was a sup-

*In SAMURAI X TRUST AND BETRAYAL **ikebana** is shown to be a subtle art, far more than just a few plants in a vase.*

porter of the **Nichibei Washin Jōyaku** and during 1858 signed the **Nichibei Shūkō Tsūshō Jōyaku** (Harris Treaty) with the United States without approval of the emperor. He also tried to arrange a marriage between the **shōgun** (AC vol. 1, p. 123) and the imperial princess Kazunomiya as part of what is known as the *kōbu gattai* (union of court and bakufu) movement. His political maneuvers placed him in conflict with the **Mito Han.** To stifle opposition to this and other actions he instituted the **Ansei no Taigoku,** which did not end until he was assassinated. His death took place at the hands of **samurai** (AC vol. 1, p. 110) from the Mito and **Satsuma** domains as he was exiting the **Edojō** by the Sakuradamon gate on a cold morning in March 1860.
Ii Naosuke is mentioned by Miaka as she studies in *Fushigi Yūgi* (ep. 17 and vol. 5, p. 9).

## 生け花
## IKEBANA (FLOWER ARRANGING)

A literal translation is "keeping flowers alive." Introduced into Japan in the early 7th century with **Buddhism** (AC vol. 1, p. 15), which has a practice of offering flowers at altars. Starting in the 15th century ikebana became a separate art form first in **Kyoto** (AC vol. 1, p. 77) among the aristocracy; by the late 17th

century ikebana had grown in popularity among the merchant classes.
Employees of the **ryokan** (AC vol. 1, p. 107) arrange flowers in *Samurai X: Trust and Betrayal*.
• Ayeka and Sasami work on ikebana for the **Bon** (AC vol. 1, p. 12) altar in *Tenchi The Movie 2: The Daughter of Darkness.*

## 池田輝政
## IKEDA TERUMASA

1564–1613. A **samurai** (AC vol. 1, p. 110) who served **Oda Nobunaga** and **Toyotomi Hideyoshi** (AC vol. 1, p. 140), who became the **daimyō** of Ōgaki Castle in Mino upon the deaths of his father and older brother in the Komaki Nagakute Campaign. Ikeda Terumasa backed **Tokugawa Ieyasu** at the **Sekigahara no Tatakai** and was given the province of Harima as a reward where he renovated **Himejijō.**
Ikeda Terumasa is mentioned in *Vagabond* (vol. 2, ch. 14).

## 池田屋事件
## IKEDAYA JIKEN

An attack in July 1864 by the **Shinsengumi,** under the leadership of **Kondō Isami,** on a meeting of **shishi** plotting against the **bakufu** held in a **Kyoto** (AC vol. 1, p. 77) **ryokan** (AC vol. 1, p. 107) named Ikedaya. Of the activists at the meeting eight died, four were wounded, and twenty were arrested. Katsura Kogorō (**Kido Takayoshi**), who was supposed to attend, missed the event because he was tricked by his lover, the **geisha** (AC vol. 1, p. 33) **Ikumatsu.** After this attack took place the **Chōshū Han** moderates changed their views, joined with the shishi, and attempted to capture Kyoto by a military action that came to be known as the **Hamaguri Gomon no Hen.**
The attack on the Ikedaya is seen in *Samurai X: Trust and Betrayal.*

## 一揆
## IKKI (PEASANT REVOLT)

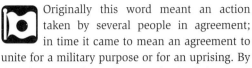 Originally this word meant an action taken by several people in agreement; in time it came to mean an agreement to unite for a military purpose or for an uprising. By the **Edo period** (AC vol. 1, p. 25) it had also come to mean any kind of peasant revolt.

🅐 The ikki known as the **Shimabara no Ran** is in *Ninja Resurrection* (ep. 1).

Ⓜ The aftermath of a peasant revolt is seen in *Lone Wolf and Cub* (vol. 1, p. 188).

## 幾松
## IKUMATSU

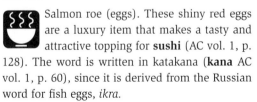 A **Kyoto** (AC vol. 1, p. 77) **geisha** (AC vol. 1, p. 33). When Katsura Kogorō (**Kido Takayoshi**) first met her, he was so impressed that he bought her contract and set her free. She then continued to work as a geisha and, after he trained her on the current political situation, as his spy. After the **Hamaguri Gomon no Hen** they hid together at a **ryokan** (AC vol. 1, p. 107) called Yoshidaya. She was Katsura Kogorō's lover and later his wife.

🅐 We see her early in *Samurai X: Trust and Betrayal*, but her name is not spoken until about midway through the show.

## イクラ
## IKURA

Salmon roe (eggs). These shiny red eggs are a luxury item that makes a tasty and attractive topping for **sushi** (AC vol. 1, p. 128). The word is written in katakana (**kana** AC vol. 1, p. 60), since it is derived from the Russian word for fish eggs, *ikra*.

🅐 Ikura is mentioned in *Kimagure Orange Road* (TV ep. 38). It is mentioned in the opening notes and later by a very hungry Kaori in *City Hunter 3* (ep. 1). Salmon roe, ark shell (**akagai**), and sweet shrimp are some of the items Onizuka orders at an expensive sushi place in *GTO* (ep. 18).

*In FLCL, we see Naota drinking from an "in" vitamin drink packet. Kids would not normally choose this as a beverage.*

© 1999 GAINAX / KGI

## IN-シリーズ
## IN SHIRĪZU

The *"in* series." A product line of supplement drinks from Morinaga and Co. in cooperation with the American company Weider Nutrition International. Most are sold in soft foil and plastic drink packets, but a few are also available in plastic bottles. All have the word *in* printed prominently on the package, with the specific version in smaller colored letters. The specific product lines and their color codings are: "Multivitamin" in green letters, "Diet" in pink letters, "Beauty" in tan letters, "Protein" in red letters, and "Energy" in blue letters.

🅐 In *FLCL*, we see the green package with the older design for "Vitamin" before it was changed to "Multivitamin."

## 井の頭恩賜公園
## INOKASHIRA ONSHI KŌEN

Also called Inokashira Kōen, Inokashira Park (Well-Head Park). A park built around an **Edo period** (AC vol. 1, p. 25) pond. The pond was constructed as part of the water supply system for the city of **Edo**. The present day park is located in both **Mitaka** and **Musashino-shi**. The park is quite substantial,

*Big, hairy, and short tempered, **inoshishi** are not to be trifled with, especially in RANMA 1/2.*

with a wooded area, a track, a shrine to **Benten** (AC vol. 1, p. 10), and a large section called the Nature Culture Park, which includes a zoo, botanical gardens, and art gallery. In October 2001, the Ghibli Museum, devoted to animation, especially the work of Studio Ghibli, opened in this park.

Ⓜ Inokashira Park and the pond appear in *GTO* (ep. 1; vol. 1, p. 134).

## 猪 OLD FORM 猪 FORMAL 猪
## INOSHISHI (WILD BOAR)

Feared in Japan as a dangerous animal, boars damage farm crops and occasionally attack people. Snakes are said to be afraid of boars, which feed on them. Travelers, if they were afraid of snakes, would sing songs that threatened to tell the boars where the snakes were.

Ⓜ A wild boar is seen trashing a village in *Ranma 1/2* (Manga vol. 1, p. 202, TV ep. 7).

## 入谷
## IRIYA

An old-fashioned neighborhood located in north central **Taitō-ku** in **Tokyo** between the Kan-eiji Cemetery and **Asakusa** (AC vol. 1, p. 6). It is served by Iriya Station, which is on the **Hibiya** Line.

Ⓐ In the *Patlabor Original Series* (ep. 1) we learn that Gotoh was born in Iriya.

## いろは
## IROHA

The rudiments, the basics. It also represents the traditional arrangement of the **kana** (AC vol. 1, p. 60) syllables, so a good translation of this meaning is simply "the ABCs."

Ⓐ In the first episode of the *Ranma 1/2* TV series there is a framed wall scroll with iroha written on it just below the **kamidana** (AC vol. 1, p. 60) in the Tendo **dōjō** (AC vol. 1, p. 23).

## 石田三成
## ISHIDA MITSUNARI

1560–1600. As a young man he was an attendant of **Toyotomi Hideyoshi** (AC vol. 1, p. 140), who was impressed with his skills in **cha-no-yu** (AC vol. 1, p. 17). With the unification of Japan he became a major figure in Hideyoshi's administration, including taking part in the invasion of Korea. After the death of Hideyoshi, he supported the Toyotomi clan, which led to his opposition to **Tokugawa Ieyasu** and eventually the battle known as **Sekigahara no Tatakai,** after which Mitsunari was captured and executed.

Ⓐ Ishida Mitsunari's role in the Sekigahara no Tatakai is mentioned in the beginning of *Ninja Resurrection* (ep. 1 "Revenge of Jubei"). • Ishida Mitsunari is mentioned by Okuni in *Samurai Deeper Kyo* (ep. 2).

Ⓜ Ōgami recounts the story that Ishida Mitsunari refused a persimmon (**kaki**) before his execution on the grounds that it would upset his stomach, in *Lone Wolf and Cub* (vol. 25, p. 16).

## 石川啄木
## ISHIKAWA TAKUBOKU

1886–1912. A writer well known for his poetry. Born in **Iwate Ken,** his life was one of poverty and separation from his family as he had to take jobs in distant cities. He continued to experiment in his writing and developed, as well as promoted, a poetic style that emphasized daily life written in simple language. He, his wife, and children contracted **kekkaku** and he died at age twenty-six.

🅐 In *Fushigi Yūgi* (ep. 42) we hear that **Morioka** is famous for Ishikawa Takuboku and **Miyazawa Kenji** (AC vol. 1, p. 86).

## 板垣退助
## ITAGAKI TAISUKE

1837–1919. Born a **samurai** (AC vol. 1, p. 110) of **Tosa Han** (AC vol. 1, p. 110), he was appointed to an official position by his **daimyō**. In 1861 he moved to **Edo** to administer the accounts and the military duties in the domain residence. He met with **Saigō Takamori** (AC vol. 1, p. 107) and agreed to oppose the **bakufu** leading Tosa troops in the **Boshin Sensō**. In 1869 he accepted a government office, which he resigned from in 1873 in protest of the government's refusal to invade Korea. He became a critic of governmental abuses and argued for greater representation of the citizens, becoming a leader of the Freedom and People's Rights Movement (Jiyū Minken Undō). In 1875, government concessions led him to again accept political office, but he would resign in protest of the centralization of power in the Grand Council of State (Dajōkan). In 1881 he assisted in the formation of the first organized political party in Japan, the Liberal Party (Jiyūtō). In 1884 the party would disband due to factionalism and government repression. Itagaki twice held the position of home minister in the 1890s before resigning from politics.

🅜 Itagaki Taisuke is mentioned by some drunken, rowdy followers in *Rurouni Kenshin* (TV ep. 4 and vol. 1, p. 129).

## 岩手県 OLD FORM 岩手縣
## IWATE KEN

A prefecture located in northern **Honshu** (AC vol. 1, p. 47) bordered by **Miyagi Ken** (AC vol. 1, p. 86), Aomori and Akita prefectures, and the Pacific Ocean. Rice farming and livestock are major agricultural activities. Forestry and fishing also add to the economy, as does some small manufacturing. The capital is **Morioka.**

🅐 We find out that Ota was born in Iwate Ken in *Patlabor the TV Series* (ep. 18). • In the *Lupin the 3rd Royal Scramble* episode called "Khan Job," we find out that Hiraizumi in Iwate Prefecture is where Goemon's ancestral grave is and where **Minamoto no Yoshitsune** (AC vol. 1, p. 84) died. • In *Fushigi Yūgi* (ep. 38) Miaka's brother takes the **Shinkansen** (AC vol. 1, p. 120) to Morioka to investigate some events that took place in Iwate Prefecture.

## いざかや OR 居酒屋
## IZAKAYA (SMALL TAVERNS)

These are informal, often noisy, neighborhood restaurants where one can enjoy a meal and a drink, or a few drinks. For some reason, ceramic **tanuki** (AC vol. 1, p. 133) are often seen in front of izakaya. In **Sapporo** (AC vol. 1, p. 111) there is a street called "Tanuki-kōji" (tanuki alley) that has a large number of bars and izakaya.

🅐 Saginomiya takes the captain to an izakaya for dinner in *801 TTS Airbats* (ep. 6).

🅜 In "Paranoiya Diary by Chief Assistant Kyochan" in *Futaba-kun Change* (vol. 4) the assistants get drunk at an izakaya while their boss suffers from writer's block.

## 出雲のお国 OLD FORM 出雲のお國
## IZUMO NO OKUNI

Okuni of **Izumo** (AC vol. 1, p. 52). A woman thought to be the founder of **kabuki**. Legend has it that she was the

## WRONG ABOUT THE ANIME

Say WHAT? Did this guy see the same picture?
Ever read a review of an anime you know well and wonder what the heck the writer thought they had seen? I'm not talking about plausible interpretations of a show. I'm talking about cases in which they are clearly wrong. With movie reviewers this is somewhat understandable. They have to rely on notes taken in the dark. Writers who have access to videos have less of an excuse.

Take for example Peter Carey, who, in his great little book *Wrong About Japan* (p. 59) describes the original *Gundam* series as involving "young soldiers in the throes of an intergalactic war." Almost every episode of the *Gundam* series takes place within the orbit of Earth's moon. He also describes *Grave of the Fireflies* as depicting the firebombing of Tokyo when in fact it is the firebombing of Kobe that we see.

Now, I have to admit that they rarely use place names that Westerners are likely to know. But the fact that the orphans have a relative living in Tokyo should have been a clue that the story does not take place there.

Several writers have asserted again and again that Major Kusanagi at the end of the first *Ghost in the Shell* movie has left her body and only exists in cyberspace. But at the end of the movie she is very much in her body looking out over the city. At no point is it suggested that she had abandoned her flesh, or cyborg, body for some neo-Platonic, non-corporeal existence.

Come on folks, please check your facts by popping the video into your player and looking over the scenes. It is easy to be wrong if you just rely on your memory. God knows how many times I have had to rewrite stuff after I found out I was wrong when I checked.

It's enough to make detail-obsessed fans like me even crazier than we already are.

daughter of Nakamura Sanzaemon, a blacksmith, and a **miko** (AC vol. 1, p. 82) of **Izumo Taisha** (AC vol. 1, p. 52). She organized a troupe of danc-

ers who performed in many parts of central Japan, including, most notably, in the riverbed of the Kamogawa in **Kyoto** (AC vol. 1, p. 77). The shows included humorous pieces based on earlier farces. In 1607 she moved to **Edo,** even performing for the **shōgun** (AC vol. 1, p. 123). Legend has it that the **kabuki mono** Nagoya Sanzaburō, a **rōnin** (AC vol. 1, p. 106), was her lover or husband at the time of his death. Okuni herself was a kabuki mono who dressed in a flashy combination of Portuguese and Japanese fashions. This is thought by some scholars to be the reason her performances were referred to as kabuki.

Ⓜ Izumo no Okuni is a significant character in *Samurai Deeper Kyo.*

# J

示現流
## JIGEN RYŪ

A sword school with special techniques for cutting with a blade. This highly aggressive **ryū** of sword fighting was the major one for members of the **Satsuma Han** such as **Saigō Takamori** (AC vol. 1, p. 107) and Tōgō Shigekata, its founder. Some of the **kata** (AC vol. 1, p. 64) of modern **kendō** (AC vol. 1, p. 66) come from the Jigen Ryū.

Ⓐ In *Samurai X: Trust and Betrayal* some members of the **Shinsengumi** discuss the possibility of a Jigen Ryū technique having been used to kill some of their comrades. • In *Samurai Deeper Kyo* (ep. 7), Tōgō Shigetaka takes part in a martial arts competition by holding his sword upright in the dragonfly stance.

Ⓜ The Jigen Ryū and its dragonfly stance are also seen in action in *Samurai Legend* (ch. 3).

歌舞伎
## KABUKI

A form of theater founded in the early 17th century by a woman known as **Izumo no Okuni**. The term kabuki means "slanted" and connotes offbeat or eccentric. Male and female roles could be played by actors of either gender. Early kabuki troupes were often largely made up of women, some of whom were prostitutes. In 1629, when the authorities forbade women from performing in kabuki, young men took over even the female roles. Once again, some of the troupes were fronts for prostitution. Further regulation in 1652 reformed kabuki, allowing it to develop into a serious theatrical art for the masses. The two main centers for kabuki were the **Kyoto** (AC vol. 1, p. 77) and **Osaka** (AC vol. 1, p. 102) area, and **Edo.** Today, kabuki is still performed only by male actors, although for a short time in the **Meiji period** (AC vol. 1, p. 81) there were some women actors.

Ⓐ Kabuki's origin is mentioned by Migeira in *Samurai Deeper Kyo* (ep. 20). Goemon sees **Sanmon Gosan no Kiri,** a play about his ancestor, at the **Kabukiza** in the beginning of *Lupin the 3rd: Dragon of Doom.* Soichiro is compared to **Bandō Tamasaburō,** the kabuki actor, by Yotsuya in *Maison Ikkoku* (ep. 7).

かぶき者
## KABUKI MONO

Kabuki people. In the late 16th and early 17th century, these were people who dressed and acted in an eccentric, flamboyant, and at times illegal manner. The government also considered the kabuki mono to be a threat to the peace as many were **rōnin** (AC vol. 1, p. 106), some from **daimyō** families, and they sometimes formed gangs. In 1607, a group of nobles disguised themselves as women to sneak into the women's quarters of the imperial palace. When they were caught and punished they were referred to as kabuki mono, a further indication that the term had a negative connotation.

Ⓜ In *Vagabond* (vol. 17–18), Muso Gonnosuke is a kabuki mono.

歌舞伎町
## KABUKICHŌ

Located in **Shinjuku-ku** (AC vol. 1, p. 120), this neighborhood is famous for its various entertainments, reputable, sleazy, legal, and otherwise. Everything from small drinking places to theaters can be found here. After WWII, when the area was being redeveloped into an entertainment district, the original plans called for a **kabuki** theater, which resulted in the name being adopted for the area. A lack of funds and the U.S. Occupation forces' distrust of kabuki's ties with traditional culture meant that the theater was never built, but the name stuck.

Ⓜ In *City Hunter* (TV ep. 1 and vol. 1, p. 43) we find that Kabukichō is one of Ryo's favorite haunts, and it shows up again and again in the series.

Ⓜ In *Dance Till Tomorrow* (vol. 6, p. 123), Aya disguises a **yakuza** (AC vol. 1, p. 146) on the

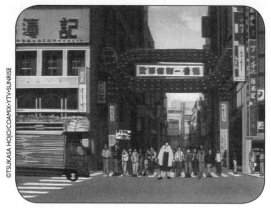

*An easily identifiable red gateway marks the entrance to **Kabukichō** as seen in* CITY HUNTER: THE MOTION PICTURE.

run so he can go to Kabukichō without being recognized.

## 歌舞伎座
## KABUKIZA

The major **kabuki** theater in **Tokyo**. Located in the present-day **Ginza** (AC vol. 1, p. 35), this theater opened in 1889. Originally the exterior was built in a Western style, but it was redecorated in an elaborate Japanese style in 1911. It burned down in a fire in the early 1920s and reopened in 1925. The theater was bombed in WWII and was rebuilt again in 1951. Seating capacity is 2,600 and the stage is nearly ninety feet wide.

Goemon sees **Sanmon Gosan no Kiri,** a play about his ancestor, at the Kabukiza in the beginning of *Lupin the 3rd: Dragon of Doom.* The Kabukiza is mentioned in *Full Metal Panic!* (ep. 11).

A performance at the Kabukiza is seen in *Astro Boy* (vol. 17, p. 86–87).

## 神楽 FORMAL 神樂
## KAGURA

A wide variety of **Shintō** (AC vol. 1, p. 121) rituals characterized by an invocation of the **kami** (AC vol. 1, p. 59), after which there is music and dance. The word is applied not only to the music and dance together but also when referring to the music or dance alone. The term is sometimes popularly, but incorrectly, used to describe any masked dance ritual at a **jinja** (AC vol. 1, p. 54). There are two main forms of kagura: *mi* kagura, which is associated with the imperial court and shrines related to the court, and *sato* kagura (village kagura), which is all the other kinds. Some add a third form called *miko-mai*, in which **miko** (AC vol. 1, p. 82) dance kagura dressed in their traditional white *chihaya* and red *hibakama*. The earliest records of kagura are from the 885 and 889, but it is widely held to be a more ancient form of worship. In fact, the prototypical kagura is usually considered to be the dance that drew **Amaterasu Ōmikami** (AC vol. 1, p. 6) from her cave.

The **kanji** (AC vol. 1, p. 61) for kagura are the same as those used in the name of kagura security in *Geobreeders*.

## 階段箪笥 FORMAL 階段箪笥
## KAIDAN DANSU

A style of **tansu** in the form of a staircase. While it is not physically attached to the structure of the building the kaidan dansu is often a part of a traditional building's design.

We see a kaidan dansu in the *Rurouni Kenshin* TV series (ep. 61) and in *Ai Yori Aoshi* (ep. 5).

## 回峯行 OR 回峰行
## KAIHŌGYŌ

The practice of circling the mountain, a type of pilgrimage of sacred sites on **Hie-izan** and some other sacred mountains in Japan. This is practiced by Tendai Buddhist monks who perform this austerity for either 100, 700, or 1,000 (*sennichi kaihōgyō*) days by running one of three set routes around the mountain, sometimes runs into **Kyoto** (AC vol. 1, p. 77), and, for those who have completed at least one 100-day practice, a special retreat called the **Katsuragawa Geango.**

While engaged in this practice the monks dress in white cotton clothing and if they have completed 300 days of kaihōgyō in their lives they are allowed to wear a narrow hat; otherwise they must carry the hat in their left hand. They wear traditional **zōri** (AC vol. 1, p. 151) that they change each day or for the longer routes several times a day as they wear out. Among the items they carry are candles, a book of sutras, and a handbook for the route they are running. They also carry a rope and a knife as they take an oath to complete the series of runs or die.

The runs begin at 1:30 in the morning, the shorter ones finishing by 7:30–9:30 A.M. As they circle the mountain the runners stop, chant, and make offerings at certain sites. But they never stop to rest or sit. The only exception to this is when they arrive at a bench under a large cedar (**sugi**), on which they sit facing the old imperial palace in Kyoto and offer a prayer for peace.

The longer periods are not done all at once but in 100-day blocks. The longest, the *sennichi kaihōgyō*, is actually part of a twelve-year retreat, the first three years of which involve the 100-days practice over a route of 30–40 kilometers each day (depending on the route), then two sets of 100 days running 30 kilometers each day for the fourth and fifth years. After the 700th day, in the fifth year, there is the *dōiri*, a nine-day period of chanting and total fasting with no sleep. The sixth year is a single set of 60-kilometer runs each day for 100 days; the seventh year consists of an 84-kilometer run each day for 100 days and later in the year doing a 30–40 kilometer run for 100 days. The final ordeal is an eight-day fast performing the *goma* ritual (in front of a fire), tossing in sticks with prayers written on them. For this, sleeping sitting up for a few hours is permitted.

While all of this may sound extreme, it is part of a practice of devotion to **Fudō-myōō** (AC vol. 1, p. 29) and related to **Shugendō** (AC vol. 1, p. 124) asceticism. The kaihōgyō is still run today pretty much the same way it was a thousand years ago, with parts of it now going over paved roads where

dirt trails used to be. Running the route of kaihōgyō once is required for all Tendai priests and nuns as part of their training.

**A** In *Samurai X: Trust and Betrayal* when Tomoe and Kenshin are walking they pass a group of kaihōgyō practitioners taking part in the Katsuragawa Geango. Note that they are all wearing their hats.

## 怪獣 OLD FORM 怪獸
## KAIJŪ (GIANT MONSTER)

Giant monsters are mostly known through kaiju films, the genre that star these large beasties. Gojira (Godzilla), Rodan, and Gamera are the most famous examples of this kind of character.

**A** Noa calls the dragon a kaiju in *Patlabor the TV Series* (ep. 19). • A marvelous take-off on kaiju films is in *Kimagure Orange Road* TV (ep. 40). *Iczer One* (ep. 1) has a reference to kaiju mecha beam cannons. • The ultimate anime homage to the kaiju genre has to be *Blue Seed,* with its regular trashing of cities and its message of humanity's need to maintain links with the earth.

## 柿
## KAKI (PERSIMMON)

An important fruit tree in Japanese history, the persimmon is a traditional autumn fruit eaten raw or dried. Many varieties are grown throughout the country, with flavors ranging from sweet to very astringent. Today most persimmons are grown in private gardens rather than in orchards. Dried persimmons are used in some New Year decorations. The wood of the tree is useful for making utensils. The leaves are sometimes used to wrap food.

**A** Green persimmons are seen in a tree outside the country house in *Samurai X: Trust and Betrayal*; later, as the seasons change, we see them ripe. • In *Tenchi Forever,* an old lady gives persimmons to Haruna.

**M** Ōgami recounts the story of **Ishida Mitsunari**

refusing a persimmon before his execution on the grounds that it would upset his stomach in *Lone Wolf and Cub* (vol. 25, p. 16).

## 角行灯
## KAKU ANDON (FOUR-LEGGED STANDING LANTERN)

A lantern set on the floor or ground that consists of a base supporting a box with a covering in the **shōji** (AC vol. 1, p. 123) style. Sometimes four legs support the shōji section; sometimes they resemble a long box set on end with the shōji section as part of the top half. Traditionally, these burned oil. Today they can be bought with electric lights in them.

**A** We clearly see a kaku andon in the country house in *Samurai X: Trust and Betrayal.*

**M** This style of lantern provides the light while Ōgami and his son eat in *Lone Wolf and Cub* (vol. 3, p. 206).

## かま OR 釜
## KAMA (COOKING POT)

An old-fashioned pot for cooking or boiling water. These are large, round, deep iron pots with a thick wooden lid and often a flange near the top that holds the kama in place when inserted into a **kamado.** The honorific

*On the floor on a firm base, the **kaku andon**, like this one from* SAMURAI X TRUST AND BETRAYAL, *is a good source of light at night.*

*What's in the **kama**? Is it rice? Is it soup? Is it done yet wonders a worker in* SAMURAI X TRUST AND BETRAYAL?

form, **okama,** has a very different meaning when used to refer to a person.

**A** In *Samurai X: Trust and Betrayal*, when Tomoe and the **ryokan** (AC vol. 1, p. 107) owner are talking about irises (**ayame**) we see for a short time another worker at a kamado with a kama in it. Later, in the country home, we see a kama over the fire in the **irori** (AC vol. 1, p. 50).

**M** Kama are used to cook rice in *Lone Wolf and Cub* (vol. 24, p. 91) and for heating water for **cha-no-yu** (AC vol. 1, p. 17) in chapter 5 of *Samurai Legend.*

## かまめし OR 釜飯
## KAMA MESHI

A dish of rice cooked in a **kama** with other ingredients, including **dashi.** This is made in a separate kama from those used for regular rice. Often miniature ceramic kama are used and the food is served in them. The dish originated in **Asakusa** (AC vol. 1, p. 6) in the 19th century. **Ekiben** (AC vol. 1, p. 26) sometimes contain kama meshi.

**M** In the "paranoia theater" segment of volume 5 of *Futaba-Kun Change,* Aro suggests kama meshi for lunch.

*You're liable to assume the **kamado** from RUROUNI KENSHIN was built in the corner of a kitchen. Actually, they're hauled to their location in one piece.*

## かまど OR 竈
## KAMADO (STOVE)

An old-fashioned wood or charcoal-burning stove or range, sometimes called *hettsui* or *kudo*. These are built directly into or are placed on the kitchen floor and look like small fireplaces with large round openings on top. Early kamado were larger and placed outside in a small hut. During the **Edo period** (AC vol. 1, p. 25) smaller ones were designed that could be placed inside the house. The openings hold **kama** for cooking rice or pots for making **misoshiru** (AC vol. 1, p. 85).

🅐 In *Samurai X: Trust and Betrayal*, when Tomoe and the **ryokan** (AC vol. 1, p. 107) owner are talking about irises (**ayame**), we see another worker at a kamado with a kama in it.

🅜 A kamado is used in *Lone Wolf and Cub* (vol. 24, p. 91) and in *Blade of the Immortal: Heart of Darkness* (pt. 4).

## 神風特別攻撃隊
## KAMIKAZE TOKUBETSU KŌGEKITAI (KAMIKAZE SPECIAL ATTACK FORCE)

The units of the famous kamikaze suicide pilots. These were named after the "divine winds" (kamikaze) that legend says helped save Japan from the Mongol invasions (see **Kōan no Eki**). In 1944, as the United States advanced on the Philippines, the Japanese Navy ordered a group of pilots to crash their bomb carrying Zero (**Zerosen**) fighters into U.S. Navy ships near Leyte. The result was so successful that the Navy organized other special units of pilots to carry out the same kind of attack. Soon the Japanese Army began creating its own units. It was not long before specially designed planes such as the **Ōka** were built for such attacks. This type of desperate attack continued until the end of the war.

🅐 In *Grave of the Fireflies* Seita says a plane flying over is a kamikaze. • The main character of *The Cockpit* story 2, "Mach Thunder Force," is a kamikaze pilot.

🅜 In *Barefoot Gen* (p. 149–), a pilot tells of being shamed into volunteering for kamikaze duty. • In a science fiction setting, the Valorous Eagles of the Glorious Youth Special Attack Squadron are given a pep talk near the end of *Drakuun* (vol. 1).

## 紙芝居
## KAMI-SHIBAI

Paper shows. Stories told with pictures inside a frame. As the story develops, each picture is removed to show the next one beneath. Storytellers set up shop in the street, often on the back of a bicycle. The storyteller is actually a candy seller who does the rounds in an area of town. When enough customers have gathered and bought candy, the tales begin. Candy buyers get the best spots in front of the storyteller. Most of the stories are serials told in short segments. This keeps customers coming back every time the storyteller stops in the neighborhood. Today this old-fashioned form of entertainment is rarely seen.

🅐 Onizuka uses this storytelling technique to explain his silly theory of the *tora-uma* in *GTO* (ep. 17).

🅜 Yama-chan asks if it is time for "the picture card show" in *Short Program* (vol. 2, p. 272). Dr. Kocohm uses kami-shibai to explain his troubles with the Empire in *Caravan Kidd* (vol. 2, p. 125).

## 金谷
## KANAYA

A town in **Shizuoka Ken.** In the **Edo period** (AC vol. 1, p. 25) Kanaya was a **shukuba machi** on the **Tōkaidō.** Today the town produces equipment for processing tea and is the location of the National Research Institute of Tea.

Ⓜ Ōgami stays in Kanaya in *Lone Wolf and Cub* (vol. 7, p. 190).

## 寛永寺
## KANEIJI

Also known as Tōeizan Kaneiji. A **jiin** (AC vol. 1, p. 53; Buddhist temple) built starting in 1624 by order of the **shōgun** (AC vol. 1, p. 123) Tokugawa Hidetada on a hill northeast of the **Edojō** in **Ueno** (AC vol. 1, p. 142) as a supernatural protector of the city. The northeast is the Kimon or Demon's Gate in **kasō** (AC vol. 1, p. 64; geomancy). This temple became an official family temple of the **Tokugawa** (AC vol. 1, p. 137) shōgun. The temple was largely destroyed in the Ueno Battle of 1868. In the **Meiji period** (AC vol. 1, p. 81) the area became **Ueno Kōen** (AC vol. 1, p. 143). There still is a Kaneiji in the area, behind the National Museum (**Tokyo Kokuritsu Hakubutsukan**). This temple, originally built in 1638, was brought from Kitain in Kawagoe in 1879. It houses the original temple's image of Yakushi Buddha. A reason for the choice of this particular building was that Kitain had once been administered by the Tendai priest Tenkai, the founder of Kaneiji. Two significant structures of the original temple remain, a five-story pagoda and the Kiyomizudō hall. One interesting note is that the famous Kinokuniya Bunzaemon established his fortune selling cypress for the construction of the new main hall of the temple.

Ⓐ Kaneiji is mentioned in episode 93 of *Rurouni*

*Ranma in* RANMA 1/2 *ties on his **kanjiki** before making his way across the snow.*

© RUMIKO TAKAHASHI/SHOGAKUKAN • KITTY FILM • FUJI TV

*Kenshin,* and in episode 94 we see a plan of the temple complex.

Ⓜ The location of the present Kaneiji is seen on a map in *Mobile Police Patlabor* (vol. 1, p. 156).

## 幹事
## KANJI

Organizer. Some businesses and organizations have staff with this title. For group events like parties and trips, one person is often chosen to be the kanji, the organizer. He handles reservations, collects funds, pays the bills, and generally sees to it that there are no complications.

Ⓐ Nakajima is the kanji for a trip to a hot spring in *You're Under Arrest* (ep. 13); however there are complications for him.

## 樏 OR かんじき
## KANJIKI (SNOWSHOES)

Footgear for walking on mud, snow, or ice. These are loops of wood or tough plant material strapped to the shoe and encircling it, often with metal cleats to reduce slipping.

Ⓐ Akane gives Ranma kanjiki in *Ranma 1/2 Anything Goes Martial Arts* (ep. 9).

## 寒天 or かんてん
## KANTEN

Agar. A jelly-like food ingredient made from cooked *tengusa* (heavenly grass), a type of seaweed. It is bought dried and soaked in water before being used. Kanten has a higher melting temperature than gelatin, so it can be eaten when the weather is hot. It is used to make many different dishes, such as **anmitsu** (AC vol. 1, p. 6).

Ⓜ Kiriko unveils a dessert that uses agar as an ingredient in *Iron Wok Jan* (vol. 5, p. 116).

## 関東大震災 old form 關東大震災
## KANTŌ DAISHINSAI (TOKYO EARTHQUAKE OF 1923)

At 11:58 A.M. on September 1, 1923, the most devastating earthquake to ever hit the **Tokyo** area took place, estimated to be 7.9 on the Japanese scale. In the quake, the aftershocks, and another major quake a day later, over half the homes in Tokyo were destroyed. The destruction was even worse in **Yokohama,** which was much closer to the epicenter. As many were preparing food at the time, fires quickly started and went out of control. The blaze was so large and hot that it generated winds of 70–80 kilometers per hour (43–50 miles per hour). By the time the fire burned itself out an estimated 142,807 people were dead or missing. Bodies littered the streets, bridges, canals, and rivers. Many had died of suffocation, about 30,000 in one locality. And thousands of Koreans, Chinese, and some Japanese were killed by rioting vigilantes due to rumors of well poisonings and arson. Elements in the military and police also took advantage of the situation to kill labor union officials and leftist activists.

Ⓐ The Great Kantō Earthquake is mentioned by Shinji in the *Patlabor* TV show (ep. 27). • The quake, and its unnatural cause, is featured in *Doomed Megalopolis.* • In *Millennium Actress* we learn that Chiyoko was born during the earthquake.

Ⓜ Inspector Nikawa tells of the death of his wife by rioters after the Kantō Earthquake in *Adolf: An Exile in Japan* (p. 162). • The shakings of the Colossal Building in Astro Boy's attempts to find the Mad Machine are compared to the Kantō quake in *Astro Boy* (vol. 3, p. 205).

## からし or 芥子
## KARASHI (MUSTARD)

*Brassica nigra, Sinapis alba, Brassica juncea*. In Japan, mustard is made from a mixture of different types of mustard seeds mixed with hot water. For this reason it is hotter than English mustard, which often includes flour as an ingredient to make it milder. When it is used as a dressing it is called *karashi-ae.*

Ⓜ In *Blade of the Immortal: Dark Shadows,* Sumino Kenei mentions that earlier in his life some of his favorite foods were *unohana* and *karashi-ae.*

## カレー
## KARĒ (CURRY)

Introduced from England into Japan in the late 19th century, Japanese curries tend to be very mild when compared with Indian curries. The powdered form is called karē-ko. Perhaps the most common form of curry dish is **karē raisu** (AC vol. 1, p. 62).

© 1999 GAINAX / KGI

*Various **kare-raisu** mixes for children come in boxes with brightly colored art. I doubt this one from FLCL really exists, but you never know . . .*

Sho gets curry for dinner in the *Bubblegum Crisis* OVA series (ep. 3). • Powdery curry, probably poorly made from karē-ko, is in *Urusei Yatsura* (TV ep. 63, st. 86). • Instant curry is mentioned in *Blue Seed* (ep. 17) and seen in *Neon Genesis Evangelion* (ep. 5). • Then there is the explosively hot 100-fold curry in *Revolutionary Girl Utena* (ep. 8). • But the ultimate curry has to be the batch made by Haruko in *FLCL*.

## 頭
## KASHIRA

Literally, the head. In a discussion of swords, the pommel at the base of a **tsuka.** These tend to be very simple in design and any ornamentation is slight to make it easier to grip. While **nihontō** (AC vol. 1, p. 95) show up in many period anime and manga, the kashira is often not clearly seen as the proper two-handed grip covers it up with the left hand.

In *Samurai X: Trust and Betrayal* we get a good view of a kashira that has a chain attached to it.

## 加藤清正
## KATŌ KIYOMASA

1562–1611. Katō was a follower of **Toyotomi Hideyoshi** (AC vol. 1, p. 140), having been born in the same village and grown up as his friend. In 1588 he and **Konishi Yukinaga** were sent to deal with a **samurai** (AC vol. 1, p. 110) uprising in Higo Province, today known as Kumamoto Prefecture, and to take over administration of the area, each man becoming **daimyō** over half the province. Yukinaga and Kiyomasa were leaders in Hideyoshi's invasions of Korea. In 1600 Katō fought on the side of **Tokugawa Ieyasu** at the **Sekigahara no Tatakai,** after which he was granted control over all of Higo Province.

Kuno refers to a story of Katō Kiyomasa wrestling a tiger in *Ranma 1/2 Hard Battle* (ep. 12).

The role of Katō Kiyomasa in the building of the Honmaru Nakamon gate of the **Edojō** is explained in *Lone Wolf and Cub* (vol. 24, p. 252).

The skin of a tiger claimed to have been captured by Katō Kiyomasa in Korea is displayed in *Vagabond* (vol. 8, ch. 77).

## 勝海舟 OLD FORM 勝海舟
## KATSU KAISHŪ

1823–99. Also known as Katsu Rintarō, Katsu Awa, or Katsu Yasuyoshi. Son of a **hatamoto** who trained in Western studies, including the military arts. He worked as a translator for foreign affairs and went to **Nagasaki** (AC vol. 1, p. 90) to be trained in the use of ships and naval techniques. He captained the ship that sailed to the United States in 1860 for the ratification of the **Nichibei Shūkō Tsūshō Jōyaku** (Harris Treaty), the first trans-Pacific voyage by a Japanese ship. When he returned he was given the rank of *gunkan bugyō* (commissioner of warships) by the **bakufu,** a rank he held when he asked **Sakamoto Ryōma** to become his assistant. Katsu negotiated the surrender of **Edo** to **Saigō Takamori** (AC vol. 1, p. 107). During the **Meiji period** (AC vol. 1, p. 81) he served in several posts. In 1887 he was granted the rank of count by the imperial court.

His role in the surrender of Edo and in foreign missions is mentioned in the *Rurouni Kenshin* TV series (ep. 79), and he also appears in the same story.

Katsu Kaishū shows up in *Vanity Angel* issue 5 and is the narrator of the tale in *Samurai Legend.*

## カツどん OR カツ丼
## KATSUDON (PORK CUTLET DONBURI)

A **donburi** (AC vol. 1, p. 24) dish made placing freshly cooked **tonkatsu** on hot rice with a sweet stock and onion mixture, then pouring a slightly beaten egg on top to cook by the heat of the food under it. A variant has the final cooking of the egg on top of the other ingredients in a pan then poured on top of the rice. Often served with a small dish of pickles.

The katsudon, or "pork cutlet rice bowl," at

Omuraan's on 2nd Street is mentioned in *Fushigi Yūgi* (ep. 1). • "Pork cutlet on rice" is requested by the students in *Urusei Yatsura* (TV ep. 14, st. 27).

Ⓜ That Manabe Johji's studio is named Studio Katsudon is mentioned in his introduction to *Outlanders* (vol. 4). • In a panic Onizuka fantasizes being offered some "pork and rice" by a police interrogator in *GTO* (vol. 7, p. 162).

## かつおぶし OR 鰹節
## KATSUOBUSHI (DRIED BONITO)

To make katsuobushi, a bonito is filleted, boiled, or steamed, and the bones removed, dried, smoked, and mold-cured with *Aspergillus glaucus*. The resulting pieces are quite hard and, with the mold, resemble a strangely shaped Italian sausage or a block of wood. In fact, in this case *bushi* means a block of wood. To use them in cooking they must be shaved—much like a piece of wood—to make **kezuribushi,** also called *hanagatsuo*. Before modern technology the shaving was done with a plane mounted in a box called a *katsuobushibako*, or katsuobushi box; the katsuobushi is moved, and the plane stays steady as the shavings fall into the box. Better restaurants and some housewives still hand-shave katsuobushi shortly before a meal is prepared in order to get the best flavor.

Ⓐ In *Grave of the Fireflies* when Seita digs up the food stash at home he finds that katsuobushi is part of it. • In *Saber Marionette J* (ep. 14) Cherry washes some katsuobushi in preparation to shaving it.

## 葛川夏安居
## KATSURAGAWA GEANGO

A special religious retreat for **kaihōgyō** practitioners who have completed at least one 100-day period of practice. Each year, these days on July 16–20, they gather on **Hiei-zan,** some walking hundreds of miles to get there. At 4:00 A.M. they start walking to Mount Hira, a journey that takes about twelve hours. There they engage in a variety of religious practices until the retreat is over.

Ⓐ In *Samurai X: Trust and Betrayal* when Tomoe and Kenshin are walking, they pass a group of kai-hōgyō practitioners taking part in the Katsuragawa Geango. How do we know this is who they are? By their robes and the special hats they wear.

## 瓦
## KAWARA (ROOF TILES)

What anime set in earlier periods, or with traditional buildings, would be complete without roof tiles? As with many other things, roof tiles came to Japan from China and Korea along with Buddhism (**bukkyō** vol. 1, p. 15). The style used in Japan is pan tiles laid in overlapping rows. In the **Edo period** (AC vol. 1, p. 25) the **bakufu** imposed regulations in **Edo** requiring thatched roofs to be converted to tile roofs as a fire-preventing measure. Tile roofs sometimes include ornamental **shachihoko** (AC vol. 1, p. 116) or **onigawara.**

Ⓐ Otaru gets a job laying tiles in *Saber Marionette J* (ep. 6). • Kyoko removes tiles to fix a leaking roof in *Maison Ikkoku* (ep. 2).

Ⓜ We see roof tiles being laid in *Lone Wolf and Cub* (vol. 12, p. 182).

*The overlapping design of **kawara** is apparent in this image from* Maison Ikkoku.

*This monk and his "encouraging stick" better be careful, Ryo packs heat in* CITY HUNTER.

## 警策
## KEISAKU OR KYŌSAKU (ZEN STICK)

"Encouraging stick" and "staff of admonition" are two ways this device is referred to in English. Both pronunciations use the same **kanji** (AC vol. 1, p. 61). The keisaku is a long stick used to aid discipline in **zazen.** A practitioner who is dozing will be struck with the stick on the back while bowing. This can be requested by the person meditating, as it is not a punishment. Each of the major schools of **Zen (Buddhism)** has its own name for this stick, either keisaku or kyōsaku.

A In *Martian Successor Nadesico* (ep. 5) Yurika is struck as a result of her thoughts drifting away while in zazen. • Ryo gets hit in *City Hunter* (ep. 21).

M Shoko is disciplined with a keisaku while engaging in something other than zazen in *Rumic Theater: One or Double* (p. 25).

## 結核
## KEKKAKU (TUBERCULOSIS)

This disease also existed in Japan and, while it does not show up much in stories in a contemporary setting, it does appear in anime and manga set in earlier times. Until the 20th century, it was the most common fatal disease. A traditional belief held that TB was a polluting disease and could stigmatize an entire family. Even today persons who have TB in their family history can sometimes have a harder time marrying.

A In *Samurai X: Trust and Betrayal* two historical personages, **Okita Sōji** and **Takasugi,** have TB; in reality both eventually died from it.

M The eighth story in *Lone Wolf and Cub* (vol. 1, p. 229) includes Izawa, a **samurai** (AC vol. 1, p. 110) suffering from TB.

## 拳法
## KENPŌ

Way of the Fist. Originally an unarmed Chinese martial art, Quanfa (Ch'uan-fa) used mainly hands and feet as weapons. It was introduced into **Okinawa** (AC vol. 1, p. 99) in the late 16th century. Karate, a more recent martial art, developed from kenpō. This is not to be confused with the occasionally used term *kenpō* that refers to swordsmanship.

A Kenpō is used in *Rurouni Kenshin* (TV ep. 10, "Aoshi"). • In the first episode of *Ranma 1/2* Akane asks if Ranma-chan practices kenpō.

## 県 OLD FORM 縣
## KEN (PREFECTURE)

In 1871 the Meiji government abolished the **han** system and replaced it by a more centralized system that divided the country into prefectures. Although they were losing their land, almost all of the **daimyō** went along with these changes. This did not happen all at once. It began in 1868 with the confiscated lands of the **Tokugawa** (AC vol. 1, p. 137) family and its allies in the **Boshin Sensō** being converted into centrally controlled prefectures. Also in 1869, the daimyō were made nonhereditary governors of their domains, subservient to the imperial government but with high salaries. With the abolition of the domains, the former daimyō retained their salaries and became part of a class of nobility called the *kazoku.* Major figures who promoted this process include **Kido Takayoshi,** Iwakura To-momi, and **Ōkubo Toshimichi.** The reforms were opposed by a very few, including **Saigō Takamori** (AC vol. 1, p. 107). The organization of the pre-fectures changed rapidly in the early days; today there are forty-seven of them. See the maps and lists on pages 124–29 for more information.

**M** Specific prefectures are commonly mentioned in many stories set in Japan.

## 剣術 OLD FORM 劍術
## KENJUTSU (SWORDSMANSHIP)

 Often translated as swordsmanship, ken-jutsu is more precisely concerned with the martial arts of the sword after it has been pulled from the sheath. For this reason is it different from **battō-jutsu,** though the two are closely related. As it is a practical military art, it is not the same as **kendō** (AC vol. 1, p. 66), which has become more of a sport.

**A** Kenjutsu is translated as swordsmanship in the first episode of the *Rurouni Kenshin* TV series. • Azumi Kiribayashi tells Ryoko she is perhaps bet-ter suited for kenjutsu than kendō in *Real Bout High School* (ep. 2).

## 欅
## KEYAKI (ZELKOVA)

A type of elm tree native to Japan. This species, which can grow to be very large, is often planted for its wood, which has many uses such as in shipbuilding. In urban areas it is often planted in parks and in **jinja** (AC vol. 1, p. 54) or **jiin** (AC vol. 1, p. 53) as it grows well in relatively narrow spaces. Keyaki are found wild in **Honshu** (AC vol. 1, p. 47), **Shikoku,** and **Kyushu** (AC vol. 1, p. 78).

**A** A zelkova tree is the center of action in an epi-sode of *Patlabor the TV Series* (ep. 8).

## けずりぶし OR 削り節
## KEZURIBUSHI (SHAVED DRIED BONITO)

Shaved **katsuobushi.** Often when you find bags of it in stores it is also called *hanagatsuo.* The shavings are used to make **dashi** or are sprinkled directly onto cold **tōfu** or cooked vegetables.

**A** The cook of a **soba-ya** is instructed that the ke-zuribushi used in her broth needed to be shaved thicker in *City Hunter 2* (ep. 36). • We get a good image of kezuribushi when Itsuko tosses a batch into water in *Rurouni Kenshin* (TV ep. 80).

**M** Being made of fish, it is no surprise that kezuri-bushi is a favorite of cats, and in *What's Michael?* (vol. 9 "The Ideal Cat," p. 18) and *Astro Boy* (vol. 23, p. 130) we see this trait as part of the story.

## きびだんご OR 黍団子 OLD FORM 黍團子
## KIBIDANGO

A type of **dango** prepared with sugar, honey, and flour made from *kibi,* a type of millet.

**A** The famous kibidango of **Okayama Ken** is mentioned in the *Urusei Yatsura* TV series (ep. 55, st. 78). • Kibidango is part of a meal in *Patlabor New Files* (ep. 9).

## 木戸孝允 OLD FORM 木戸孝允
## KIDO TAKAYOSHI

1833–77. Also known as Katsura Kogorō and Kido Kōin. One of the major figures who brought the **Meiji period** (AC vol. 1, p. 81) into existence. He was born in **Hagi**, a castle town of the **Chōshū Han.** When he was seven he was adopted by the Katsura family, whose name he kept until 1865. As a young man he studied under **Yoshida Shōin,** who influenced his pro-imperial views. He moved to **Edo** in 1852 where he studied **kenjutsu** and met pro-imperial **samurai** (AC vol. 1, p. 110) from the **Mito Han.** In 1862 he was transferred to **Kyoto** (AC vol. 1, p. 77), partly due to suspicions concerning his contacts with the Mito samurai. In Kyoto he was the chief domain officer for the Chōshū Han. After the **Hamaguri Gomon no Hen** he went into hiding with the **geisha** (AC vol. 1, p. 33) **Ikumatsu,** whom he later married. When the pro-imperial forces in the Chōshū domain under the leadership of **Takasugi Shinsaku** took control of the domain, Kido became one of the domain leaders and negotiated an alliance with the **Satsuma Han.**

During the Meiji period he played an important role in the new government. He traveled to the United States and England as an associate ambassador in 1871–73, where he studied Western political systems and education theory. In 1874 he resigned from the government to protest a Japanese military attack on Taiwan promoted by **Saigō Takamori** (AC vol. 1, p. 107). He returned to government office in 1875 and spent the last years of his life supervising the education of the Meiji emperor.

**A** Katsura Kogorō is a major character in *Samurai X: Trust and Betrayal.*

## 奇兵隊
## KIHEITAI

Irregular militia. A volunteer militia organized in 1863 by **Takasugi Shinsaku** in the **Chōshū Han.** The Kiheitai consisted of roughly 300 to 400 men from all classes with ranks based entirely on skill. Training included modern Western weapons. The Kiheitai was disbanded at the beginning of the **Meiji period** (AC vol. 1, p. 81). The example set by the Kiheitai was a factor leading to universal conscription, which replaced traditional hereditary military roles.

**A** We see the Kiheitai training in *Samurai X: Trust and Betrayal*

## きんぴらごぼう OR 金平牛蒡
## KINPIRA-GOBŌ

Finely sliced **gobō,** sometimes mixed with sliced carrots (**ninjin**), lightly fried then simmered with red pepper, sugar, **shōyu** (AC vol. 1, p. 124), and **sake** (AC vol. 1, p. 109). Sesame seeds are often sprinkled on top.

**A** While translated simply as "burdock" in the beginning of episode 4 of *Rurouni Kenshin*, what Kenshin actually says is kinpira-gobō. • The man-

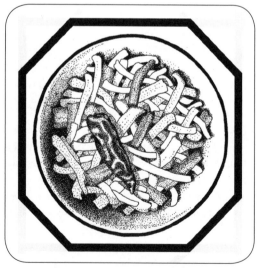

*Kinpira-gobō is a deceptively simple dish. Perhaps we'll add some pepper for spice.*

ager gives a plate of kinpira-gobō to Hideki in *Cho-bits* (ep. 1).

Ⓜ In *Survival in the Office* (vol. 2, p. 110), after an **OL** (AC vol. 1, p. 100; office lady) invites a young man up to her apartment and tells him to help himself to a snack, he finds kinpira in the fridge.

## 弘安の役
## KŌAN NO EKI (KŌAN WAR)

The Kōan War of 1281, the second at-tempted invasion of Japan by the Mon-golians. A total of 140,000 men in two invading fleets attacked. One fleet of 40,000 at-tacked Tsushima, Iki Island, and then the port of Hakata in **Kyushu** (AC vol. 1, p. 78). The other fleet of 100,000 attacked Hirado, also in Kyushu. The Japanese had built a long wall at Hakata and fought the invaders there and in night raids on their island camps and boats for weeks The Mon-gols retreated to the area of Takashima island in Ōmura Bay near **Nagasaki** (AC vol. 1, p. 90) to regroup for another invasion attempt. The fleets were dispersed and destroyed by a **taifū** (AC vol. 1, p. 130; typhoon) on August 23, 1281. Some in-vaders took refuge on Takashima island and were massacred. The rest fled on the remaining ships. Estimates are that 60–90 percent of the invaders died in the invasion attempt and storm.

Ⓐ The Koan War is mentioned in the movie *Kima-gure Orange Road: I Want to Return to That Day.*

## 小林一茶
## KOBAYASHI ISSA

1763–1827. Poet known for being one of the great masters of haiku. Born the son of a farmer, he lost his mother at age two. When he was fourteen he moved to **Edo**, where he was homeless for a time until he found work as an apprentice. At the age of fifty-one, following his father's death, he returned to his village where he married a much younger woman. Their four children died in childhood, and he was a widower at the age of sixty-two. His compositions, which

are written in vernacular, often dealt with poor people and the sorrows of the weak.

Ⓜ In *The Return of Lum Feudal Furor* (p. 143) we see Kobayashi greeting **Bashō.**

## 神戸 [市] OLD FORM 神戸
## KŌBE

The capital of **Hyōgo Ken** and a major port since the 8th century. Originally the city was known as Hyōgo. The name Kōbe is relatively recent. For much of its history Kōbe was a major Japanese port for trade with China. Today it is the second busiest port in Japan.

Ⓐ *Grave of the Fireflies* begins with the firebomb-ing of Kōbe by the United States in WWII.

Ⓜ In *Sanctuary* we see Kōbe's Chinatown (vol. 5, p. 51) and harbor (vol. 6, p. 8). • A great deal of the story in Tezuka's *Adolf* series centers around Kōbe and its Jewish population.

## 高知県 OLD FORM 高知縣
## KŌCHI KEN

A prefecture in southern **Shikoku** bor-dered by Ehime and Tokushima prefec-tures and the Pacific Ocean. In the **Edo period** (AC vol. 1, p. 25) this area was known as the **Tosa Han.** As the climate is quite warm, two rice crops are grown annually in some places. Fishing and forestry contribute to the economy, as does a small amount of papermaking and wood-working. Tourists visit the coastal areas as well as the inland mountains.

Ⓜ In *Sanctuary* (vol. 3, p. 150) new **Kokkai** (AC vol. 1, p. 72) member Yoshikawa Hidemaru intro-duces himself as being from Kōchi Prefecture.

## 石
## KOKU (VOLUME MEASUREMENT)

A volume measurement usually used for rice or other grains. In the **Edo period** (AC vol. 1, p. 25) it was the equivalent of 5.12 U.S. bushels (0.18 cubic meters or 180.39 liters), an amount considered to be enough to feed one person for a year. The exact size of the koku varied until it was standardized by **Toyotomi Hideyoshi** (AC vol. 1, p. 140). The koku was also used to measure the productivity of cropland, which was needed for taxation, as well as to describe the salaries of **samurai** (AC vol. 1, p. 110) and the wealth of **daimyō**.

Ⓜ In *Lone Wolf and Cub* vol. 1, p. 72 and many other places the wealth of a **han** is stated in koku.

### 国立科学博物館
### KOKURITSU KAGAKU HAKUBUTSUKAN (NATIONAL SCIENCE MUSEUM)

This **Tokyo** museum is located in **Ueno Kōen** (AC vol. 1, p. 143) in **Taitō-ku.** Founded in 1877 as the Kyōiku Hakubutsukan, it was renamed in 1949. It contains exhibits on science and conducts research on natural history.

Ⓜ The National Science Museum is seen in *Mobile Police Patlabor* (vol. 1, p. 147).

### 独楽 OLD FORM 獨樂
### KOMA (SPINNING TOP)

Long a popular toy worldwide, tops were introduced to Japan in the 8th century from the Korean kingdom of Koguryō, which at that time was also known as Koma. Like many things introduced into Japan around then, koma were used mainly by the nobles. They had became popular with the common populace by the 17th century, and eventually tops came to be considered a children's toy. Playing with tops is one of the pleasures associated with New Year's celebrations.

Ⓐ When we first see Shinta in *Samurai X: Trust and Betrayal* he is carrying a top, a top that Kenshin keeps until the end of the story.

Ⓜ Daigoro learns to spin a top in *Lone Wolf and Cub* (vol. 3, p. 81).

*Ranma-chan and the kids in* RANMA 1/2 *compete to see whose* **koma** *can stay up the longest.*

### こんぶ OR 昆布
### KONBU (KELP)

A type of kelp, specifically Laminaria. One of many edible seaweeds widely used in Japanese cooking, essential for making **dashi** and important in **shōjin ryōri.** Teas and medicinal drinks are also made with konbu. Konbu is even used in New Year's decorations and as **Shintō** (AC vol. 1, p. 121) offerings. Konbu grows well in cold waters, and the best comes from **Hokkaido** (AC vol. 1, p. 46). Konbu contains a high amount of natural monosodium glutamate, which adds to its usefulness in cooking. It also is a good source of vitamins and minerals. To use it for making dashi, place it into a pot of cold water, place the pot over a flame, and remove the konbu as soon as the water begins to boil.

Ⓐ A piece of konbu tied into a knot is seen in a **bento** (AC vol. 1, p. 10) in the opening sequence of the *Patlabor New Files* (ep. 10). • Konbu seaweed ties are also seen at lunch in *Here Is Greenwood* (ep. 6).

Ⓜ We find that the mother of Murota died while attempting to harvest konbu in *Strain* (vol. 2, p. 166).

## 近藤勇
## KONDŌ ISAMI

1834–68. Born a farmer's son from Musashi Province, in 1863 he joined the **Shinsengumi** and became its commander. In 1864 he led the attack against pro-imperial **shishi,** which became known as the **Ikedaya Jiken.** In 1868 he formed and led a military unit, the Kōyō Chinbutai, against pro-imperial armies. He was executed after his capture in battle in the same year.

◭ Kondō Isami is a significant character in *Samurai X: Trust and Betrayal* and in *Peacemaker.*

## コンドーム
## KONDŌMU (CONDOM)

The most commonly used contraceptive device in Japan. In the 1980s something like 80 percent of couples used condoms. Until recently the Pill was heavily regulated and unavailable to most women, who turned to the condom as their major form of contraception. Many women buy their condoms from women who sell the product door to door.

◭ Sousuke comments on how one condom can hold a liter of water in *Full Metal Panic!* (ep. 1).

Ⓜ In volume 1 of *Peach Girl*, Momo finds a condom in Toji's wallet, not knowing someone slipped it in when he dropped it in class. • Makoto manages to save a girl from some thugs with the use of condoms in *IWGP: Ikebukuro West Gate Park* (vol. 1, p. 16). • Uchiyamada wonders about a distressingly familiar round outline in Onizuka's back pocket, just as Onizuka is talking to his daughter in *GTO* (vol. 18, ch. 144).

## 小西行長
## KONISHI YUKINAGA

?–1600. Yukinaga became a follower of **Toyotomi Hideyoshi** (AC vol. 1, p. 140) in 1577. Konishi Yukinaga was also known to Europeans by his Christian name of

**THE EXOTIC OCCULTISM OF THE WEST**

Ever wonder about those pentagrams, the diagrams in the opening of *Neon Genesis Evangelion*, and the stereotypical robed sorcerers in anime and manga?

Wonder no more; they are there because the West is so darned exotic! Just as some Western writers will use Asian elements in a story to make it exotic, the Japanese do the same. And just as Western writers get it wrong from a historical or cultural standpoint, so do the Japanese. In both cases this has never stopped anyone from tossing in a bunch of cool stuff from another society to make the story more colorful. In fact, many of the images the Japanese use come from Hollywood or old Hammer films. Perhaps that's why some of it looks so tacky.

Dom Agostinho. His father, a merchant, had also served Hideyoshi. His early service included a role as a naval commander in 1585 and 1587. In 1588 he and **Katō Kiyomasa** were sent to deal with a **samurai** (AC vol. 1, p. 110) uprising in Higo Province, today known as Kumamoto Prefecture, and to take over administration of the area, each becoming **daimyō** over half the province. Yukinaga and Kiyomasa were leaders in Hideyoshi's invasions of Korea. Yukinaga's army reached P'yongyang before being repulsed by the Chinese army. In 1600 he fought against the forces of **Tokugawa Ieyasu** at the **Sekigahara no Tatakai.** He could not commit **seppuku** (AC vol. 1, p. 115) after being defeated due to Christian prohibitions against suicide, so he was captured and executed in **Kyoto** (AC vol. 1, p. 77).

◭ Konishi Yukinaga's defeat at the battle of Sekigahara is mentioned early in *Ninja Resurrection* (ep. 1).

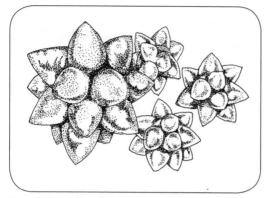

*Konpeitō: small, spiky, and sweet. How the heck do they make these things?*

## 金平糖
## KONPEITŌ

A simple candy in the form of small spiky balls made from sugar and cornstarch.
**A** The soot balls in the furnace room are fed with colored konpeitō in *Spirited Away.* • Kaori used a large mace with konpeitō written on it in *City Hunter 3* (ep. 1).

## コロッケ
## KOROKKE (CROQUETTE)

Introduced to Japan by the Portuguese, this fried food became very popular after WWII as a treat in those hard times. These days they can be bought in supermarkets, butcher shops, and even small korokke-ya. Croquettes are a mixture of any of a large variety of minced ingredients, formed into balls, then deep-fried. The ingredients include eggs as a binder, bread crumbs as a coating, and often flour or cooked grains. Corn and rice are used in some recipes.
**A** A croquette is burned by Mihoshi in the *Tenchi Universe* TV series (ep. 13). • Asuma asks for a croquette in the *Patlabor Original Series* (ep. 5).
**M** Near the end of volume 1, Nana makes croquettes for Eikichi in *GTO: Great Teacher Onizuka.*

## 高速道路
## KŌSOKU DŌRO (EXPRESSWAY)

Japan began building its expressway system in the 1960s with the first portion, the Meishin Expressway between Nagoya and **Kōbe,** opening in 1965. Given the geography of Japan with flat land being scarce and often occupied, construction costs are high, as are the tolls charged users.
**A** Shinobu is taking an expressway, the **shuto kōsoku wangan sen,** on her way to the **Yokohama bei buriji** early in *Patlabor 2.*

## コスプレ
## KOSUPURE (COSTUME PLAY)

Cosplay, or costume play. The act of dressing up in public as your favorite character. You can choose from anime, manga, rock stars, **aidoru** (AC vol. 1, p. 3), live-action shows, or game characters, or even make one up. One popular place to cosplay is **Harajuku** (AC vol. 1, p. 41), where on Sundays cosplayers gather to show off their costumes and get photographed.
**A** The ultimate example of cosplay has to be *Otaku no Video,* in which the activity is often mentioned and seen. • Nagisa wonders if Iczer One is doing cosplay in *Iczer One* (ep. 1). • Not knowing who she really is, Oji asks Yuki if she likes to cosplay when he first sees her in uniform in *The Legend of Black Heaven* (ep. 2).

## 江東区 OLD FORM 江東區
## KŌTŌ-KU

This ward of **Tokyo** is bordered on the north by Sumida Ward, on the east by **Edogawa-ku** and the **Sumidagawa, on** the south by **Tōkyō Wan,** and on the west by the Arakawa river, **Minato-ku,** Chūō Ward, and **Chiyoda-ku.** The **Fukagawa** district is in Kōtō Ward. This area still has a significant lumber industry, with several timber docks on the bay. Much of the southern part of Kōtō Ward is landfill, which led to the "great garbage war" of the early 1970s.

With two-thirds of Tokyo's garbage landfill taking place along the bay in Kōtō Ward, the local council passed a resolution in 1971 against being a dumping ground. The governor of Tokyo proposed that each ward set up treatment centers for its own garbage. The two wealthy wards of Suginami and Meguro opposed such plans for their areas. In 1973 the council of Kōtō Ward passed a resolution to use force to block trucks from Suginami Ward. In 1974 a processing plant was built in Suginami Ward.

**A** Near the end of the first *You're Under Arrest* episode, we see the diagram of the chase route, including through a timber dock, superimposed over a map of Kōtō Ward.

## 熊手 OR くまで
## KUMADE (BAMBOO RAKE)

 An ordinary bamboo rake. It is sometimes decorated to be a good-luck charm that literally "rakes in good luck." The rakes have various charms or depictions of desired objects attached to them. The good-luck charms are sold at **tori no ichi,** and the price of the rake goes up the fancier it gets. Traditionally, if you buy one you have to get a larger one the next year.

**A** We see a kumade good-luck charm on the altar in the *Irresponsible Captain Tylor* TV series (ep. 9).

**M** We also see one in *The Return of Lum Feudal Furor* in the upper left corner of page 71.

## 鎖帷子
## KUSARI-KATABIRA (CHAIN-MAIL VEST)

Part of the standard armor worn under the more ornate and visible plate armor of a warrior. Occasionally, kusari-katabira would be worn under regular clothes, a practice used by the police in the **Edo period** (AC vol. 1, p. 25) and by ninja.

**A** Kenshin comes up against opponents wearing kusari-katabira under their regular clothes in *Samurai X: Trust and Betrayal.*

**EXPRESSWAYS OF JAPAN**

On **Hokkaidō** (AC vol. 1, p. 46):
Dōō Expressway
Dōtō Expressway
Sasson Expressway

On **Honshū** (AC vol. 1, p. 47):
Akita Expressway
Ban'etsu Expressway
Bayshore Expressway (Shuto Kōsoku Wangan Sen)
Chūgoku Expressway
Chūō Expressway
Hachinohe Expressway
Hanwa Expressway
Higashi Kantō Expressway
Higashi Meihan Expressway
Hokuriku Expressway
Jōban Expressway
Jōshinetsu Expressway
Kan'etsu Expressway
Meishin Expressway
Nagano Expressway
Nishi-Meihan Expressway
San'yo Expressway
Tateyama Expressway
Tōhoku Expressway
Tōkai-Hokuriku Expressway
Tōmei Expressway

On **Kyushu** (AC vol. 1, p. 78):
Kyūshū Expressway
Kyūshū-Odan Expressway
Miyazaki Expressway
Ōita Expressway

On **Okinawa Ken** (AC vol. 1, p. 99):
Okinawa Expressway

On **Shikoku:**
Matsuyama Expressway
Takamatsu Expressway
Tokushima Expressway

*Sasuke in RANMA 1/2 may not be the coolest-looking ninja, but watch out for his **kusarifundo**.*

🅼 In *Lone Wolf and Cub* (vol. 3, p. 174), Ōgami points to the fact that his accusers came with kusari-katabira under their clothes as proof that the evidence found was not just discovered but planted.

鎖分銅
## KUSARIFUNDŌ (WEIGHTED CHAIN)

 A long length of chain weighted at each end with a piece of metal. Several techniques were developed to use this concealable weapon in both an offensive and defensive manner even against an opponent on horseback.

🅰 We see such a weighted chain, used by Sasuke, in *Ranma 1/2 Anything Goes Martial Arts* (ep. 17) and in *Dagger of Kamui*.

🅼 Less than savory fellows use this weapon in *Lone Wolf and Cub* (vol. 1, p. 220) and *The Legend of Kamui: Perfect Collection* (vol. 1, p. 27).

鎖鎌
## KUSARIGAMA (CHAIN AND SICKLE)

A weapon consisting of a sickle (*kama*) with a chain (*kusari*) attached to it. The chain could be wrapped around an opponent's weapon or body. The sickle could be used

to cut or kill the opponent. This weapon was popular not only with some warriors but with practitioners of **ninjutsu** (AC vol. 1, p. 95) and the police. There are variants that use a rope rather than a chain.

🅰 A variant of this weapon with a rope rather than a chain is seen in *The Legend of the Dog Warriors The Hakkenden* ep. 11. • A more traditional version is seen in the *Urusei Yatsura* TV series (ep. 55, st. 78). • In the opening animation of the *Rurouni Kenshin* TV series we see such a weapon used.

🅼 In *Vagabond* (vol. 12 and 13) we see this weapon used in the combat between Shishido Baiken and **Miyamoto Musashi** (AC vol. 1, p. 86).

くさそてつ or 草蘇鉄
## KUSASOTETSU (OSTRICH FERN)

A popular **sansai** (wild food plant). Boiling or simmering are two ways of preparing it for eating. The fiddlehead of the kusasotetsu is also called *kogomi* (こごみ or 屈み).

🅼 Ostrich ferns are for sale at the village market in *The Legend of Kamui: Perfect Collection* (vol. 1, p. 10). • In *Vagabond* (vol. 2, ch. 15), Otsu shows a large double handful of *kogomi* she has found.

串団子 OLD FORM 串團子
## KUSHI-DANGO

**Dango** skewered on a stick and grilled, then dipped in a mixture of sugar and **shōyu** (AC vol. 1, p. 124). This is a very common form of dango and is the one most likely to be seen in anime and manga.

🅼 Ataru enjoys kushi-dango in his typical inelegant manner in *Urusei Yatsura: The Return of Lum, Urusei Yatsura: Sweet Revenge* (p. 77) and the *Urusei Yatsura* TV series (ep. "Spring Special 2").

🅰 Botchan has kushi-dango after his bath near the red-light district in *Botchan* (pt. 1). • In *Saber Marionette J Again* (ep. 4), a plate of dango sits

*In* Samurai X Trust and Betrayal *using animals to till a small field is impractical, so a* **kuwa** *does the job.*

on the counter next to a platter with sauce as everyone talks in the restaurant. Further down the counter is a plate of kushi-dango.

🅜 Mr. Yotsuya enjoys some kushi-dango at a stand on the beach in *Maison Ikkoku* (vol. 6, p. 198).
• Mrs. Kakei brings over kushi-dango when she visits in *Rumic Theater* (p. 20).

鍬
## KUWA (HOE)

A hoe, the head of which could be made either entirely of metal or of wood with a metal blade attached to the end. The later type would require less metal and be more affordable. When seen in anime or manga, this implement is used to till small fields. In the famous novel *Musashi* (see **Yoshikawa Eiji**), there is a scene in the chapter called "The Hōzōin" in which **Miyamoto Musashi** (AC vol. 1, p. 86) feels great fear from an old monk tilling a field with a *kuwagara*, the long-handled hoe.

🅐 In *Metal Fighter Miku* (ep. 11), a nun using a hoe to till a field terrifies Miku, an obvious reference to the scene in *Musashi*. • Kenshin uses a *kuwagara* to prepare a plot of land for him and Tomoe in *Samurai X: Trust and Betrayal*. • Tenchi uses one to till land for carrots in *Tenchi Muyo! Special: The Night Before the Carnival* (OVA 7).

🅜 In *Vagabond* (vol. 4, ch. 37), Takehiko Inoue's adaptation of the *Musashi* novel, we also see the scene with the old monk.

くずもち OR 葛餅 OLD FORM 葛餅
## KUZU MOCHI (ARROWROOT CAKE)

White cakes (**mochi**, AC vol. 1, p. 87) made from the starch of the kuzu root (kudzu, often translated as "arrowroot"), usually cut into triangular shapes and served sweetened.

🅐 Kuzu mochi, translated as "arrowroot cake," is eaten by Kaoru in the sweet shop in **Asakusa** (AC vol. 1, p. 6) in *Rurouni Kenshin* (TV ep. 89).

京都所司代 FORMAL 京都所司代
## KYŌTO SHOSHIDAI (KYOTO DEPUTY)

An appointed governor of **Kyoto** (AC vol. 1, p. 77). Originally, this position was created by **Oda Nobunaga**. In the **Edo period** (AC vol. 1, p. 25), he also had administrative responsibilities in adjacent provinces and kept an eye on the activities of the Western **daimyō**. Every five years he would go to **Edo** and report to the **shōgun** (AC vol. 1, p. 123).

🅐 The Kyōto Shoshidai is mentioned in *Samurai X: Trust and Betrayal* and in the *Rurouni Kenshin* TV series (ep. 28).

🅜 A report by the Kyoto Shoshidai that has been intercepted is read in *Lone Wolf and Cub* (vol. 11, p. 259).

京都守護職 FORMAL 京都守護職
## KYŌTO SHUGOSHOKU (KYOTO MILITARY COMMISSIONER)

This position was established by the **bakufu** in September 1862 with police control of **Kyoto** (AC vol. 1, p. 77) and **Osaka** (AC vol. 1, p. 102) to oppose the pro-imperial forces in the area. The Kyōto Shugoshoku continued to exist until the end of the **Edo period** (AC vol. 1, p. 25).

🅐 The Kyōto Shugoshoku is mentioned in *Samurai X: Trust and Betrayal*.

portant for silk trading and manufacturing, which continued to be a major industry until after WWII. Lumber, electronics, and transport equipment are the major industries today.

🄰 Noa and Asuma go to Maebashi in *Patlabor: The New Files* (ep. 16), "All Quiet at the Second Unit."

## ロッテ
## LOTTE CO., LTD.

A major candy, drink, and dessert manufacturer headquartered in **Tokyo.** The company was founded in 1948 and today has major subsidiaries, including a fast-food chain (Lotteria), a deli chain (Mutter Rosa), a baseball team (Chiba Lotte Marines), and an electronics division. Its headquarters is located in **Shinjuku-ku** (AC vol. 1, p. 120).

🄰 Lotte is the manufacturer of **Green Gum.** In *Fushigi Yūgi* (ep. 3 and 4) we see Miaka chew Green Gum ,and later Tamahome attempts to auction some off as a rare item to a crowd.

## メルヘン or メルヒェン
## MÄRCHEN (MAGICAL FOLK TALE)

A German term universally used by folklorists to designate tales with magic or the supernatural as a motif. Often this is translated as "fairy tales," but this is not quite accurate as most such tales do not have fairies in them. A common element in Märchen is triumph over adversity. The earliest book to attempt the serious study of Märchen was *Kinder-und Hausmärchen* by the Brothers Grimm.

🄰 In *Urusei Yatsura Movie 3 Remember My Love* an amusement park named Tomobikicho Märchenland plays key a role in the story. • In *Otaku no Video* (pt. 2, 2nd anim. seq.) the character Märchen Doll Maki is unveiled. • Many works by Miyazaki Hayao fall into the category of Märchen. Some examples include *My Neighbor Totoro, Kiki's Delivery Service,* and *Spirited Away.*

## 前橋 [市]
## MAEBASHI

The capital of **Gunma Ken** in central **Honshu** (AC vol. 1, p. 47). In the 8th century Maebashi was a locally significant city. In the **Edo period** (AC vol. 1, p. 25) it became im-

## 丸
## MARU

A suffix added to some names. The use of maru at the end of names has historically been used for boys names and for items one is fond of such as swords, flutes, hawks, etc. The parts of a castle also often end in maru, as do the names of many businesses and ships. Adults with certain skills often would have the ending on their name. Interestingly enough, prisoners would have it added to their names by their captors to signify an almost parental authority over them. The origin of this ending is disputed, with many possible origins conjectured by scholars; a likely one is that it comes from *maru*, meaning "round."

Ⓜ The most famous business name ending in maru is the Chachamaru bar in *Maison Ikkoku.* • Then there is the ship in *Plastic Little,* also named the Chachamaru.

Ⓜ In *Shadow Star* (vol. 1), Hoshimaru's name is given to him by Shiina, who explains that it is a combination of star (*hoshi*) and round (maru).

## 将門塚 FORMAL 將門塚
## MASAKADO-ZUKA (MASAKADO'S MOUND)

The burial place of the head of **Taira no Masakado** in what is now **Tokyo,** specifically in **Chiyoda-ku.** Legend has it that upon his death in battle in 940, his head flew to the spot where it was respectfully buried by the locals, who considered Taira no Masakado a hero. They also placed a stone marker in front of the mound and worshipped him at Kanda Myōjin. In the 13th century, a Tendai temple was built near the mound. Locals blamed the plague and calamities of the time on the temple because the construction was seen as an insult to Taira no Masakado. In the **Edo period** (AC vol. 1, p. 25) Kanda Myōjin was moved, but the mound remained in a garden built for a **daimyō.** The Meiji government built a new building for the Finance Ministry on the location in 1869, again leaving the mound unmolested. In the **Kantō Daishinsai** of 1923 the mound was destroyed and the stone damaged. A few years later, after a series of suicides by local business managers in the area, the stone was replaced and the suicides stopped. Today the stone stands behind an office building. Flowers, incense, and occasional **sake** (AC vol. 1, p. 109) offerings seem to keep the spirit of Taira no Masakado happy.

Ⓐ In *Doomed Megalopolis,* several attempts are made at the Masakado-zuka to raise the spirit of Taira no Masakado to destroy **Tokyo.** This OVA series opens with the modern setting of the mound. • Clancy refers to the tomb of Masakado in *Patlabor the TV Series* (ep. 19).

## THEY DON'T LOOK JAPANESE!

Of course they don't look Japanese. They don't even look human!

They are cartoon characters, and the level of detail in animated art or comics is abstracted for simplicity. Scott McCloud in his classic *Understanding Comics* writes, and draws, about the way we perceive drawings that are not realistic as still being faces, etc. Sure Sakura (pretty much any Sakura in any anime) does not look Japanese, but she does not look European either. She is a character represented by a drawing. What makes her Japanese is the setting of the story.

Now, there are artists who aim for a more realistic look, such as Otomo in his *Akira* manga and anime. But even there, abstraction is part of the process. The more realistic Japanese artists may have been influenced by some of the European artists, whose graphic novels have a very different style from those of Japan. In some cases the artists seem to be drawing characters that are more Caucasian.

However, something happened to me years ago that makes me wonder about such claims. I live in the San Francisco Bay Area where we have subtitled Japanese shows on regular broadcast on Saturday evenings. I was watching a *dorama* about work in a modern restaurant with a couple of friends, neither of whom had ever watched Japanese TV before. One of my friends pointed to an actor and said, "He doesn't look Japanese!" The other friend, who is an artist and a fan of Japanese woodblock prints, replied "Sure he does. Just look at that long nose. It could have come from an Edo-period print." So it's not just anime characters but real people being accused of not looking Japanese. Perhaps we need to review our perceptions of what it means to "look Japanese," especially when we are looking at drawings or an actual Japanese person in Western clothing.

Does the artist draw with a European influence and make his characters look non-Japanese? Is the actor of mixed ancestry? Are we just interpreting what we see according to preconceptions that don't apply?

## 枡屋
## MASUYA

A shop in **Kyoto** (AC vol. 1, p. 77) run by a merchant named Kiemon, a pseudonym for the **samurai** (AC vol. 1, p. 110) Kotaka Shuntarō of the **Chōshū Han**. In 1864, Masuya was raided by the **Shinsengumi. Teppō** (AC vol. 1, p. 135) and ammunition were found hidden in a secret compartment. As was the case with almost all shops, the owner lived in the same building; thus Kotaka was captured and tortured. The shop had been discovered by following a servant of **Miyabe Teizō**, who had also been living at the shop. Less than a week later the **Ikedaya Jiken** took place.

△ We hear a Shinsengumi member mention the weapons found at Masuya in *Samurai X: Trust and Betrayal*.

## めんるい OR 麺類
## MEN RUI (NOODLES)

A wide variety of noodles is available in Japan, both native styles and types originating in China and other countries. Some of the common ones include **hiyamugi, sōmen** (AC vol. 1, p. 46), **rāmen** (AC vol. 1, p. 105), **soba,** and **udon.**

△ In a stand-and-eat noodle place in **Tomakomai,** Kai orders a bowl of noodles without **negi** and adds **shichimi tōgarashi** from a small red shaker in episode 5 of *Patlabor Original Series.*

## 三重県 OLD FORM 三重縣
## MIE KEN

A prefecture located in **Honshu** (AC vol. 1, p. 47) on the Kii Peninsula. The famous **Ise Jingū** (AC vol. 1, p. 51) is here. Mie's economy is based on forestry in the south and industry in the north, as well as agriculture, including high-quality beef. This area is also known for a national park system that draws many visitors every year.

△ In *Blue Seed* (ep. 17) part of the story takes place in **Ise** (AC vol. 1, p. 51) in Mie Prefecture.

## 密教 OLD FORM 密敎
## MIKKYŌ (ESOTERIC BUDDHISM)

A type of Mahayana Buddhism with special teachings said to have come from Dainichi, the Dharma-kaya Buddha. A series of initiations is required to learn these teachings. Mikkyō originated in India and neighboring areas between the 2nd and 8th centuries. Mikkyō incorporated many influences from Hinduism and local religions in its practices. A major practice of mikkyō is the use of prayers or incantations for practical ends, which resulted in the religion gaining a reputation for magic. It entered Japan from China through the teachings of Kūkai, who is also known as Kōbō-daishi, and is practiced by the Shingon sect. Japanese Tendai also incorporated mikkyō teaching and practices in Japan, practices that were not part of T'ien-t'ai teaching in China. Today this type of Buddhism is practiced almost exclusively in Japan; in other parts of the world it has vanished or been supplanted by other schools of Buddhism.

△ In *Phantom Quest Corps* (ep. 4), Ayaka gets some competition in the form of a mikkyō sect. • Sanosuke wonders if Yukyuzán Anji is a mikkyō practitioner when he first meets him in *Rurouni Kenshin* (ep. 38). • Mikkyō is translated as tantric, which is not quite accurate, in *Spirit Warrior* (ep. 1). • In *Lupin the 3rd: The Pursuit of Harimao's Treasure* Harimao is said to be a believer in mikkyō.

## 港区 OLD FORM 港區
## MINATO-KU

A ward of **Tokyo** located on the edge of **Tōkyō Wan**, bordered by **Shinagawa-ku** to the south, **Shibuya-ku** to the west, and to the north by **Shinjuku-ku** (AC vol. 1, p. 120), **Chiyoda-ku,** and Chūō Ward. Minato-ku is the location of many embassies, businesses, and expensive homes. Noted areas in this ward include **Azabu Jūban** (AC vol. 1, p. 8), **Akasaka,** and **Roppongi** (AC vol. 1, p. 106). Famous landmarks include **Aoyama Reien** (AC vol. 1, p. 6), **Tokyo Tawā** (AC vol. 1, p. 138), the **Rainbow Bridge,** the World Trade Center, and the Tōgū Palace.

🅐 A meeting takes place in a traditional restaurant in Akasaka, Minato Ward, in *Otaku no Video* (pt. 2, 2nd anim. seq.). • Yoko is from Minato Ward in *Kimagure Orange Road* TV (ep. 27).

## みそラーメン or 味噌ラーメン
## MISO-RĀMEN

A **rāmen** (AC vol. 1, p. 105) dish with **miso** (soy bean paste; AC vol. 1, p. 84) added to the broth. This variety of rāmen originated in **Sapporo** (AC vol. 1, p. 111).

🅐 On the signs handwritten on a restaurant wall we see miso rāmen, shio rāmen, and **gyōza** (AC vol. 1, p. 37) in *GTO* (ep. 15).

Ⓜ In *Survival in the Office* (vol. 1, p. 48), an **OL** (AC vol. 1, p. 100) orders noodles (**men rui**) in miso soup (miso-rāmen). • In *GTO* (vol. 11, p. 135) we read that miso rāmen and **takoyaki** (AC vol. 1, p. 132) are Tomoko's favorite foods.

## 三鷹 [市]
## MITAKA

A city in **Tokyo** Prefecture. Until the **Shōwa jidai,** Mitaka was a farming area on the Musashino Plain. Heavy industrialization took place in this area during WWII. Today Mitaka is a residential city. The Ghibli Museum is located here.

🅐 Misako wore a Musashino Seika Girl's school uniform and is probably from Mitaka in *Here Is Greenwood* (ep. 4).

Ⓜ Mitaka-shi Tokyo is mentioned in *Voyeur* (vol. 1, p. 35), and Mitaka Station is seen in *Video Girl Ai* (vol. 5, p. 46).

## 水戸藩 old form 水戸藩
## MITO HAN

An **Edo period** (AC vol. 1, p. 25) **han** in parts of the provinces of Hitachi and Shimotsuke. It was first granted to Tokugawa Yorifusa, the eleventh son of **Tokugawa Ieyasu** and the father of **Tokugawa Mitsukuni.** The Mito domain was famous for its **Shintō** (AC vol. 1, p. 121) and Confucian (**Jukyō,** AC vol. 1, p. 56) scholarship. The **daimyō** of this domain inherited the position of vice-shōgun and could not become **shōgun** (AC vol. 1, p. 123). He usually resided in **Edo** and did not have to participate in the **sankin kōtai. Tokugawa Yoshinobu,** the last shōgun, was from Mito Han.

Ⓜ Ōgami carries out an assassination of a pro-imperial official in the Mito domain in *Lone Wolf and Cub* (vol. 1, p. 130), and a note in the text (vol. 9, p. 71) mentions the exception from the sankin kōtai.

## 三菱
## MITSUBISHI

A major business founded in the **Meiji period** (AC vol. 1, p. 81) by Iwasaki Yatarō. When the **Tosa Han** shipping company was reorganized in 1871 due to the abolition of the **han** system, Iwasaki's company obtained some of its former facilities and eleven ships. A few years later, in 1873, the company was renamed Mitsubishi Shōkai. Mitsubishi diversified into mining, banking, ship building, real estate, and eventually aircraft building. Two of their most famous planes were the **Betty** and the **Zerosen.** After WWII Mitsubishi was broken up by the U.S. Occupation authorities into several companies that are independent but continue to be affiliated.

🅐 The Mitsubishi logo is clearly visible on a round building in the first episode of the *City Hunter 1* TV series when the killer is chasing after Ryo, and Mitsubishi is on a sign in *Dirty Pair Project EDEN.* • We also see a large Mitsubishi Fuso truck in the second episode of *Neon Genesis Evangelion.*

## 宮部鼎蔵 OLD FORM 宮部鼎蔵
## MIYABE TEIZŌ

Former chief military instructor in the castle town of Kumamoto in Higo Province. In 1861 he left, becoming a **rōnin** (AC vol. 1, p. 106), to join the other **shishi** in **Kyoto** (AC vol. 1, p. 77). In 1864 he was living in **Masuya** and gathering fighters; his plan was to capture the Imperial Palace and have the emperor order the destruction of the **bakufu** and appoint the lord of the **Chōshū Han** as the Protector of Kyoto. This scheme involved the use of fire as a weapon to create a diversion and was opposed by many other shishi leaders.

🅰 Miyabe is often mentioned but never seen in *Samurai X: Trust and Betrayal.*

## 盛岡 [市]
## MORIOKA

Capital of **Iwate Ken** located on the Kitakamigawa river. In the **Edo period** (AC vol. 1, p. 25) this was the castle town for the Nanbu family. This city has been famous for centuries for its Nanbu ironware and is the location of Iwate University.

🅰 In *Fushigi Yūgi* (ep. 42) we hear that Morioka is famous for **Ishikawa Takuboku** and **Miyazawa Kenji** (AC vol. 1, p. 86).

## 無外流
## MUGAI RYŪ

A sword school (**ryū**) with a philosophical basis in Chinese Yin Yang theories. While the school has an aggressive combative style, strong moral and spiritual discipline is a key part of its teachings. The founder, Tsuji Gettan Sukemochi, was the son of farmers and started the Mugai Ryū after more than thirty years of training, including the study of Chinese classics and **zazen.**

🅰 The Mugai Ryū style is mentioned in *Samurai X: Trust and Betrayal*

Ⓜ One of Ōgami's opponents states that even the Mugai Ryū would be no match for his technique in *Lone Wolf and Cub* (vol. 5, p. 63).

## 麦茶
## MUGICHA (BARLEY TEA)

A simple drink made from roasted barley. In the summer this is a popular cold beverage. The golden brown color makes it easy to spot in anime. You can buy it in tea bags, loose, or in bottles and cans.

🅰 Barley tea is passed in an interesting way in *Mahoromatic* (ep. 3).

Ⓜ Kosaku offers a visitor barley tea in vol. 1 of *One Pound Gospel* (p. 169). • Rin orders **warabi** sweet cake and barley tea at a roadside tea house in *Blade of the Immortal: Cry of the Worm.* • It's hot and Onizuka decides to treat the entire school to barley tea in *GTO* (vol. 18, ch. 143). To do this he uses up the school's supply for an entire year.

## 武者修行 OLD FORM 武者修行
## MUSHA SHUGYŌ (WARRIOR PILGRIMAGE)

The period in a young warrior's life when he would travel, honing his skill at other **dōjō** (AC vol. 1, p. 23) and **taryū-jiai**. These could be solitary voyages, or the warrior could be accompanied by followers. The word **shugyō** is also used for religious pilgrimages, and the warrior's pilgrimage thus has a connotation of the spiritual as well as the martial. One of the most famous persons to have undertaken such a training journey was the 16th-century sword master **Tsukahara Bokuden,** who made three such journeys in his life.

Ⓜ In *Vagabond* (vol. 2, ch. 15) we see the combat between the young Takezō and **Arima Kihei,** a swordsman who is on a musha shugyō. Later in volume 3 we see **Miyamoto Musashi** (AC vol. 1, p. 86) beginning his own musha shugyō.

# N

that specialize in this dish called nabemono-ryōri-ya. Nabemono is a popular dish during the colder times of the year.

 The class makes a nabemono together using some very questionable mushrooms Cherry has picked in *Urusei Yatsura* (ep. 86, st. 109).

 When Otsu returns from gathering **sansai** for the nabemono, **Takuan** is very pleased in *Vagabond* (vol. 2, ch. 15).

## なべ OR 鍋
## NABE (IRON POT)

A pot or pan for cooking, usually made of iron. Nabe come in a variety of shapes and sizes, some specialized for certain foods such as **sukiyaki** (AC vol. 1, p. 126). In traditional homes they would often be seen hanging from a **jizaikagi** (AC vol. 1, p. 55). Food dishes cooked in a nabe are referred to as **nabemono.** Ceramic nabe are called **donabe.**

 A good view of such a pot is near the end of *Ranma 1/2 Anything: Anything-Goes Martial Arts* (ep. 9).

 In *Inu-Yasha* (vol. 8, p. 172), we see a nabe with an **otoshibuta** in it as Kaede and Kikyo speak. • Kaii shares a meal cooked in a nabe with Itto and Retsudō in *Lone Wolf and Cub* (vol. 24, p. 104). • **Takuan** is very pleased when Otsu brings the **sansai** she has gathered for the nabemono in *Vagabond* (vol. 2, ch. 15).

## なべもの OR 鍋物
## NABEMONO (ONE POT MEALS)

Meals in which all the ingredients have been cooked in the same pot, either a **nabe** or **donabe.** Usually these are vegetables, meat, and fish boiled or simmered together in water or **dashi.** There are also many specific types of nabemono, though they are often difficult to identify in anime or manga. Some **ryokan** (AC vol. 1, p. 107) serve this dish so it is cooked on the **chabudai** (AC vol. 1, p. 17) in front of the guests. There is even a category of restaurants

## 鍋焼きうどん OLD FORM 鍋燒うどん
## NABEYAKI-UDON

A **nabemono** of **udon** usually with seafood, vegetables, and meat. Occasionally a large **tenpura** shrimp or slice of hard-boiled egg will be added. This is considered a winter dish and is commonly served in the **donabe** in which it was cooked.

 A donabe, containing nabeyaki-udon, is brought by Kyoko to Godai as he studies in *Maison Ikkoku* (vol. 7, p. 83).

## 長屋
## NAGAYA (ROW HOUSE)

One-story wooden apartment buildings often with ten to twenty rooms. These were usually organized in blocks with a

*There's not much room in the **nagaya** seen here in* RUROUNI KENSHIN, *but those who lived in them didn't have much to clutter them up.*

©NOBUHIRO WATSUKI/SHUEISHA • FUJI-TV • ANIPLEX INC.

separate entrance to the complex. Inhabitants of *nagaya*, usually families, would form small communities, often assisting each other in times of need. The interior of an apartment would commonly include a combined **genkan** (AC vol. 1, p. 34) and kitchen consisting of an earthen floor just inside the entrance. The living area would usually be four-and-a-half to six **tatami** (AC vol. 1, p. 134) mats in size. **Futon** (AC vol. 1, p. 32) would be stored in a corner when not in use, and the space would also double as a workshop. The entrance was usually separated from the living area with a wide wooden step under which was storage and by a **shōji** (AC vol. 1, p. 123) screen. The tatami, futon, shoji, and any small items of furniture were provided by the tenant, who would take them when he moved. Water was supplied by a well and there was a common privy, the waste from which would be sold by the landlord to farmers for fertilizer. During the **Edo period** (AC vol. 1, p. 25), nagaya were a common form of housing for workers and tradespeople, something like 70 to 80 percent of townspeople in **Edo** lived in them. Not all dwellers in nagaya were ordinary city dwellers. At **daimyō** residences the interior of the outer walls were actually nagaya for low-ranking **samurai** (AC vol. 1, p. 110).

🄰 Many of Sanosuke's friends in the *Rurouni Kenshin* TV series live in nagaya; an excellent view of the interior of one is in episode 23. • In *Saber Marionette J* Otaru is seen living in a nagaya.

🄼 Shira hires a few thugs in a nagaya in *Blade of the Immortal* (vol. 12). • In *Uzumaki*, the nagaya scattered around town turn out to have an interesting history, a very nasty history.

## 内務省
## NAIMUSHŌ (MINISTRY OF THE INTERIOR)

Created November 1873 and headed by **Ōkubo Toshimichi** to deal with matters of domestic security and industrial development. Its offices were built on the former estate of the Sakai family, the former lords of **Himejijō**. Starting in the 1880s, under a new head,

the Naimushō began to take a more active role in suppressing human rights. After WWII it was abolished by the Occupation forces.

🄼 Ōkubo Toshimichi, who headed up the Naimushō, is in *Rurouni Kenshin* (TV ep. 30 and vol. 1, p. 129).

## 中野区 OLD FORM 中野區
## NAKANO-KU

A ward of **Tokyo** located on the Musashino plateau and bordered on the north and west by **Nerima-ku,** on the south by Suginami Ward, and on the east by **Shinjuku-ku** (AC vol. 1, p. 120). During the **Edo period** (AC vol. 1, p. 25) this was a farming area and was also set aside by **Tokugawa Iemitsu** as a hunting preserve for the **shōgun** (AC vol. 1, p. 123) After the **Kantō Daishinsai,** many residents of the city moved to the Nakan area. Today it is mainly a residential community.

🄰 This is where Koji lives in *Metal Skin Panic— MADOX-01*.

## 中山道 OR 中仙道
## NAKASENDŌ

One of the Gokaidō, or five main highways, of the **Edo period** (AC vol. 1, p. 25). The Nakasendō is sometimes referred to as the Kiso Kaidō or the Kisoji. Constructed originally in 702, during the Edo period this road was controlled by the **bakufu**, who maintained sixty-seven **shukuba machi** along its 500 kilometers (310 miles). In the Edo period this road began at **Nihonbashi** (AC vol. 1, p. 94) in **Edo** and led to **Kyoto** (AC vol. 1, p. 77) by way of the central Japan mountains. Because it was mountainous, it had less traffic than the **Tōkaidō.**

🄰 Sanosuke mentions the Nakasendō in *Rurouni Kenshin* (ep. 38). • Tokugawa Hidetada on the Nakasendō is mentioned by Sanada Nobuyuki in *Samurai Deeper Kyo* (ep. 7).

🄼 In the first chapter of *Blade of the Immortal: The Gathering* Hyakurin mentions the Nakasendō when speaking to Manji. • The sixth chapter of *Lone Wolf and Cub* (vol. 1, p. 159) takes place on the Nakasendō. • Some bloody events take place on the Nakasendō in chapter 2 of *Samurai Legend*.

## 奈良 [市]
## NARA

 The Japanese capital from 710–84. After the new capital was established in **Kyoto** (AC vol. 1, p. 77), Nara continued to be an important center for cultural and religious developments. Today it is the capital of Nara Prefecture in central **Honshu** (AC vol. 1, p. 47). Nara avoided damage from bombing in WWII and contains a rich collection of some of Japan's most important ancient and historical buildings. Nara park is famous for its tame **shika** (AC vol. 1, p. 117).

One *Urusei Yatsura* story takes place in Nara (TV ep. "Spring Special 2" and *The Return of Lum: Sweet Revenge* (p. 69–).

An episode of *Blue Seed* (ep. 14) also takes place in Nara.

Jiro goes to Iga from Nara in *Dagger of Kamui* and **Miyamoto Musashi** (AC vol. 1, p. 86) heads for Nara in volume 4 of *Vagabond*.

## ねぎ OR 葱
## NEGI (SPRING ONION)

*Allium fistulosum*. A type of onion, often referred to as leek (which it is not), spring onion, or welsh onion, even though it has nothing to do with Wales. It is often sliced very thin as a condiment for **men rui** (noodle) dishes, soups, and in **nabemono.** In the Kantō region, the white part is usually favored; in the Kansai region the green part is preferred. It grows year round but is said to be better in winter.

In a noodle stand in **Tomakomai** Kai orders a bowl of noodles without negi and adds **shichimi tōgarashi** from a small red shaker in episode 5 of *Patlabor Original Series*. • In *City Hunter: Million*

### NEWTONS IN ANIME

Before there was the BlackBerry, even before there was the Palm, there was the Newton, the first PDA with handwriting recognition. From 1993 to 1998, Apple sold these handy devices until the smaller, less expensive Palm was introduced and the market for the Newton shrank. Many Newton owners still use their machines, which says something about the robustness of the hardware. If you see someone flip open what looks like a large Palm handheld and start using a stylus, sneak a peek and try to spot Apple's old rainbow logo below the screen.

Where can we find the Newton in anime?

*801 T.T.S. Airbats.* In episode 4, we see Isurugi use an Apple Newton, either a 100, 120, or 130, to look up information on a **Zerosen** in a database.

*Neon Genesis Evangelion.* In episode 21, during the flashbacks to when Gehirn existed, a guard uses a Newton with an attached card reader to verify Ritsuko's identity. You can even read the buttons on this ancestor of today's PDA. Thanks go to Leonid G. Bashkirov of Mactime.ru for letting me know about this one. And in episode 23, Ritsuko uses a Newton MessagePad 100 as her remote control unit when she is explaining the secret of the dummy plugs. There may be more examples out there. If you spot one, let me know.

*Dollar Conspiracy,* we see Umibozu buying negi at a good price.

## 練馬区
## NERIMA-KU

A ward of **Tokyo** bordered on the west by Hōya city, on the south by Musashino city, Suginami Ward, as well as **Nakano-ku,** on the east by Toshima and Itabashi wards, and on the north by Saitama Prefecture. It is mainly a residential area for the metropolitan part of Tokyo.

🅐 Much of the *All Purpose Cultural Cat Girl Nuku Nuku* OVA series takes place in Nerima.. • Nerima is where Ataru uses a pay phone in the *Urusei Yatsura* TV series (ep. 6, st. 11).

🅜 At the end of *Dark Angel* vol. 1, we see Asamiya and some of his assistants hard at work playing **pachinko** (AC vol. 1, p. 104) near the studio in Nerima. • In the supplemental story at the end of *Outlanders* (vol. 2), we see an enterprising street vendor selling extract of viper juice from the savage jungles of Nerima. • In *Caravan Kidd* (vol. 1, p. 52), Babo eats at a **yatai** (AC vol. 1, p. 147) and complains that "in the old days Nerima was a lively place."

## 鼠小僧
## NEZUMI KOZŌ

A famous **Edo** thief from the 1820s. He was known for bold assaults on the homes of the rich. This audacity made him very popular with the people of the city. After he was captured and executed he became the subject of **kabuki** plays and fiction. His tomb is at Ekōin, a Buddhist temple, in Sumida Ward not far from the **Ryōgokubashi** bridge.

🅐 Nezumi Kozō, translated as Rat Boy, is mentioned and shown in an **Edo period** (AC vol. 1 p. 25) print, and his descendant is a character in *Lupin the 3rd—Mission: Irresistible* (ep. "Rats to You").

🅜 Nezumi Kozō is mentioned in a song composed by O-Maki in *Blade of the Immortal: Dreamsong* (pt. 2).

## 日米修好通商条約 OLD FORM 日米修好通商條約
## NICHIBEI SHŪKŌ TSŪSHŌ JŌYAKU (JAPAN-U.S. FRIENDSHIP AND COMMERCE TREATY)

The United States Japan Treaty of Amity and Commerce, also known as the Harris Treaty, the Japan-U.S. Trade and Commerce Treaty, and the Japan-U.S. Friendship and Commerce Treaty. This treaty on trade was signed in Kanagawa, now a part of **Yokohama,** on July 29, 1858, between representatives of the **bakufu** and the United States with Townsend Harris, consul general, representing the United States. This treaty expanded the number of ports open to the United States to include Yokohama, **Kōbe**, and **Nagasaki** (AC vol. 1, p. 90); at that time the only ports open were **Shimoda** and **Hakodate.** It also allowed for the exchange of diplomats, upheld religious freedom in Japan, made it possible for Japan to have ships built in the United States, and appointed the United States as mediator in disputes with European countries. The treaty went into effect on July 4, 1859. The fact that this treaty was signed without the consent of the emperor fueled the conflicts of the **bakumatsu.**

🅐 The Japan-U.S. Trade and Commerce Treaty is mentioned by Madoka as she and Kyosuke quiz each other in *Kimagure Orange Road: I Want to Return to That Day.* • The Japan-U.S. Friendship and Commerce Treaty is mentioned by Miaka as she studies early in episode 17 of *Fushigi Yūgi.*

## 日米和親条約 OLD FORM 日米和親條約
## NICHIBEI WASHIN JŌYAKU (TREATY OF KANAGAWA)

The Treaty of Peace and Amity Between the United States and The Empire of Japan, also known as the Treaty of Kanagawa. This treaty was signed in Kanagawa, now a part of **Yokohama,** on March 31, 1854 between representatives of the **bakufu** and the United States, with **Matthew Calbraith Perry** representing the United States. The treaty called for the opening of the ports of **Shimoda** and **Hakodate, the** provisioning of ships visiting those ports, the treatment of shipwrecked sailors, and the establishment of an American consulate in Shimoda. This is the treaty that ended Japan's long isolation of the **Edo period** (AC vol. 1, p. 25).

🅜 The Nichibei Washin Jōyaku is mentioned by Miaka as she studies in *Fushigi Yūgi* (TV ep. 17 and vol. 5, p. 9).

## 日本海 OLD FORM 日本海
## NIHONKAI (SEA OF JAPAN)

The sea between Japan and the Asian continent. It is a significant source of seafood and, in the winter, winds blowing from the northwest pick up moisture and drop it as large amounts of snow along the coastal areas of **Honshu** (AC vol. 1, p. 47), giving the famous Snow Country its name.

**A** A radio weather report states that a typhoon (**taifū** AC vol. 1, p. 130) is expected to cross Honshu and enter the Sea of Japan in *Patlabor New Files* (ep. 12). • Episode 9 of the *Patlabor the TV Series* partly takes place in **Sakata** on the shores of the Nihonkai.

## にんじん OR 人参 OLD FORM 人参
## NINJIN

Carrot. Western carrots and a Japanese variety that is more reddish are available in markets. They are commonly simmered. One cultural aspect of carrots is that many Japanese children and adults do not like them. This is a humorous element in some series, much like American jokes about children who do not like peas.

**A** In *Haibane Renmei* (ep. 3), the kids strongly express their dislike of carrots. In *Gundam 0083*, Kou often requests no carrots when eating in the mess hall. Naturally, the servers often give him extra.

## 庭番
## NIWABAN

Garden guards. Special attendants who supervised the guardians at the **Edojō** of the **Tokugawa** (AC vol. 1, p. 137) **shōgun** (AC vol. 1, p. 123). This position was established by **Tokugawa Yoshimune**, who brought the original niwaban with him from the Kii domain. They also escorted the shōgun in the gardens and occasionally worked as secret agents.

**A** The Niwaban-shu is suspected of having sent an assassin in *Samurai X: Trust and Betrayal*.

**M** In *Lone Wolf and Cub* (vol. 1, p. 288) the niwaban are referred to as a type of ninja.

## 能
## NŌ

A theatrical dance form originating in the 14th century. Nō is a highly stylized combination of music, chant, and restrained dance.

The background of Nō is a complex blend of elements. Its origins go back to professional troupes affiliated with **Shintō** (AC vol. 1, p. 121) shrines (**jinja** AC vol. 1, p. 54) and Buddhist temples (**jiin** (AC vol. 1, p. 53). The style of these performances were called *dengaku* Nō and *sarugaku* Nō. The masks come from an earlier style of dance drama called *gigaku*.

The themes of Nō are influenced by Buddhism, and the music consists of drums and flute with a chorus usually of six or eight members. The music is from Shintō **kagura,** Buddhist worship services, popular 10th-century songs called *imayō*, and 13th-century party music called enkyoku. The dance is influenced by 7th-century dance and music called **bugaku** and by an 11th-century dance style called *furyū*, which also used flute and drum. Added to all of this is the 12th-century dance and song drama style called *shirabyōshi*.

In the **Muromachi period** (AC vol. 1, p. 90) *sarugaku* Nō was transformed into what we now call Nō by a famous writer/performer named Kan'ami and his son, Zeami, who founded the Kanze school of Nō, which was originally patronized by the Ashikaga shōguns. During the **Sengoku jidai** (AC vol. 1, p. 113) the **bakufu** was preoccupied with survival and Nō began to be patronized by other classes, especially the **samurai** (AC vol. 1, p. 110). In 1571, the Kanze school performed for **Tokugawa Ieyasu**. Among the viewers was **Toyotomi Hideyoshi** (AC vol. 1, p. 140), who was to become a major supporter of Nō, even learning the techniques so he could perform the dramas

*A brew, a light meal, and camaraderie—a **nomi-ya** provides it all in* CITY HUNTER.

he commissioned about himself. During the early **Edo period** (AC vol. 1, p. 25) **Tokugawa Iemitsu** established regulations concerning Nō that strictly limited its form. Among the formalized traditions of Nō are a specific design of the wooden stage, **kata** (AC vol. 1, p. 64) for movements and poses, and bulky costumes, especially those worn by the major character actor (*shite*), who wears at least five layers of clothing

🅐 Nō plays a major role in *Gasaraki*, with a performance taking place in the first episode.

🅜 Watanabe no Tsuna's cutting off the demon's arm in the Nō play *Rashomon* is mentioned by Mustachio in *Astro Boy* (vol. 16, p. 65).

## 飲み屋
## NOMI-YA

 Small inexpensive bars that also serve simple food and snacks. These range in size from large enough to have a few tables to so small they only have a counter and a few stools. Many can be recognized by an **Aka-chōchin** (AC vol. 1, p. 4) at the entrance.

🅐 A nomi-ya in **Shinjuku-ku** (AC vol. 1, p. 120) is the location of the opening of episode 37 in the *City Hunter 1* TV series.

## 覗き
## NOZOKI (PEEPING TOM)

A problem for those seeking privacy outdoors or even indoors. Nozoki are a long-established problem in Japan and are even seen in **Edo period** (AC vol. 1, p. 25) shunga spying on couples.

🅜 Perhaps the most brazen nozoki in anime and manga is Yotsuya-san in *Maison Ikkoku*.

## ニュー・ハーフ
## NYŪ HĀFU (SHE-MALE)

Sometimes used to refer to men who professionally cross-dress as women, in erotic anime and manga it often refers to intersexed characters. In such stories they may be men who have been surgically altered to look like women while keeping their penis, hermaphrodites with a functional set of both male and female sexual organs, or characters transformed by supernatural means. In non-erotic manga it usually refers to cross-dressing entertainers. Other names used for this phenomenon when applied to "hostesses" (**hosutesu,** AC vol. 1, p. 47), performers, and those in the sex industry include *shī mēru* (she-male), *misutā redī* (Mr. Lady), and *shisutā bōi* (Sister Boy).

*Uh oh! Umi-chan from* CITY HUNTER: THE MOTION PICTURE *gets an unexpected gift from a **nyū hāfu** hostess . . . er, host . . . er, hostess . . .*

🅜 Several of the stories in *Countdown* include men who have been altered to pass as women.

🅐 Miyuki, a cross-dressing piano player, is not someone to trifle with in *Suikoden Demon Century*. • In the third *F3* anime story, a male **yūrei** (AC vol. 1, p. 149) possesses one of the women, who takes on certain physical masculine characteristics, to both the terror and delight of some of the other characters. • The character Erica in *City Hunter: The Motion Picture* is an example of the cross-dressing hostess. • In *Fushigi Yūgi* (ep. 30), Nuriko tells Miaka he prefers to be called a "new half."

🅜 In *Futaba-Kun Change*, Futaba's family name is Shimeru, the Japanese pronunciation of the English term she-male. • Minako in *Rumic Theater: One or Double* (p. 220) is another example of the "hostess" class of nyū hāfu, as are the employees of the bar in *3x3 Eyes*. • Hermaphrodites show up in some of the stories of Yui Toshiki contained in *Hot Tales* (vols. 1 and 2).

織田信長
## ODA NOBUNAGA

1534–82. At the end of the **Sengoku jidai** (AC vol. 1, p. 113), Oda Nobunaga rose to power and unified one-third of Japan under his rule. It is this rise to power that ushered in the Azuchi-Momoyama period with its great flourishing of the arts.

O-

Many words begin with the honorific O. If you cannot find a term that begins with O just try under the next letter.

But Nobunaga was not only a patron of the arts, he was a ruthless warlord who, with the aid of his vassals, **Toyotomi Hideyoshi** (AC vol. 1, p. 140) and **Tokugawa Ieyasu,** rose from obscurity to be the most powerful figure of his time. His reputation for brutality can be seen in the slaughter of Buddhist sectarian opponents and the destruction of the Enryaku-ji temple on **Hieizan** outside of **Kyoto** (AC vol. 1, p. 77). At one point he surrounded 20,000 opponents—men, women, and children—in Nagashima and, after fencing the area in, set fire to the buildings and killed everyone inside. He also used **teppō** (AC vol. 1, p. 135) to defeat more powerful opponents in many key battles.

In 1582, one of Nobunaga's generals rebelled against him, attacking the Honnōji temple where he was staying. After being wounded in combat he chose to commit **seppuku** (AC vol. 1, p. 115) deep inside the burning temple rather than be captured. Eleven days later, the rebel was killed in battle with the forces of Toyotomi Hideyoshi. Oda Nobunaga, Toyotomi Hideyoshi, and Tokugawa Ieyasu are often referred to as the "Three Heroes" for their role in unifying Japan.

🅐 In *Yotoden*, Oda Nobunaga is portrayed as aligned with demonic forces. • Oda Kazusanosuke Nobunaga is exposed as "The Lord" in *Samurai Deeper Kyo* (ep. 14). • In *Mirage of Blaze,* he is mentioned as one of the leaders in the struggle.

## お台場海浜公園
## ODAIBA KAIHIN KŌEN (ODAIBA SEASIDE PARK)

A **Tokyo** park located in **Minato-ku** on an island composed mainly of landfill in **Tōkyō Wan** at one end of the **Rainbow Bridge**. Before the landfill project, part of the area included islands that were fortified by the **bakufu** in the mid-19th century. The ruins of these fortifications are part of the park. The park includes a beach and trails for walking. Nearby is the Decks Tokyo Beach mall, the Fuji Television studios, and the Odaiba Kaihin Kōen Station. This is a popular area for dates and meeting friends.

▲ The first *You're Under Arrest* episode ends in Odaiba Park near the Rainbow Bridge.

## 小栗忠順
## OGURI TADAMASA

1827–68. Also known as Oguri Kōzuke no Suke. A major official for the **bakufu**. Born in **Edo** of a **hatamoto** family, in 1860 he was part of the delegation to the United States. From 1865 to 1868 while serving as commissioner of finance (*kanjō bugyō*) he attempted to reform Japan's finances and the military. He also played a major role in foreign affairs. He developed strong relations with French minister Leon Roches, who promised military and financial assistance to the government. He also founded companies to trade internationally and shipyards in **Yokohama** and **Yokosuka**. His strong support of military action against the supporters of the emperor led to his being dismissed by **Tokugawa Yoshinobu**. He was captured by imperial forces in 1868 and executed, the only major government official to suffer this fate.

▲ Oguri Kozunosuke shows up near the end of *Dagger of Kamui*, where he speaks of his dealings with the French.

*Kenshin in* RUROUNI KENSHIN *looks surprised. This* **ohagi** *must be really good.*

## 御萩
## OHAGI (EQUINOX BEAN CAKE)

A type of **mochi** (AC vol. 1, p. 87) with *an* on the outside rather than inside. These are sometimes called "inside-out cakes." The name comes from that of bush clover (*hagi*). When they are made in the spring, they are referred to as *botan mochi*. These are traditionally also eaten and offered to the ancestors at the gravesite or on the **butsudan** (AC vol. 1, p. 16) at the fall and spring equinoxes.

Ⓜ Megumi makes a large batch of ohagi to celebrate Yahiko's recovery in *Rurouni Kenshin* (TV ep. 9 and vol. 3, p. 86).

▲ In *Ranma 1/2: Anything Goes Martial Arts* (ep. 18) we see Happosai scarfing down a pile of "equinox bean cakes."

## おはじき OR 御弾き OLD FORM 御弾き
## OHAJIKI

A game played with flat, roundish objects such as small stones, shells, or glass "coins." To play, place a variety of pieces on a flat surface, such as the floor or ground, then take turns flicking one against the others, removing them as you hit them. Whoever has the most pieces at the end of the game wins. Ohajiki is based on a Chinese game called *dangi*. Originally played in the Japanese court in the 8th century, it eventually spread and became a children's game. Originally it was played with small stones and was called *ishihajiki*, or "stone flicking."

**A** Midori and her friends play a game using colored shells in *Growing Up.* • Setsuko has some of the glass game pieces in *Grave of the Fireflies.* • In *Haunted Junction* (ep. 1) Haruto plays the game with the girl in the mirror. • And, of course, it is one of the traditional feminine skills Aoi knows in *You're Under Arrest* (ep. 5).

## 桜花 OLD FORM 櫻花
## ÔKA (OHKA)

Full name: Kūgishō Navy Special Attacker Ōka. Ōka is another word for the cherry blossom (**sakura,** AC vol. 1, p. 110). Commonly referred to by allied soldiers as the "Baka Bomb." Basically it is a small plane carrying a high explosive charge and designed to be crashed into a target by its kamikaze pilot (**Kamikaze Tokubetsu Kōgekitai**). It would dive at a very high speed, making it hard to hit with antiaircraft fire. The Ōka were used only in the final months of the war. The planes had a very short range, so they were carried under a **Betty** until they were close enough to their targets to fly on their own.

**A** The main character of *The Cockpit* story 2, "Mach Thunder Force" is an Ōka pilot.

## 御釜 OR おかま
## OKAMA (MALE HOMOSEXUAL; DEROGATORY)

A general slang term for a male homosexual. Some consider the word to be derogatory, much like fag in English. The term is derived from **kama,** rice pot, with the honorific *o* added. A less rude form is *okama-san.* However, more enlightened people prefer the term *gei* (gay). The view of gay men in Japan holds that they want to be women. This is the major reason that gays are often portrayed as highly feminine, even cross-dressing.

**A** Tamahome refers to Noriko as an okama when he introduces him to his fellow villagers in *Fushigi Yūgi* (ep. 8). • In *Tokyo Godfathers,* Gin refers to Hana as an okama when they bicker; "she" also refers to himself as an okama. The subtitles use "fag" or "homo" depending on who is speaking. • The most flamboyant cross-dressing okama in anime has to be Ms. Aki in *Magical Shopping Arcade Abenobashi,* who shows up in a variety of interesting (and disgusting) outfits as the show progresses.

**M** In *Ogenki Clinic* (vol. 1, "Medical record 17") when a beautiful client lifts her/his skirt to show his/her penis, Dr. Ogekuri uses the word okama and a kama is actually pictured in the word balloon.

## おから OR 雪花菜 OLD FORM 御殻
## OKARA (TŌFU LEES)

When soy milk is processed to make **tofu,** the bran is filtered out, resulting in the lees. As okara has little flavor of its own, it is often served mixed with shredded vegetables. Also known to culinary professionals as *kirazu* or politely referred to as *unohana.*

**M** In *Blade of the Immortal: Dark Shadows* (pt. 1), Sumino Kenei mentions that earlier in his life some of his favorite foods were *unohana* and *karashi.*

## 岡山県 OLD FORM 岡山縣
## OKAYAMA KEN

A prefecture in western **Honshu** (AC vol. 1, p. 47) that is bordered by Tottori and Hiroshima prefectures, **Hyōgo Ken,** and the **Seto Naikai.** The terrain ranges between plains, highlands, and mountains. The economy is largely agricultural, but also includes ceramics, petrochemicals, steel, and machinery manufacturing.

©NOBUHIRO WATSUKI/SHUEISHA · FUJI-TV · ANIPLEX INC.

*Okita in Samurai X Trust and Betrayal is a master swordsman at an early age. He cut short the lives of many opponents.*

Ⓐ The famous **kibidango** of Okayama Prefecture is mentioned in *Urusei Yatsura* (TV ep. 55, st. 78).

## 沖田 総司
## OKITA SŌJI

?–1868. Also known as Okita Sōshi. A young member of the **Shinsengumi** in **Kyoto** (AC vol. 1, p. 77). As a teen he gained a reputation as a great swordsman. He died an early death from **kekkaku.**

Ⓜ Okita is a major character in *Peacemaker.*

Ⓐ Okita is seen in *Samurai X: Trust and Betrayal*, along with symptoms of his disease.

Ⓜ Melon mentions Okita Sōji in *Vanity Angel,* issue 5.

## おこさまランチ or お子様ランチ
## OKOSAMA-RANCHI (CHILD'S PLATE)

A mixed-food plate for children. These inexpensive meals for children contain a variety of foods on a single plate, including desert. Usually a flag is inserted into one of the servings as a decoration. Sometimes dishes shaped like trains, boats, or other objects are used.

Ⓐ Yumeji seems to be enjoying his okosama-ranchi and its variety of ingredients in *Saber Marionette*

*J Again* (ep. 4). • Okosama-ranchi is translated as "kid's lunch" in *Magical Shopping Arcade Abenobashi* (ep. 7).

Ⓜ In *Marionette Generation* (vol. 1, p. 76), Izumi's explanation for why he named the doll "Lunch" involves okosama-ranchi.

## 大久保利通
## ŌKUBO TOSHIMICHI

1830–78. Born in Kagoshima, the castle town of the **Satsuma Han**, the son of a low-ranking **samurai** (AC vol. 1, p. 110) retainer of the **daimyo**. Toshimichi gained recognition and promotion to government posts for his talents. In the late 1850s, he began to promote moderate anti-**bakufu** policies, including the *kōbu gattai* (union of court and bakufu) movement. In 1863, he began advocating the overthrow of the bakufu. In 1866 he and **Saigō Takamori** (AC vol. 1, p. 107) met with **Kido Takayoshi** to form a secret alliance between the Satsuma Han and the **Chōshū Han.** During the **Meiji period** (AC vol. 1, p. 81), he helped form many of the policies of the government, including foreign relations, tax reform, **haitōrei,** and the end of official discrimination against outcasts. He became head of the **Naimushō,** making him possibly the most powerful figure in the government. He commanded the conscript army that put down the **Seinan Sensō** in January 1877. He was assassinated by former samurai from Satsuma on May 14, 1878 and was buried in **Aoyama Reien** (AC vol. 1, p. 6).

Ⓜ Ōkubo Toshimichi appears in *Rurouni Kenshin* (TV ep. 30 and vol. 1, p. 129).

## オムライス
## OMURAISU (OMELET RICE)

A thin shell of omelet surrounding a rice filling; the filling can contain chicken, pork, or other ingredients. Ketchup is often used to decorate the top.

Ⓐ Marine makes omuraisu for everyone including drawings done with the ketchup in *Saber Marionette J Again* (ep. 6).

## 鬼瓦
## ONIGAWARA (DEMON-FACED EDGE TILE)

Decorated tiles at the ridge ends of **kawara**-covered roofs. The tiles usually have grotesque faces on their ends. Earlier in history, boards with demon masks on them were placed at the ridge edge, but in time these were replaced by the onigawara. The demon-like face actually represents Kahaku, a river deity. The image was considered to be protection against fire.

**A** Such a tile is seen in *Rurouni Kenshin* (TV ep. 3), on the roof of the bathhouse in *Spirited Away,* and in *Saber Marionette J* (ep. 1) when the spy is moving across the rooftops.

**M** In *Lone Wolf and Cub* (vol. 8, p. 180) such a tile is seen on the Yagyū residence.

## 女誑し or 女たらし
## ONNATARASHI (PLAYBOY)

In a very negative sense, the term literally means "women deceiver." The word is sometimes abbreviated to *tarashi*. One also hears the English word "playboy" used in some anime.

**A** Listen carefully and you will hear Ryoga call Ranma an onnatarashi, among other insults, during the conversation he has with Miss Hinako in the restaurant in *Ranma 1/2* (OVA 4). • In the *Castle of Cagliostro,* the term is justifiably applied to both the Count and to Lupin. • In *Revolutionary Girl Utena,* several of the main male characters are onnatarashi; the English word "playboy" is often used in the series.

## 折紙
## ORIGAMI

Paper folding as an entertainment and art form. Doing origami for fun did not exist in ancient Japan, as paper was scarce. There are examples of origami used in religious rituals in the distant past but these are the exception. Origami is believed to have developed as an entertainment in the **Heian period** (AC vol. 1, p.

**DON'T CALL THEM SOAPS!**

Wanna push my buttons? Call an anime or a manga a soap opera.

Soap operas are a specific type of serialized drama. Not all drama series are soaps. What makes soaps different from other TV dramas is that soaps focus on social elites, highly paid professionals, wealthy businessmen, and people with large inheritances. An interesting thing about soaps is that they are an almost exclusively American phenomenon, that is, the United States and Latin America. In England and Australia, drama series usually are neighborhood oriented, *East Enders,* for example. In Japan the home or workplace is often the setting. Examples from anime and manga include *Maison Ikkoku, Chobits, Patlabor, Hot Gimmick,* and *Ai Yori Aoshi,* none of which focus on social elites.

So the next time you show a series to someone and they call it a soap opera, you can correct their error. But do it diplomatically.

44) and taken its present form of using just folds and no cutting in the **Muromachi period** (AC vol. 1, p. 90). In the **Edo period** (AC vol. 1, p. 25) it increased in complexity and by the **Taishō jidai** the number of established patterns was around 150. There are non-entertainment examples of origami in traditional folded-paper ornaments, gift wrappings, and even functional items like paper wallets. A famous example of origami is the **senbazuru** (origami paper cranes; AC vol. 1, p. 113).

**A** Mayuka is taught how to do origami in *Tenchi The Movie 2: The Daughter of Darkness.*

## 押し入れ or 押入れ
## OSHIIRE (FUTON STORAGE CLOSETS)

Closets for storing **futon** (AC vol. 1, p. 32) during the day when they are not laid out for sleeping Other items can also be stored in these deep and spacious closets.

©NOBUHIRO WATSUKI/SHUEISHA • FUJI-TV • ANIPLEX INC.

*Don't have a zen? Then use an* **oshiki** *for your meals, like this one from* SAMURAI X TRUST AND BETRAYAL.

**A** A certain degree of activity takes place in Godai's oshiire in the first episode of *Maison Ikkoku*. • We get to see Bloodberry putting futon in the oshiire in *Saber Marionette J Again* (ep. 1). • They are also seen in *My Neighbor Totoro* and *Spirited Away*.

## おしき OR 折敷
## OSHIKI (FLAT SERVING TRAY)

A rectangular tray used for meals on the floor. The tray would sit in front of the eater with the dishes arrayed on it. Oshiki were often used by people of low status or wealth; higher-status persons would often, but not always, use **zen.** Today they are not used much as most Japanese use **chabudai** (AC vol. 1, p. 17).

**A** Oshiki are used when Ashitaka eats with the herders in *Princess Mononoke*. • Kenshin and Tomoe eat their meals from oshiki in *Samurai X: Trust and Betrayal*.

**M** Manji eats his meal from one in the very beginning of *Blade of the Immortal: The Gathering*.

## おとしぶた OR 落とし蓋
## OTOSHIBUTA (DROP LID)

A drop lid, that is, a lid that sits inside a pot directly on whatever is being cooked. Traditionally made of wood, it is useful when simmering vegetables, as the lid holds the vegetables in place so they don't bounce around and fall apart.

**A** Kuno refers to **Tsukahara Bokuden** using a stew pot lid to block an attack in *Ranma 1/2: Hard Battle* (ep. 12).

**M** In *Inu-Yasha* (vol. 8, p. 172), we see a **nabe** with an otoshibuta in it as Kaede and Kikyo speak.

## 大津
## ŌTSU

A town in Shiga Prefecture. Ōtsu was a **shukuba machi** on the **Tōkaidō** highway. The town is located east of **Kyoto** (AC vol. 1, p. 77) and south of **Hieizan.** In 1600, Kyōgoku Takatsugu defended Ōtsu Castle against opponents of **Tokugawa Ieyasu.** While the castle was eventually surrendered, it held out long enough for Ieyasu to win the **Sekigahara no Tatakai.**

**A** Kenshin and Tomoe move to Ōtsu in *Samurai X: Trust and Betrayal*.

## パンこ OR パン粉
## PANKO (BREAD CRUMBS)

These are used in cooking several Western-style fried dishes including **korokke** and **tonkatsu.**

**M** In *Ogenki Clinic* (vol. 2), the doctor illustrates a point with a pun involving panko.

## ペリー, M. C.
## PERRY, MATTHEW CALBRAITH

1794–1858. The U.S. Naval officer who led an expedition to Edo Bay (**Tōkyō Wan**), arriving on July 8, 1853, to negotiate with Japan to open its ports. The twelve steam-powered warships he used were termed the "black ships" by the Japanese. His arrival was not a surprise, as the Dutch had already informed the **bakufu** that Perry would be coming. He carried a letter from the U.S. president to the emperor, which he presented to the bakufu. In 1854 he returned for an official answer to the letter and demanded negotiations be started or he would sail to **Edo** itself. The Japanese agreed to meetings and built a special building at Kanagawa for this purpose. On March 13, 1854, the **Nichibei Washin Jōyaku** was signed between the United States and Japan.

Miaka mentions the arrival of the black ships while studying in *Fushigi Yūgi* (TV ep. 17 and vol. 5, p. 9).

Perry's arrival off the coast of Uraga is mentioned in *Hikaru no Go* (vol. 1, p. 41).

## ピンク映画
## PINKU EIGA (PINK MOVIE, SEX FILMS)

The term *pinku eiga* goes back to a review in 1962 where it was said to describe the large amount of exposed female skin in the film *Flesh Market*. Ōkura Studios, which released *Flesh Market,* took up the term in its promotional literature and applied it to many of its other products. In time the term became commonly used for any film with lots of sexual content.

A **Kabukicho** retailer of videos, including pinku eiga, turns out to also provide information to Ryo in *City Hunter: The Motion Picture.*

## ポカリスエット
## POCARI SWEAT

Perhaps the best known, outside of Japan at least, Japanese sports drink. The distinctive blue-and-white label with the

### THE PERSON IN THE MIDDLE OF A PHOTOGRAPH WILL DIE

A superstition dating back to the 19th century says that if three people have their picture taken together, the one in the middle will die or have something bad happen to them. In *Urusei Yatsura* (OVA 3, pt. 2) it is not a person that has this unfortunate problem but a goat, a goat whose ghost years later causes problems on the Mendou estate. In *Rurouni Kenshin* (TV ep. 22) a character references the superstition that being photographed sucks away one's soul. Needless to say such a belief has long been dead in camera-happy Japan, where even cell phones have been able to take photographs for years.

unusual name is easy to spot even if you can't see the letters. Made by the Otsuka Pharmaceutical Company since 1980, Pocari Sweat is designed to restore electrolytes lost through activity. • Pocari Sweat cans are on the table in *Otaku no Video* (pt. 2, 1st anim. seq.) as Tanaka is talking about the creation of garage kits.

Shinohara opens a can of Pocari Sweat in *Mobile Police Patlabor* (vol. 1, p. 184). Hikaru gets a can from a **jidō-hanbaiki** (AC vol. 1, p. 53) in *Hikaru no Go* (vol. 1, p. 58). Ken helps himself to a bottle of Pocari Sweat when he is at Saki's in *Between the Sheets* (p. 21).

## ポッキー
## POCKY

A snack made by the Glico Company. Pocky are often described as a straight pretzel dipped in chocolate. This is misleading because, while Pocky are about the same diameter as a small pretzel, they are not covered in salt or glazed. Also Pocky comes in several flavors, not just chocolate. I have seen chocolate, strawberry, almond, marbled chocolate, and plain. There is even a special Men's Pocky that uses a less sweet chocolate. And, no, they are not thicker.

Note: Other snacks are made in this stick-like shape, so don't assume that all thin snacks are Pocky.

M *Please Teacher (Onegai Teacher)* is the ultimate Pocky story as it is Mizuho's favorite snack.

M In *Cardcaptor Sakura* (vol. 1, p. 50), we see Kero-chan enjoying Pocky.

In MAGICAL SHOPPING ARCADE ABENOBASHI, *a group of neighborhood residents exercise at the local shrine.*

# R

## レインボーブリッジ
## RAINBOW BRIDGE

The Rainbow Bridge (reinbō buriji) links reclaimed islands, mostly part of **Kōtō-ku,** in **Tōkyō Wan** with **Minato-ku** in central **Tokyo.** The bridge opened in 1993, allows foot traffic, and includes a visitors' center. The Rainbow Bridge is a suspension bridge with two towers, each 126 meters tall. The Tokyo Metropolitan Expressway is on the upper of the two decks of traffic.

A The first *You're Under Arrest* episode begins with a lone car driving on the bridge and ends with the main characters in Odaiba Kaihin Kōen at its base. It is also in the opening sequence and background on the menu screen of the DVD discs.

M Ai and her assistants return to Japan by materializing next to the Rainbow Bridge in *Time Traveler Ai* (vol. 1, p. 192).

## ラジオ体操 OLD FORM ラヂオ體操
## RAJIO TAISŌ (RADIO CALISTHENICS)

NHK (**Nippon Hōsō Kyōkai**, AC vol. 1, p. 96) broadcasts a radio exercise program four times a day, the earliest being at 6:30 A.M. These programs began in 1928. The only period they were not broadcast was during the U.S. military occupation after WWII. The broadcasts are incorporated into the daily schedule of many schools, factories, and businesses. Groups of people even gather at local parks to exercise together with their neighbors. Students on vacation are encouraged to participate and in some areas can win prizes for perfect attendance.

A We see an elderly group exercising to rajio taisō at the local shrine in *Magical Shopping Arcade Abenobashi* (ep. 1). • In the first episode of *The Legend of Black Heaven* the three girls unintentionally choose to do their exercises in a way that draws plenty of attention.

M In *Shadow Star* (vol. 1, "Razor's Edge") Shiina's dad asks her over breakfast if she is still "exercising along with that program on the radio" as they eat breakfast.

## ラムネ
## RAMUNE

An old brand of carbonated lemonade, and a few other flavors, in a distinctly shaped bottle. The top of the bottle has a bulge containing a marble. The pressure of the

*Arumi finishes off her bottle of **Ramune**, in MAGICAL SHOPPING ARCADE ABENOBASHI.*

carbonation holds the marble against the top of the bottle sealing the drink inside. Once the marble is forced down with a special plunger the beverage can be drunk with the marble clinking back and forth as you tilt the bottle.

🅰 Satoshi and Arumi enjoy Ramune while hanging around their neighborhood in *Magical Shopping Arcade Abenobashi* (ep. 1). Toukairin buys Ramune for some kids in *You're Under Arrest* (ep. 46).

## れんげ OR 蓮華
## RENGE (CHINESE SPOON)

Usually made of ceramic with a flat bottom, these are provided when you order a Chinese noodle dish such as **rāmen** (AC vol. 1, p. 105) or something like **yakimeshi,** which is difficult to eat with **hashi** (AC vol. 1, p. 42). They are also called *chirirenge*, which is the full name. This spoon design was introduced into Japan in the **Heian period** (AC vol. 1, p. 44).

🅰 Notice that Noa uses a renge to eat her yakimeshi in *Patlabor the TV Series* (ep. 12), an example of the Japanese view that foods should be eaten with utensils from their country of origin.

Ⓜ Yakimeshi is also eaten with a renge by Shiina and Hiro in *Shadow Star: Shadows of the Past.* • In *GTO* (vol. 5, ch. 33), Tomoko plays with her food, making a mini rāmen in her renge.

## 蓮根
## RENKON (LOTUS ROOT)

*Nelumbo nucifera.* The rhizomes of the lotus plant are harvested in the fall when they are large enough to provide a good food source. When slices are cooked they are crispy. Renkon can be found in salads, simmered dishes, and in **tenpura.** A cross section of renkon resembles a spoked wheel with a series of holes around a solid center.

🅰 Lotus root is one of the foods Cherry mentions in *Urusei Yatsura* (TV ep. 36, st. 59).

Ⓜ "Battle lotus root!" is the name of a cooking competition in *Iron Wok Jan* (vol. 3, p. 131–).

## レズビアン
## REZUBIAN (LESBIAN)

In Japan, the native terms associated with lesbians often have derogatory connotations. Examples include *kai awase* (shellfish combo), *doseiai* (same-sex love, a technical term that has a connotation of mental illness), and *onabe* (a pun on **okama** using **nabe**). As a result, Japanese lesbians simply adopted the English word rezubian (lesbian). Sometimes this is abbreviated *rezu*, which has come to have some negative connotations, too. Within the lesbian community, another terminology has arisen with

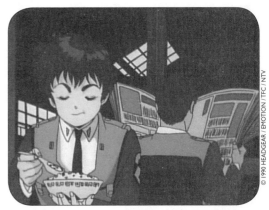

*Noa in PATLABOR uses a **renge**, a simple and functional eating utensil.*

such terms as *tachi* or *otachi* (from *tachiyaku*, a lead **kabuki** actor playing a male role) used for the more masculine or dominant partner and *neko* (cat) or *nenne* (ingenue) for the more feminine partner. Then there is *sukadachi* for masculine women who dress in a feminine manner and *zuboneko* for feminine women who dress in a masculine style. Many of these terms are slang and best avoided in conversation with Japanese.

**A** In the *El Hazard* OVA series the delightful Alielle often gets a little too close to other women for their comfort. • Akane in the *Kimagure Orange Road* OVAs is a very sympathetic lesbian character who develops a one-sided interest in another woman. • The lesbian subtext in the *Revolutionary Girl Utena* TV series becomes much more explicit in the movie. • Of course, there are erotic anime with lesbian and bisexual women such as *F3, Tokyo Private Police,* and *Stainless Nights.*

**M** The princess Rosalia, who does not consider herself a lesbian, escapes her captors by seducing a female guard in *Drakuun* (vol. 2) only to be tracked down and protected by the same woman. • In the *Ghost in the Shell* manga there is a very hot threesome that was not included in the first U.S. edition but was restored for the second edition.

蝋燭 FORMAL 蠟燭
## RŌSOKU (CANDLE)

These were not commonly used until the middle of the **Edo period** (AC vol. 1, p. 25). Japanese traditional candles are made of vegetable wax from a particular species of tree. The wick is a hollow roll of paper, allowing the candle to be easily attached to a spike that simply fits inside the bottom of the wick. The tip of the wick on a new candle is a sharp hard point. This allows candles that have nearly burned to the end to simply be set at the top of a new candle. This economical design means that all of the candle is used.

**A** Tomoe writes in her diary by candlelight in *Samurai X: Trust and Betrayal.* • We get a good view of a rōsoku in *Samurai Deeper Kyo* (ep. 4).

*Unlike an oil lamp, a rōsoku won't spill. Still, Tomoe in* SAMURAI X TRUST AND BETRAYAL *must be careful with fire in her wooden home.*

両国橋 OLD FORM 兩國橋
## RYŌGOKUBASHI

The Ryōgoku Bridge. Built in 1657 in **Edo** after the Meireki Fire, this was the first bridge to span the **Sumidagawa.** It allowed increased development on the other side of the river such as in **Fukagawa** and Honjo. It also provided an escape route in case of future fires. Originally it was named the Ōhashi, meaning "great bridge," as it was the longest bridge in Japan, with a length of 175 meters. In time, it became known as Ryōgokubashi, meaning "two provinces bridge," since it connected the provinces of Musashi on the west bank and Shimōsa on the east. Actually, the land on the east bank had already become part of Musashi by that time. The bridge is the original site of the famous summer fireworks shows on the Sumidagawa.

**M** The bridge shows up several times in *Lone Wolf and Cub*, most notably when Nagasakiya crosses it with his load of *tōtekirai* (vol. 22, p. 20), when we see it being repaired after the flood (vol. 24, p. 133) and when Okan crosses it on her way to send the signal (vol. 25, p. 57).

凌雲閣
## RYŌUNKAKU (ASAKUSA TWELVE STORIES)

A famous twelve-story octagonal tower that stood in Asakusa (AC vol. 1, p. 6). It was the tallest building in Tokyo when it was was opened in 1890. While officially named Ryōunkaku, Cloud Surpassing Pavilion, it was commonly referred to as Jūnikai, or Twelve Stories. The bottom ten stories were made of brick and the top two were wooden. An observation deck provided a view from the top. Its elevator, Japan's first, operated for only a few months before officials decided it was unsafe. Most of the building was devoted to shops with an art gallery on the ninth floor. The building was demolished after being damaged in the **Kantō Daishinsai.**

**A** The tower is seen from a distance and from the observation deck in *Doomed Megalopolis* and in the first *Sakura Wars* OVA series.

竜 FORMAL 龍
## RYŪ (DRAGON)

Dragons in Asia are not the same as those fire-breathing beasties found in Western legends. Asian dragons are associated with water. They traditionally live in lakes, ponds, streams, rivers, and the sea. It is said that a dragon rising from the sea will create a mass of vapor that forms large clouds. Some may even see the tip of the dragon's tail as it rises. Dragons are thus prayed to as bringers of rain. These prayers can be accompanied with the launching of fireworks, the ringing of bells, and Buddhist songs.

**M** One of the best-known dragons in anime and manga is Shenlong from Toriyama's famous *Dragon Ball* series.

**A** We see a dragon cloud in episode 11 of *The Legend of the Dog Warriors The Hakkenden*.

流 FORMAL 龍
## RYŪ (MARTIAL ARTS STYLE)

In martial arts, a ryū is a "school" or "style" of a particular martial art. In the **Edo period** (AC vol. 1, p. 25) the number of ryū has been estimated to be around one thousand. The majority of ryū at that time were sword styles. While many of the ryū from the pre-WWII era no longer exist, there are still about one thousand ryū active in Japan today.

**A** Some of the ryū seen in *Samurai X: Trust and Betrayal* include the **Hokushin Ittō Ryū, Jigen Ryū,** and **Mugai Ryū.**

**M** Several action-oriented historical manga commonly have more ryū in them. Some examples include *Lone Wolf and Cub, Vagabond,* and *Blade of the Immortal.*

西遊記
## SAIYŪKI (*THE JOURNEY TO THE WEST*)

The Japanese pronunciation for the Chinese story *Xi You Ji* (Hsi-yu Chi), known in English as *The Journey to the West.* Inspired by an actual voyage by Xuan Zang (Hsüantsang) in the 7th century, this is a fanciful tale of a Buddhist monk traveling to India (the West) to obtain sutras. In the *Saiyūki* the main character is **Son Goku,** the Monkey King, who has become immortal by stealing and eating the peaches of immortality in Heaven. To pay for his crime, he is ordered to accompany the monk as a servant and bodyguard. On the way they make allies, including a fallen celestial warrior incarnated in a pig's body, and fight many demons who wish to eat the holy monk's flesh. A complete edition of the original tale is available from the University of Chicago Press in four volumes translated into English by Anthony C. Yu as *Journey to the West.*

**Ⓜ** The original plan for the Dragon Ball series was a retelling of the *Saiyūki* story, but it got out of hand. • There is a more recent *Saiyūki* series that is available in English.

**Ⓐ** There have been several anime adaptations of this tale, starting as early as the 1920s. Tezuka even did a *Saiyūki* anime in 1967, which was redubbed with many name changes and released in U.S. theaters as *Alakazam the Great.* A later, surreal, Tezuka version on TV, *Goku no Daiboken,* was cut short after complaints from the PTA about its humor and language. Matsumoto Leiji took the tale into space in 1978 with his *Starzinger,* released in English as *Spaceketeers* on U.S. television.

**Ⓜ** In *Return of Lum Sweet Revenge,* two plays, one about Sugata Sanshiro and the *Journey to the West,* get tangled up.

### 坂本竜馬 FORMAL 坂本龍馬
### SAKAMOTO RYŌMA

1836–67. A **shishi** who in more than one way played a major role in the **Edo period** (AC vol. 1, p. 25) to an end. Born in the **Tosa Han** castle town of Kōchi, Ryōma was living in **Edo** studying **kenjutsu, Hokushin Ittō Ryū,** when **Perry** arrived with the black ships. Around the time of the **Ansei no Taigoku,** he joined the anti-**bakufu** forces in Tosa led by Takechi Zuizan. He left the Tosa domain to become a **rōnin** (AC vol. 1, p. 106). He went to the home of the bakufu official **Katsu Kaishū** to assassinate him but was so impressed with Katsu's vision of a Japan with a strong Western-style navy that he became his assistant, recruiting other shishi to assist in the project. Even working for an official was not enough to protect him, and he had to flee to **Sat-**

**suma Han** to avoid capture by bakufu authorities. In March 1866 he played a role in establishing the **Satchō Dōmei.** With the collapse of the bakufu looking more likely, he was welcomed back by the Tosa Han. It was a proposal by Ryōma that was indirectly communicated through domain officials to **Tokugawa Yoshinobu,** which led to the restoration of power to the emperor. He often carried a gun and traveled using assumed names to confuse his enemies. Ryōma was killed in December 1867 in **Kyoto** (AC vol. 1, p. 77) by pro-bakufu assassins.

**Ⓜ** An interesting depiction of Sakamoto Ryōma is in *Peacemaker.* He wears a cowboy hat, boots, and a six shooter, not all of which is inaccurate.

**Ⓐ** Sakamoto Ryōma is seen acting as an intermediary during a meeting between Satsuma and the **Chōshū Han** in *Samurai X: The Motion Picture.*

### 酒田
### SAKATA

A seaport and manufacturing city located in Yamagata Prefecture on the **Nihonkai** at the mouth of the Mogamigawa river. Historically this port was important for shipping local rice.

**Ⓐ** Goto requests that Izumi and Shinohara bring him back **hatahata** as a **miyage** (AC vol. 1, p. 86) of their unofficial trip to Sakata in *Patlabor the TV Series* (ep. 9).

### 桜餅 OLD FORM 櫻餅
### SAKURA MOCHI

A **mochi** (AC vol. 1, p. 87) filled with *azuki-an* wrapped in **sakura** (AC vol. 1, p. 110) leaves that have been salt pickled. These are traditionally served during the **Hina Matsuri** (Doll Festival) (AC vol. 1, p. 45); in **Kyoto** (AC vol. 1, p. 77) they are a springtime seasonal treat.

**Ⓐ** Ran feeds Rei sakura mochi in the *Urusei Yatsura* OVA "I Howl at the Moon."

**Ⓜ** Sakura mochi is ordered by a customer at a

Go ahead and eat **sakura mochi**, leaf and all. The filling is very sweet.

roadside tea shop in *Blade of the Immortal: Cry of the Worm*.

## さねもりさま OR 実盛様 OLD FORM 實盛樣
## SANEMORI-SAMA

Large, straw, human-shaped figures made for the ritual protection of crops. They would be carried around the rice fields by villagers playing drums to repulse evil spirits and crop-eating insects. Afterward, the figure is burned or thrown in a river.

**A** We see the making, procession with, and burning of a Sanemori-sama figure in the *The Legend of the Dog Warriors The Hakkenden* (ep. 5).

## サンカ OR 山窩
## SANKA (A NOMADIC PEOPLE)

A nomadic people of uncertain origin found at one time from **Kyushu** (AC vol. 1, p. 78) to as far north as the **Kantō chihō** (AC vol. 1, p. 61). Their name means mountain cave. They wandered according to the seasons, hunting, fishing, and gathering food. On occasion they traded the objects they made, including excellent basketry, for items that they needed but could not make. Sanka were still practicing their traditional ways until quite recently, but by the early 1960s they had largely settled down and

were being absorbed into the rest of Japanese society. Another name for these people is *pon*.

**M** Some of the characters in *The Legend of Kamui: Perfect Collection* (vol. 2, p. 40, 42) are sanka.

## 参勤交代 FORMAL 参勤交代 OR 参觀交代
## SANKIN KŌTAI (ALTERNATIVE ATTENDANCE)

A system instituted by **Tokugawa Iemitsu,** the third **shōgun** (AC vol. 1, p. 123). During the **Edo period** (AC vol. 1, p. 25) **daimyō** were required to live in **Edo** either during alternative years or, for those living in the nearby provinces, for six month-periods. Their wives and children had to stay permanently in Edo, effectively as hostages. To allow the to do this, daimyō maintained estates in Edo, which, combined with the cost of travel every year, strained the budgets of their **han** and reduced the chance of rebellion. As there were 260 daimyō this meant a constant flow of funds into Edo. The Matsumae Han, the furthest from Edo, was exempted from this requirement as they protected the northern borders of the country. In 1862 the **bakufu** ended this requirement as a conciliatory gesture to the daimyō.

**M** In *Lone Wolf and Cub*, we first hear of sankin kōtai in vol. 8 (p. 265) and again later in other stories.

*Seen in* THE LEGEND OF THE DOG WARRIORS: THE HAKKENDEN *these ritual figures, Sanemori-sama, are also known as Sanemori-ningyō.*

*Mmm, **sanma**! Fire up the grill and pass the soy sauce!*

## さんま or 秋刀魚
## SANMA

Saury. A long, slender fish that is caught in large quantities in the fall as it migrates to the seas around Japan. A cheap fish, it is common in home cooking. The meat is oily and it is usually grilled. Occasionally it is eaten raw.

🅐 The local policeman eats and complains about the sanma, translated as saury, that had been stored frozen for some time in *Kaze no Yojimbo* (ep. 10).

## 楼門五三桐 or 楼門五山桐 OLD FORM 樓門五三桐
## SANMON GOSAN NO KIRI

*The Temple Gate and the Paulownia Crest.* A famous **kabuki** play originally titled *Kinmon Gosan no Kiri*. First performed in **Osaka** (AC vol. 1, p. 102) in 1778, the title was changed when it was first performed in **Edo** in 1800. The play is about the famous thief **Ishikawa Goemon** (AC vol. 1, p. 51) encountering his enemy **Toyotomi Hideyoshi** (AC vol. 1, p. 140), who is referred to as Hisayoshi in the play; the *kiri* or paulownia crest was the symbol of Toyotomi. The play was the first of the genre known as Ishikawa Goemon mono. (An English translation is in Volume 2 of the Kabuki Plays on Stage series from the University of Hawai'i Press.)

🅐 Goemon sees this play about his ancestor at the **Kabukiza** in the beginning of *Lupin the 3rd: Dragon of Doom*.

## 山菜
## SANSAI (MOUNTAIN VEGETABLES)

Any of a variety of edible wild greens, some commercially grown, that can be used in cooking. Sansai are an important ingredient in traditional rural cooking in Japan. The uses they are put are as varied as those for cultivated vegetables. In the wild, these greens are gathered in the hills and alongside fields. Many types are boiled in water first and then drained to remove bitterness. Examples include **warabi** and **kusasotetsu**.

🅜 **Takuan** is pleased when Otsu brings wild greens for the **nabemono** in *Vagabond* (vol. 2, ch. 15).

## さんしょう or 山椒
## SANSHŌ (SZECHWAN PEPPER)

*Zanthoxylum piperitum*, Japanese pepper, sometimes called Szechwan pepper, of which it is a close relative. They are really the seed pods of the Japanese prickly ash. The pods, not the bitter seeds, are ground then used much like pepper. Sometime the pod is used whole. Light green in color, it is one of the ingredients in **shichimi tōgarashi** and is commonly used with grilled **unagi** (AC vol. 1, p. 144) and chicken.

🅐 Megumi gives Akito a stamina drink made from **dokudami**, sanshō, **shiitake,** burdock (**gobō**), lotus root (**renkon**), snapping turtle (**suppon**) and pit viper blood, plus a few other ingredients in *Martian Successor Nadesico* (ep. 10).

## 三途の川 or 三途川
## SANZU NO KAWA (RIVER STYX)

The river to the other world. Often translated as River Styx or just Sanzu River. The Sanzu no Kawa traditionally divided this world from the next. On or before the seventh day after death, the dead must cross this river. Sanzu means three paths ,and the Sanzu no Kawa had three levels of difficulty for crossing. The easiest was for the doer of virtuous deeds, the hardest for doers of evil. In some areas of Japan when the dead were buried, coins, or images of coins, were buried with them for the ferry man.

🅰 We see the "Sanzu River" from the air in *Yu Yu Hakusho* (ep. 1).

Ⓜ In *Blade of the Immortal: Cry of the Worm*, Magatsu Taito points out that the distance between him and Manji is the Sanzu no Kawa, after he traps Manji against a tree in a bog during their duel. • The fourth chapter of *Lone Wolf and Cub* (vol. 1, p. 99) is titled "Baby Cast on the River Styx" and at the end of the chapter a woman remarks, "A baby carriage on the River Sanzu."

## 札幌雪まつり
## SAPPORO YUKI MATSURI (SAPPORO SNOW FESTIVAL)

This **matsuri** (AC vol. 1, p. 81) is held for a week in early February in **Sapporo** (AC vol. 1, p. 111). Its origin was in 1950 when a group of high school students playing in Ōdōri Park sculpted six piles of snow for the fun of it. It has grown into a major event, drawing tourists from around the world and involving hundreds of volunteers to make the sculptures. Three parks, Ōdōri, Makomanai, and Susukino, are the locations for the event each year. Some of the sculptures are extremely large. For example, in 1984 a full-scale reproduction of Buckingham Palace was built.

🅰 The Sapporo Winter Festival is the location of episode 16 of *Patlabor the TV Series*.

## さしみ OR 刺身
## SASHIMI (SLICED RAW MEAT)

Sashimi made of seafood or other meats is served in a variety of ways, from a simple slab of tuna or sliced scallop to a whole **tai** cut up and artistically arranged with garnishes on a platter, perhaps shaped like a wooden boat. At times the sashimi is so fresh it is still moving, in which case it is a style called *ikizukuri*. A famous food served as sashimi is **fugu** (AC vol. 1, p. 29), which is sliced so thin as to be transpar-

**WHAT VOLUME IS THIS?**

Ever notice how some titles don't have clear volume numbers on them. With American comic books and cartoons this is less of an issue because they usually don't have a long, continuing story line. But with anime and manga, the volume number is very important. It is easy to pick up a volume and not know what is going on because you haven't read the previous one, or three. I have had to turn to the Web for lists so I could start buying a title that has been out for some time and lacks volume numbers. I don't want to have to guess where I should begin or which volume to buy next. In some cases I learned to read the product codes in those tiny letters at the bottom of a video case, or to look at the verso of the title page of a manga.

This problem isn't as bad as it used to be. Nowadays, companies are a bit more savvy and include volume numbers on the spine of manga or DVD disc cases, or at least the episode number on the back of the case. This is one reason you no longer see long titles in this book as you did in Volume 1 of the *Anime Companion*. Titles like *Ranma 1/2: Anything Goes Martial Arts, Cat-Fu Fighting* (ep. 1) are now simply *Ranma 1/2: Anything Goes Martial Arts* (ep. 5), which is a little shorter and clearer. If you have Volume 1 of the book and would like to know where something from an older unnumbered VHS series is on the DVD, just check my Website. I have tables comparing the two for quick and easy reference.

ent. Sometime thin strips of **daikon** (AC vol. 1, p. 21) are served with sashimi as a contrast in color and flavor, as well as to clean the palate. Often a little **wasabi** is placed on the sashimi before eating. **Shōyu** (AC vol. 1, p. 124) is used as a dip for sashimi. Sashimi is served raw, except for **tako** (AC vol. 1, p. 131), which is usually cooked first; however, **ika** (AC vol. 1, p. 48) is not. In all cases, slicing the food with a knife is a key "ingredient," so plain raw oysters are not classified as sashimi.

🅐 Sashimi and **sake** (AC vol. 1, p. 109) are illicitly enjoyed by Ryoko in a high school class in *Tenchi Universe* (ep. 12 st. 2). • A whole-fish sashimi in a boat-shaped tray with the head still attached is seen in *Patlabor New Files* (ep. 9). In episode 81 of the *Rurouni Kenshin* TV series, we see one in the *ikizukuri* style. • In *Mirage of Blaze* (ep. 4), old friends who have not seen each other in years celebrate at a restaurant that serves raw horse sashimi.

## 薩長同盟
## SATCHŌ DŌMEI (SATSUMA-CHŌSHŪ ALLIANCE)

In 1866, the previously opposed **Satsuma Han** and **Chōshū Han** formed a military alliance against the **bakufu**. A major player in organizing the alliance was **Sakamoto Ryōma**, a **rōnin** (AC vol. 1, p. 106) from the **Tosa Han** who arranged a meeting between **Ōkubo Toshimichi** and **Saigō Takamori** (AC vol. 1, p. 107) of the Satsuma domain and **Kido Takayoshi** of Chōshū Han.

🅐 Sakamoto Ryōma is seen acting as an intermediary during a meeting between Satsuma and Chōshū in *Samurai X: The Motion Picture.*

## 薩摩藩
## SATSUMA HAN

Also known as the Kagoshima Han. An **Edo period** (AC vol. 1, p. 25) domain comprising Satsuma and Ōsumi provinces, as well as part of Hyūga Province. Today that would include all of Kagoshima Prefecture and part of Miyazaki Prefecture. The domain was given to Shimazu Iehisa by **Tokugawa Ieyasu** for his support at the **Sekigahara no Tatakai.** Originally a backer of the **bakufu** against the **shishi,** this domain changed sides, becoming instrumental in creating the **Meiji period** (AC vol. 1, p. 81). The famous **Saigō Takamori** (AC vol. 1, p. 107) and **Ōkubo Toshimichi** were from the Satsuma Han.

🅐 The Satsuma domain plays a role in *Dagger of Ka-*

*mui.* • That Togo Shigetaka is from Satsuma domain and is mentioned in *Samurai Deeper Kyo* (ep. 7).

## 鞘
## SAYA (SCABBARD)

The sheath or scabbard for a **nihontō** (AC vol. 1, p. 95). Usually these are made of lacquered wood but metal ones also exist.

🅐 We see saya in any anime or manga in which swords are used. In *Samurai X: Trust and Betrayal,* we actually see Kenshin viciously attack an opponent's face with his saya.

Ⓜ In chapter 108 of *Vagabond* (vol. 12), **Miyamoto Musashi** (AC vol. 1, p. 86) defeats several opponents with just his saya.

## 成人の日
## SEIJIN NO HI (COMING-OF-AGE DAY)

A national holiday celebrated on January 15 when young people who have turned twenty years old in the past year visit shrines and receptions organized by their local government. In Japan, turning twenty means you can vote and legally smoke and drink alcohol.

Once there was a ceremony called **genpuku** for boys and one called *mayu-harai* for girls who were coming of age.

Ⓜ Coming-of-Age Day is mentioned in *Maison Ikkoku* (ep. 20 and vol. 11, p. 131).

## 西南戦争 OLD FORM 西南戰爭
## SEINAN SENSŌ (SATSUMA REBELLION)

The last significant armed rebellion against the Meiji government. This conflict lasted from January 29 to September 24, 1877. Former **samurai** (AC vol. 1, p. 110) of the **Satsuma Han** led by **Saigō Takamori** (AC vol. 1, p. 107) seized weapons from military storehouses. This act resulted in Saigō leading an army of about 40,000 men against the government's army of conscripted commoners. The major battle, last-

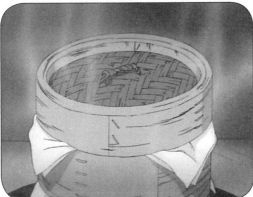

*What's in this **seirō** from* Ranma 1/2? *Shūmai, perhaps?*

ing about fifty days, took place in Kumamoto. When government reinforcements arrived, the Satsuma army retreated, fighting their way to Kagoshima, where the remaining 400 men charged their attackers and Saigō committed **seppuku** (AC vol. 1, p. 115).

**A** The Seinan wars are mentioned by a passerby in *Rurouni Kenshin* (TV ep. 31).

## せいろう OR せいろ OR 蒸籠
## SEIRŌ (FOOD STEAMER)

A food steamer made of bamboo or wood. The bamboo ones are of Chinese design and are called *chūka* seirō. The wooden ones are either square or round with a perforated wooden base and called *kaku* seirō or *wa* seirō. Both designs allow for several steamers to be stacked, allowing for many items to be cooked at the same time.

**A** Yahiko uses a kaku seirō in *Rurouni Kenshin* (ep. 64). • A chūka seirō is a normal item in the kitchen of Shampoo in *Ranma 1/2: Hard Battle* (ep. 3) and it is also seen in *Spirited Away*.

**M** It should come as no surprise that we commonly see chūka seirō in *Iron Wok Jan*.

## 関ヶ原の戦い
## SEKIGAHARA NO TATAKAI (BATTLE OF SEKIGAHARA)

This battle at Sekigahara in Mino Province (now **Gifu Ken**) solidified the power of **Tokugawa Ieyasu,** enabling him to eventually become **shōgun** (AC vol. 1, p. 123). The fighting began early on October 21, 1600, with over 100,000 soldiers taking part. In the afternoon several **daimyō** defected to Ieyasu, ensuring his victory over the troops led by **Ishida Mitsunari.** The two sides are commonly referred to by geographical terms, with Ieyasu's called the Eastern Army and his opponents the Western.

**A** This battle is described at the beginning of *Ninja Resurrection* (ep. 1, "Revenge of Jubei"). • *Samurai Deeper Kyo* begins during the battle itself.

**M** *Vagabond* begins with the aftermath of the battle when defeated troops were being hunted down and executed.

## せきはん OLD FORM 赤飯
## SEKIHAN (RICE WITH RED BEANS)

Reddish rice made by steaming rice with with *azuki* beans or *sasage* (black-eyed peas). The *sasage* turns the rice pinkish. This is a common dish for celebrations, including birthdays and weddings. Sekihan is also called *okowa*.

**M** Futaba's father asks if the sekihan is ready yet during the discussion of what is happening to Futaba-kun in *Futaba-Kun Change* (vol. 1); later (vol. 5), when Futaba-chan has her first period, sekihan is made as part of the celebration.

## 千住
## SENJU

In the **Edo period** (AC vol. 1, p. 25), Senju was the first **shukuba machi** on the Ōshū Kaidō where it crossed the **Sumidagawa.** By the early 18th century there were over seventy-two inns here, and an unlicensed brothel area. It was here that **Bashō** began his famous travel on foot described in the *Narrow Road to the Deep North.* Today it is part of **Tokyo.** Most of the Senju area lies in **Adachi-ku** and **Arakawa-ku.**

Ⓜ Senju is mentioned in the *Patlabor Original Series* (ep. 1) and in *Mobile Police Patlabor* (vol. 1, p. 128).

## 戦争文学
## SENSŌ BUNGAKU (WAR LITERATURE)

This body of literature is very different from the earlier tradition, which tended to focus on heroic warriors. The modern literature focuses on ordinary individuals, often draftees, their suffering, and struggles. The political views of these writers ranged from anti-war to nationalistic. Even the nationalistic works did not spare their authors from censorship during WWII, as some were considered not nationalistic enough. After the war, such works continued to be published, often looking at the suffering of civilians. The eras of the Korean and Vietnam wars produced several novels dealing with those conflicts.

Ⓜ *Barefoot Gen* is an example of a work focusing on the sufferings of civilians. It was a manga that was adapted into an anime.

Ⓐ Anime versions of writings depicting the sufferings of children living in WWII also include *Rail of the Star* and *Grave of the Fireflies.* • Other anime adaptations of stories about soldiers in WWII include *The Harp of Burma* and *The Cockpit,* a collection of three stories.

## 戦争犯罪に関する裁判
## SENSŌ HANZAI NI KANSURU SAIBAN (TOKYO WAR TRIALS)

In a series of thousands of trials of Japanese for war crimes in the late 1940s, just fewer than a thousand were condemned to death. Many of the rest were sentenced to prison. This series of trials climaxed with the most famous group of prosecutions, known as the International Military Tribunal for the Far East (Kyokutō Kokusai Gunji Saiban), also known as the Tokyo War Trial. Beginning in May 1946 and lasting until November 1948, twenty-eight military and civilian leaders were tried. The eleven judges were from each of the allied states plus one each from the Philippines and India. The only judge trained in international law was Radhabinod Pal from India. The judge from the Philippines was a survivor of the Bataan Death March, and the Soviet judge did not understand English or Japanese, the two official languages of the proceedings. The convicted had their appeals turned down by General MacArthur and the U.S. Supreme Court. Those sentenced to death were hung on December 23, 1948.

Ⓜ Two former prison inmates who were convicted, probably during one of the minor trials and not the Tokyo War Trial, meet in *Sanctuary* (vol. 6, p. 203).

## 瀬戸内海 OLD FORM 瀬戸内海
## SETO NAIKAI (SETO INLAND SEA)

Literally: "Sea Within Channels." A large body of water with **Honshu** (AC vol. 1, p. 47) to the east and north, **Kyushu** (AC vol. 1, p. 78) to the west, and **Shikoku** to the south. Included in this area are over 1,000 islands. From prehistoric days this sheltered sea has been an important area for fishing and transportation. The two major ports of **Kōbe** and **Osaka** (AC vol. 1, p. 102) are located here. In 1934 the entire area was designated a national park.

Ⓜ The opening of the second volume of *The Legend of Kamui: Perfect Collection* is in the Seto Naikai.

## 渋谷区 OLD FORM 澁谷區
## SHIBUYA-KU

A ward of **Tokyo.** While mainly residential, Shibuya is famous for its entertainment and shopping areas that are popular with young people. A quick look at a map of the area shows a tangle of streets due to the hilly nature of much of the land. The famous statue of **Hachikō** (AC vol. 1, p. 37) is just outside Shibuya Station. Other famous landmarks include **Meiji Jingū** (AC vol. 1, p. 81), the NHK Broadcast Center (**Nippon Hōsō Kyōkai** AC vol. 1, p. 96), the Gotō Planetarium, Yoyogi Park, and Yoyogi National Stadium in the **Harajuku** (AC vol. 1, p. 41) district. This area also includes many embassies.

🅰 Shibuya shows up often in *Serial Experiments Lain* and is where Chisa Yomoda committed suicide (ep. 1). • In *Patlabor the TV Series,* Shibuya is mentioned and is seen in more than one episode (eps. 1, 13, 22).

Ⓜ In *GTO* (vol. 15), Onizuka gets into trouble in a night club in Shibuya, while in *Dance Till Tomorrow* (vol. 6, p. 149) a **yakuza** (AC vol. 1, p. 146) says that it is "Gettin' like Shibuya around here . . ." when he runs into a costumed actor.

### しちみとうがらし OR 七味唐辛子
### SHICHIMI TŌGARASHI (SEVEN-SPICE MIX)

A mix of spices whose name literally means "seven tastes" or "seven flavors." It is known as *nanairo tōgarashi* in the **Tokyo** area. The ingredients are zest from a citrus fruit (often **mikan,** AC vol. 1, p. 82, or yuzu), **sanshō,** *goma* (sesame), *keshi* (poppy seeds), *asanomi* (hemp seeds), *hoshinori* (dried **nori,** AC vol. 1, p. 97), and *tōgarashi* (chile pepper). It is even possible to get special blends made up at some dealers. Most often, one sees it sprinkled on noodle dishes and **nabemono.**

🅰 In episode 5 of *Patlabor Original Series* at a noodle stand in **Tomakomai,** Kai orders a bowl of noodles (**men rui**) without **negi** and adds shichimi tōgarashi from a small red shaker. Note the different sizes of the pieces that come out of the shaker.

*A child's name is written on special decorated paper and hung up during* **shichiya** *like this one in* TENCHI THE MOVIE: TENCHI MUYO IN LOVE.

### 七夜
### SHICHIYA (NAMING A BABY)

Seventh night, often called *oshichiya.* A celebratory event during which the name of a child is written on paper and posted. It is customary for relatives and close friends to be invited when doing this. **Sekihan,** a whole **tai** (one without a head is bad luck), and **sake** (AC vol. 1, p. 109) are usually served on this occasion.

🅰 We see a sheet of paper with Tenchi written on it at the end of *Tenchi The Movie: Tenchi Muyo in Love.*

### しいたけ OR 椎茸
### SHIITAKE

A common type of Japanese mushroom that is widely cultivated, mainly in Ōita, **Shizuoka,** and Miyazaki Prefectures. Shiitake are usually dried for storage. The flavor is distinctive and works well in a variety of dishes. It is used in **tenpura, nabemono,** or, in the dried form, for making vegetarian **dashi** for **shōjin ryōri.**

🅰 Megumi gives Akito a stamina drink made from **dokudami, sanshō,** shiitake, burdock (**gobō**), lotus root (**renkon**), snapping turtle (**suppon**), and pit viper blood, plus a few other ingredients in *Martian Successor Nadesico* (ep. 10). • Shiitake is mentioned in *Cowboy Bebop* (ep. 17).

## 四国 OLD FORM 四國
## SHIKOKU

The smallest of the four main islands of Japan. It is located south of both the **Seto Naikai** and **Honshu** (AC vol. 1, p. 47) and east of **Kyushu** (AC vol. 1, p. 78). The island is mainly composed of high mountains and has a spare population engaged mainly in farming. It is connected to Kyushu by ferries and to Honshu by both ferries and bridges. As smaller islands are included in the same administrative structures, the entire area is sometimes called the Shikoku region (Shikoku chihō). The **Awa Odori** (AC vol. 1, p. 8) comes from this island.

**A** Shikoku is the place where Ryoga defeats the boar when we first see him in the *Ranma 1/2* TV series (ep. 7).

**M** In *Sanctuary* (vol. 6, p. 149), **yakuza** (AC vol. 1, p. 146) from Shikoku take part in a power struggle. • In *Lupin III* (vol. 3, p. 26), the character Sandayu the Wind is from Shikoku.

## 島原の乱 OLD FORM 島原の亂
## SHIMABARA NO RAN (SHIMABARA UPRISING)

An **ikki** beginning on December 11, 1637, led by **Amakusa Shirō,** a charismatic young man. The Christian peasants of this area had been heavily overtaxed and brutally persecuted for their beliefs before they revolted. They were supported by many **rōnin** (AC vol. 1, p. 106) who had followed **Konishi Yukinaga** before his death. The uprising ended with the deaths of over 37,000 men, women, and children on April 12, 1638.

**A** The suppression of the Shimabara no Ran is seen in *Ninja Resurrection* (ep. 1).

## 新橋
## SHINBASHI

A district of **Tokyo** located in **Minato-ku,** southwest of the **Ginza** (AC vol. 1, p. 35). The name comes from the "new bridge" built there on the **Tōkaidō**. In the **Meiji period** (AC vol. 1, p. 81) and **Taishō jidai** this was a well-known **geisha** (AC vol. 1, p. 33) district frequented by politicians and business leaders. Today it is mainly office buildings, small restaurants, and bars.

**A** Shinbashi is where Orin's geisha house is in the *Theater of Life.* • In *Patlabor 2*, the phantom subway station is located in this area.

## 新橋駅 OLD FORM 新橋驛
## SHINBASHI EKI (SHINBASHI STATION)

The original Shinbashi train station, in **Shinagawa-ku,** was the location of the **Tokyo** terminus of the first **tetsudō** in Japan until 1914, when **Tokyo Eki** (AC vol. 1, p. 138) opened, becoming the new terminus. The building was designed in the **Meiji period** (AC vol. 1, p. 81) by the American Architect R. P. Bridgens and, while it was often photographed and millions passed through it each year, little is known about the building as no plans survive. In 1924, a new Shinbashi Station was built on a site to the north in **Minato-ku.** Preserved as a historical monument to the original train line, within the Shiodome Freight Station railyard is the terminal section of track along with the "zero" marker post and a section of the platform.

**A** The original Shinbashi Station is seen at the beginning of an episode of the *Rurouni Kenshin* TV series (ep. 22).

## 下諏訪 [町]
## SHIMO SUWA

A hot spring town located in Nagano Prefecture on the shores of **Suwako.** In the **Edo period** (AC vol. 1, p. 25) it was a **shukuba machi.** In the **Meiji period** (AC vol. 1, p. 81) the silk reeling industry expanded here.

**A** Shimo Suwa is mentioned in Sanosuke's childhood memories in the *Rurouni Kenshin* TV series (ep. 5), and later in the series Sanosuke actually goes to Shimo Suwa (ep. 38).

Ⓜ Shimo Suwa is mentioned in *Lone Wolf and Cub* (vol. 1, p. 78).

## 下田 [市]
## SHIMODA

A city on the Izu Peninsula in **Shizuoka Ken.** This was a busy port during the **Edo period** (AC vol. 1, p. 25) for ships trading between **Osaka** (AC vol. 1, p. 102) and **Edo.** The **Nichibei Washin Jōyaku** (Kanagawa Treaty) opened the port to U.S. ships and designated the city as the location of the American consulate. It only served as the location of the consulate for a year, as the city was rather remote for diplomatic activity. Today Shimoda is a fishing port with seafood and tourism industries. Each year, the Kuro Fune Matsuri (Black Ship Festival) commemorates the arrival of the U.S. fleet under the control of **Matthew Calbraith Perry.**
Ⓐ The story in *The Izu Dancer* ends in Shimoda.

## 下関 [市] OLD FORM 下關
## SHIMONOSEKI

Located in western **Honshu** (AC vol. 1, p. 47) in **Yamaguchi Ken,** the city of Shimonoseki has long been a political center and port city. The **Dannoura no Tatakai** (AC vol. 1, p. 21) was fought near here. At the end of the **Edo period** (AC vol. 1, p. 25), the city was attacked by foreign warships in retaliation for the shelling of foreign merchant vessels by the **Chōshū Han.** Today Shimonoseki is an important deep-sea fishing port.
Ⓐ Shimonoseki is mentioned in the *Wandering Days* and is one of the cities seen at noon in *Blue Seed* (ep. 25). • In *Urusei Yatsura* (ep. 55, st. 78), everyone meets at Shimonoseki near the end of the story.

## 品川区 OLD FORM 品川區
## SHINAGAWA-KU

A ward of **Tokyo** along **Tōkyō Wan.** This area includes buildings dating back as far as the **Kamakura period** (AC vol. 1, p. 59). During the **Edo period** (AC vol. 1, p. 25), Shinagawa was a **Tōkaidō** post-station town just outside the city. In the **Meiji period** (AC vol. 1, p. 81), the lower parts of the area were industrialized and remain so today, with a large upland residential area housing a population of over 300,000.
Ⓐ Shinagawa is mentioned in the *Rurouni Kenshin* TV series (ep. 15) and in *Tokyo Godfathers.*
Ⓜ Shinagawa is also mentioned in the *Blade of the Immortal: Dark Shadows* (pt. 1) by Anotsu when he talks with Magatsu.

## 新宿駅 OLD FORM 新宿驛
## SHINJUKU EKI (SHINJUKU STATION)

The main train station for the **Shinjuku** (AC vol. 1, p. 120) Ward of **Tokyo.** In fact, it is the busiest train station in Tokyo. Built in 1885 on the Shinagawa Line at Tsunohazu, a village then just outside of what was then Shinjuku, the station grew as more lines came through, and by 1928 Shinjuku Station was busier than **Tokyo Eki** (AC vol. 1, p. 138). This station is also known for being confusing. People often get lost in it or take the wrong exit. Local landmarks include **My City** (AC vol. 1, p. 90) and **Studio ALTA.**
Ⓐ The message board at Shinjuku Station is where you leave a message if you wish to contact Saeba Ryo, the main character of *City Hunter.* • Godai and Sakamoto get off a train at Shinjuku Station in *Maison Ikkoku* (ep. 40).
Ⓜ In *Voyeurs, Inc.* (vol. 2, p. 185), Shinjuku Station, south section, department store B1 mall is mentioned, which means the locality of the Keio Department Store. • Haruo has to deal with a crowded train at Shinjuku Station in *Club 9* (vol. 1).

## 新撰組 OR 新選組
## SHINSENGUMI

A special police unit in **Kyoto** (AC vol. 1, p. 77) composed of **rōnin** (AC vol. 1, p. 106) with the purpose of fighting opponents of the **shōgun** (AC vol. 1, p. 123). Originally the group was formed, in 1863, under the name Rōshigumi in **Edo** to guard the shōgun during a visit to Kyoto. Some of the members were recalled due to their pro-imperial views, and the remaining members reorganized as the Shinsengumi with **Kondō Isami** and **Hijikata Toshizō** as leaders. Major events involving this group include the **Ikedaya Jiken** and the **Hamaguri Gomon no Hen.**

**Ⅿ** The Shinsengumi is seen in the *Rurouni Kenshin* OVA *Samurai X: Trust and Betrayal* and commonly mentioned in the *Rurouni Kenshin* manga. • In *Millennium Actress* we see a short sequence set in Kyoto with the Shinsengumi.

## 志士
## SHISHI (MEN OF HIGH PURPOSE)

A term applied to principled warriors. During the **bakumatsu** the name was given to opponents of the **bakufu.** At that time, most of these men were low-ranking **samurai** (AC vol. 1, p. 110) who supported the restoration of power to the emperor. This movement came into existence toward the end of the **Ansei no Taigoku.** They were known for their attacks on government officials and foreigners.

**Ａ** In *Samurai X: Trust and Betrayal*, shishi is translated as "patriots," and in the *Rurouni Kenshin* TV series as "imperialists."

## 静岡県 OLD FORM 靜岡縣
## SHIZUOKA KEN

A prefecture located on the island of **Honshu** (AC vol. 1, p. 47) on the Pacific coast. Most of the area is mountainous, including part of the slope of **Fuji-san** (AC vol. 1, p. 30). Noted products include tea, **mikan** (AC vol. 1, p. 82), forest products, fish, eels, textiles, paper, musical instruments, oil refining, and manufacturing along the coast. With many **onsen** (AC vol. 1, p. 102), as well as its proximity to national parks and **Tokyo,** this is a popular area with tourists.

**Ａ** Shizuoka is at the center of damage when it is hit by a **tsunami** in *Blue Seed* TV series (ep. 24). • Shun's family runs the Kisaragi Inn in Shizuoka Ken in *Here Is Greenwood* (ep. 2).

## しょうちゅう OR 焼酎 OLD FORM 燒酎
## SHŌCHŪ (HARD LIQUOR)

Shōchū by law cannot exceed 36 percent alcohol and is made from sweet or common potatoes or grains. It can be drunk straight but is usually mixed with hot water, called *yuwari*, or served in cocktails. Like many hard liquors in the West, it can range from very low quality to excellent. Various fruit liquors, called *kajitsushu*, are made at home using shōchū, a common one being **umeshu** (AC vol. 1, p. 143).

**Ⅿ** Kei pours rice spirits on Toge's wound in *Adolf: The Half-Aryan* (p. 23). • Onizuka's corrupt cop buddy offers him a choice of **bīru** (AC vol. 1, p. 10), shōchū, or **sake** (AC vol. 1, p. 109) in *GTO* (vol. 8, ch. 60).

## 彰義隊
## SHŌGITAI

In March 1868, about 2,000 former retainers of the **Tokugawa** (AC vol. 1, p. 137) **shōgun** (AC vol. 1, p. 123) banded together in **Edo** to resist the new government. Headquartered in the **Kaneiji** temple in **Ueno** (AC vol. 1, p. 142), they acted as an informal police force for the city while it was under threat of invasion by imperial forces. They resisted the imperial forces after the city was surrendered and eventually were defeated in the Battle of Ueno on July 4, 1868. The battle, which included modern artillery, ended with the temple burned to the ground. Several survivors escaped and eventually fought in the **Goryōkaku no Tatakai.**

**Ａ** In the *Rurouni Kenshin* TV series (ep. 2) we

*Before there were posters, there were **shōheiga**. This one in SAMURAI X TRUST AND BETRAYAL IS much more attractive than bare walls.*

find that Yahiko's father died while a member of the Shōgitai.

## 障屏画 OLD FORM 障屏畫
## SHŌHEIGA (SCREEN AND WALL PAINTING)

Paintings done directly on walls and screens. This traditional art includes paintings on interior stationary walls, **fusuma** (AC vol. 1, p. 32), and **byōbu**.

**A** Such paintings are seen in the **ryokan** (AC vol. 1, p. 107) in *Samurai X: Trust and Betrayal*, and stunning examples of this art are seen in *Spirited Away*.

## しょうじんりょうり OR 精進料理
## SHŌJIN RYŌRI (VEGETARIAN COOKING)

**Buddhist** (AC vol. 1, p. 15) vegetarian cooking was introduced into Japan in the 6th century, and it uses no meat, seafood, or eggs. Such cooking spread in the 13th century along with the expansion of **Zen** Buddhism in Japan, since Zen views cooking and food as aspects of one's spiritual training. Shōjin ryōri is a very sophisticated cuisine that does not attempt to mimic meat dishes, but instead focuses on the natural flavors and textures of the ingredients.

One does not need to join a temple as a monk or nun to enjoy this food; some temples serve it to outsiders and there are often restaurants near major temples that specialize in shōjin ryōri.

**A** In *Tenchi The Movie 2: The Daughter of Darkness*, Sasami prepares shōjin ryōri for dinner during the **Bon** (AC vol. 1, p. 12) festival.

## 少女
## SHŌJO (YOUNG WOMAN)

While shōjo is usually translated as girl, young woman would better apply. Generally, the word does not refer so much to very little girls as to girls and teens. A check of some Japanese sources turns up ages ranging from seven to ten at the youngest to about eighteen at the oldest. There is a large market for **manga** (AC vol. 1, p. 80) and anime aimed at this group, which is increasingly being translated into English. Stories in the shōjo genre range from innocent girl's stories to much stronger material for older readers. Many of the tales are as adventurous or action-oriented as in any other genre. Certain stylistic elements are associated with shōjo as a genre, such as beautiful or pretty male characters, abstracted layouts and dialogue, an emphasis on the feelings of characters, and exotic settings, usually European. These elements are not always present because the shōjo genre is diverse and has blended with more masculine forms of writing.

**M** Well-known shōjo stories, or stories with strong shōjo elements, which every fan should be familiar with, include *Fushigi Yūgi, Banana Fish, Revolutionary Girl Utena, Here Is Greenwood, The Vision of Escaflowne,* and *Sailor Moon*.

**A** Ruri is called a *kodomo* (child) by Yurika and responds that she is a shōjo in *Martian Successor Nadesico* (ep. 5).

## THE TOKUGAWA SHŌGUN

All dates are from when each Tokugawa Shōgun assumed office until he left it.

**Tokugawa Ieyasu**, 1603–5
Tokugawa Hidetada, 1605–23
**Tokugawa Iemitsu**, 1623–51
Tokugawa Ietsuna, 1651–80
Tokugawa Tsunayoshi, 1680–1709
Tokugawa Ienobu, 1709–12
Tokugawa Ietsugu, 1713–16
**Tokugawa Yoshimune**, 1716–45
Tokugawa Ieshige, 1745–60
Tokugawa Ieharu, 1760–86
Tokugawa Ienari, 1787–1837
Tokugawa Ieyoshi, 1837–53
Tokugawa Iesada, 1853–58
Tokugawa Iemochi, 1858–66
**Tokugawa Yoshinobu**, 1867

## 昭和時代
## SHŌWA JIDAI (SHŌWA PERIOD)

1926–89. Literally "Enlightened Peace." This period of Japanese history was the longest reign of any emperor in Japanese history. At its beginning, Japan was becoming more democratic. But with the Great Depression, right-wing forces gained more power and, in the name of suppressing communism, smashed many democratic movements. In the 1930s, the military took a stronger role in government policy, leading to acts of aggression against other Asian states and eventually the attacks that led the United States to enter WWII. After the bombings of **Hiroshima** (AC vol. 1, p. 45) and **Nagasaki** (AC vol. 1, p. 90), the government was deadlocked on what to do. The prime minister turned to the emperor, who urged surrender. The post-war years of the Shōwa jidai saw Japan go from an impoverished

occupied state that had lost a significant percentage of its male population to a highly democratic economic superpower.

A The death of the Shōwa emperor is mentioned in *Otaku no Video* (pt. 2). • In the *Kimagure Orange Road* TV series (ep. 11), the Shōwa-period war with the United States is mentioned by the teacher. • Years in Japan are often expressed as the year of the reign of the emperor at the time, so *Geobreeders* (ep. 1) opens in Shōwa 73 and *The Cockpit* story 2, "Mach Thunder Force," takes place during the twentieth year of the Shōwa Era.

## 昭和天皇
## SHŌWA TENNŌ (SHŌWA EMPEROR)

1901–89. Hirohito, the 124th *tennō* (emperor) of Japan. His father was Crown Prince Yoshihito, later Emperor Taishō, and his mother was Princess Sadako. The future Shōwa Tennō became Crown Prince in July 1912 when his father became emperor, ushering in the **Taishō jidai.** In 1921, he traveled to Europe, and upon his return became regent because his father was ill. In December 1926, at the age of twenty-five, he became emperor and the **Shōwa jidai** began. He largely stayed out of politics, letting the cabinet rule the nation. Two instances in which he did take action were the ordering of the suppression of the military rebellion of **February 26, 1936** (AC vol. 1, p. 29) and accepting the demand that Japan unconditionally surrender in August 1945. As part of that surrender, he made a special radio broadcast to the entire nation notifying them of the end of the war. After the end of the war, he devoted himself to ceremonial roles, botanical research, and good-will tours to Europe (1971) and the United States (1975). He died on January 7, 1989, after a long illness. (Note: It is not customary in Japan to refer to the emperor by his personal name. Thus, Hirohito is almost always referred to as "the Shōwa Emperor." Both forms are used in English-language texts, however.)

A The death of the Shōwa Emperor is mentioned in *Otaku no Video* (pt. 2).

M The emperor's surrender radio broadcast is heard in *Barefoot Gen: Out of the Ashes* (p. 2).

## 宿場町
## SHUKUBA MACHI (POST STATION TOWN)

Post station towns, also known as *shukueki*. Designated stopping points that provided rest facilities for travelers, these towns were not only found on major roads such as the **Nakasendō** and the **Tōkaidō**, but on lesser routes. In the **Edo period** (AC vol. 1, p. 25) they were controlled by the **bakufu,** and residents had to provide a certain number of horses and transport workers for official use. Some shukuba machi mentioned in this book include **Adachi-ku, Araichō, Hachiōji, Utsunomiya, Ōtsu, Shimo Suwa, Senju,** and **Kanaya.**

M Ōgami stays in Kanaya in *Lone Wolf and Cub* (vol. 7, p. 190).

## シューマイ OR シウマイ OR 焼売 OLD FORM 燒賣
## SHŪMAI (DIM SUM)

One of many Chinese foods that have become part of Japanese life. Shūmai are made of seasoned meats, usually pork, but even shrimp and beef are used, encased in a thin wheat wrapping and steamed rather than fried. These are often eaten with **rāmen** (AC vol. 1, p.

*A delicious looking dish from* Fushigi Yugi. *Just imagine these* **shūmai** *with a shrimp filling. Waiter, more tea!*

105) or **yakisoba** (AC vol. 1, p. 145) when they are not enough to be a full meal. A common decoration is a single pea placed on top of each shūmai.

A Miaka dreams of shūmai at the beginning of *Fushigi Yūgi* (ep. 1). • Onizuka tells a scary story about shūmai rumored to have been made with human flesh in *GTO* (ep. 5).

## 春画 OLD FORM 春畫
## SHUNGA (EROTIC ART)

Erotic prints, illustrations, or paintings, the word shunga literally translates as "spring pictures." It is believed that the earliest shunga images were paintings by artists done for the fun of it. In the Nara period (710–94), the first illustrated sex manuals were produced. Shunga did not become a widespread art until the development and spread of printing. In the **Edo period** (AC vol. 1, p. 25), urban society came to be an audience for the prints. Some of the greatest print makers of the period produced shunga as part of their work. Later shunga often degenerated into crude pornographic works and by the 19th century little was being produced. The term shunga has fallen out of favor with many Japanese, and the more acceptable term *higa* (secret pictures) is now often used.

A Kenshin meets Sanosuke at a print seller and teases him, asking if he is looking for shunga in *Rurouni Kenshin* (TV ep. 23).

## 手裏剣 OLD FORM 手裏劍
## SHURIKEN (THROWING STARS)

Small knives, darts, or many-pointed throwing weapons. While associated with **ninjutsu** (AC vol. 1, p. 95) in the West, usually in the form of stars, shuriken have been used by other fighters in Japan and come in a variety of shapes. The martial art of throwing these is called *shurikenjutsu*.

A In *Samurai X: Trust and Betrayal* shuriken are tossed through a wall. • The star-shaped form is seen in *Urusei Yatsura* (TV ep. "Spring Special

2"). • Swastika-shaped ones are used by Kaede in *City Hunter 2* (ep. 24).

## 首都高速湾岸線
## SHUTO KŌSOKU WANGAN SEN (BAYSHORE EXPRESSWAY)

The Bayshore **kōsoku dōro,** also known as the Expressway Bayshore Line, the Shuto Expressway Wangan Line, and the Wangan Expressway. A major expressway that goes along **Tōkyō Wan** from **Yokohama,** across the **Yokohama Bei Buriji,** through **Tokyo Kokusai Kūkō** (AC vol. 1, p. 138; Haneda airport), through the parts near the bay of Ota Ward, **Shinagawa-ku, Kōtō-ku, Edogawa-ku,** and on past **Tokyo Dizunīrando** into **Chiba Ken** (AC vol. 1, p. 18).

**A** Shinobu is taking the Bayshore Expressway on her way to the Yokohama Bay Bridge early in *Patlabor 2.* • Toward the end of the first *You're Under Arrest* episode, we hear the Bayshore mentioned. • In *City Hunter* (ep. 25), the Wangan Expressway is mentioned by Ryo.

## そば or 蕎麦
## SOBA

Specifically, the buckwheat plant itself. The term is commonly used for the thin, brown noodles (**men rui**) made from buckwheat flour. Soba are used in both hot and cold dishes. When they are served cold, and often when served hot, they are dipped in a **shōyu** (AC vol. 1, p. 124) based sauce. Soba eaten at midnight on New Year's while the bells are still ringing (**joya no kane** AC vol. 1, p. 55) is called **toshikoshi soba.** There is even a greenish variety made with green tea. Restaurants specializing in soba are called soba-ya.

**M** Ryoga gives Akane a souvenir box of soba from his travels in *Ranma 1/2: Anything Goes Martial Arts* (ep. 16 and vol. 7, p. 76).

**A** The ultimate appearance of soba in anime has to be episode 36 of *City Hunter 2,* which shows the various stages of making soba noodles and

several ways of serving them, as well as discusses the aesthetics of eating them. • Soba is eaten by Sanshiro Sugata in *Sanshiro the Judoist* (pt. 1).

**M** A soba-ya is seen in the background of the street scene in *The Return of Lum Urusei Yatsura: Creature Features* (vol. 7, p. 9).

## 孫悟空
## SON GOKŪ

The Monkey King. In Chinese, he is known as Sun Houzi (Sun Hou-tzu). He is the main character of the **Saiyūki,** in which he has great magical powers and becomes immortal after stealing and eating the peaches of immortality while on a visit to heaven. He carries a staff that he can make longer or shorter at will and flies on a cloud.

**M** Son Goku is the hero of *Dragon Ball.* He is also the inspiration of the title character of Buichi Terasawa's *Goku Midnight Eye* series, a character who also carries a staff of variable length.

**A** There have been several anime adaptations of the *Saiyūki* story in which you can see Son Goku. Some of these have been released in English.

**M** There is even a short appearance of Son Goku in Masamune Shirow's *Black Magic* (p. 72).

## 尊王攘夷
## SONNŌ JŌI (REVERE THE EMPEROR, EXPEL THE BARBARIANS)

A late **Edo period** (AC vol. 1, p. 25) movement that sought to restore the emperor to ruling status and to expel foreigners from Japan. The concept originated in **Mito Han** scholarship in the early 19th century and later became the rallying cry for the overthrow of the **bakufu.** One of the advocates of sonnō jōi was **Yoshida Shōin.**

**A** Translated as "imperial reverence barbarian expulsion movement," you can hear the words sonnō jōi spoken by Miaka as she studies in *Fushigi Yūgi* (ep. 17).

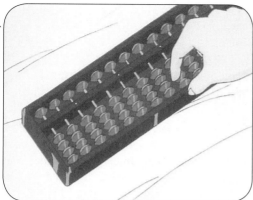

*Some people are faster with a soroban, like this one in Ranma 1/2, than others are with an electronic calculator.*

## 算盤
## SOROBAN (ABACUS)

The abacus did not enter Japan from China until the 16th century but was rapidly adopted for calculating and became part of the educational curriculum. In 1927, the teaching of the soroban was made an official part of the curriculum. The common Japanese abacus has an upper and lower section consisting of twenty-three or twenty-seven rods with beads on each one. The upper section has one bead, the lower section has four. Each year 3–4 million Japanese take the annual proficiency test held by the Japanese Chamber of Commerce and Industry. Even with the development of electronic calculators it is common to see Japanese use a soroban to quickly handle fairly complex calculations. As soroban users are less likely to make errors, some businesses restrict the use of calculators.

**Ⓐ** We see a soroban used in the first season of *Ranma 1/2* (ep. 14) • Akira uses one in the first episode of *Clamp School*. • The air pirate Dora uses one to calculate the influence of the winds on their travel time in *Castle in the Sky.*

**Ⓜ** Babo rattles a soroban while lecturing Wataru about making money in *Caravan Kidd* (vol. 2, p. 140).

## スタジオアルタ
## STUDIO ALTA

A building located in the **Shinjuku** (AC vol. 1, p. 120) Ward of **Tokyo.** The distinctive features of this landmark are the name in large Roman letters, a large clock, and a large video screen on the side facing **Shinjuku Eki.**

**Ⓜ** In *City Hunter,* Studio ALTA is a common landmark outside Shinjuku Station.

**Ⓐ** Studio ALTA with its large screen is visible in the *Urusei Yatsura* OVA "The Electric Household Guard," behind Shuichi Sakura as he campaigns in the *Sanctuary* anime, in *Megazone 23* (ep. 1), and in *Fushigi Yūgi* (ep. 51)

**Ⓜ** Studio ALTA is also seen in *3 x 3 Eyes: Curse of the Gesu* (ch. 1).

## 菅原道真
## SUGAWARA NO MICHIZANE

845–903. A noted scholar, poet, and calligrapher of the **Heian period** (AC vol. 1, p. 44). He was fifty-four when he attained high government office. A conflict with the powerful Fujiwara clan resulted in his being falsely accused of plotting against the emperor. He was exiled to **Kyushu** (AC vol. 1, p. 78), where he died in poverty two years later. After a series of unpleasant events happened to the court and capital it was decided that his angry spirit was responsible. He was posthumously pardoned and given the highest court rank. He was deified as Tenman Tenjin and shrines to him were built in **Kyoto** (AC vol. 1, p. 77; Kitano-tenmangū jinja) and Dazaifu (Dazaifu jinja). Today there are many shrines in his honor in Japan where students go to pray for success in exams.

**Ⓐ** Sugawara Michizane is among the characters that appear in *Haunted Junction* (ep. 5).

**Ⓜ** Ataru's mother gives him an **omamori** (AC vol. 1, p. 100) of Sugawara Michizane in *Return of Lum: Ran Attacks!* (p. 23).

## 杉
## SUGI (CEDAR)

Japanese cedar trees grow in a conical shape and can get quite large. Their wood has long been used in construction, for furniture, and for smaller utilitarian items such as **masu** (AC vol. 1, p. 80).

Ⓜ We get an impressive view of the sugi at **Togakushi Jinja** in *Mai the Psychic Girl* (Perfect Collection vol. 1, p. 88). • In *Vagabond* (vol. 2, ch. 17), Takezō is tied to a large sugi. • A very old solitary sugi is used as a landmark in *Lone Wolf and Cub* (vol. 2, p. 78).

## すいか OR 西瓜
## SUIKA (WATERMELON)

Watermelon is popular as a summer treat. An interesting game involving a watermelon, a baseball bat or stick, and a blindfold is called **suika-wari** (AC vol. 1, p. 126). You will notice that watermelons in Japan are round, not oblong as they usually are in the United States.

Ⓐ Kaji raises watermelons in *Neon Genesis Evangelion* (ep. 17). • Watermelon is eaten, played with, and, when it is angered, fled from (yes, fled from) in *Urusei Yatsura* (TV ep. 40, st. 63), and in *Beautiful Dreamer*, Lum cools a watermelon by running cold water from a tap over it.

Ⓜ Tamuro and Yura are treated to watermelon in

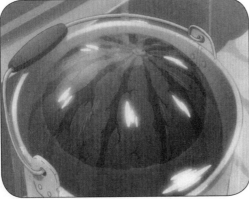

*A simple and easy way to cool off* **suika** *is by running water over it like this one in* Aɪ Yori Aoshi.

part 3 of "Wasted Minds" in the *Rumic World Trilogy* (vol. 2, p. 108).

## 水滸伝 FORMAL 水滸傳
## SUIKODEN (OUTLAWS OF THE MARSH)

The famous Chinese epic *Shui hu zhuan* (*Shui hu chuan*), known in English under more than one title but usually as *The Water Margin* or *Outlaws of the Marsh*. This tale is set in the early 12th century. Some of the events and characters in the tale are real, and their exploits the inspiration for tales by professional storytellers. Scholars claim that in the 14th century the work was edited by Shi Nai'an (Shih Nai-an) and Luo Guanzhong (Lo Kung-chung) into the story we know today. This massive tale of 108 heroes who band together to resist corrupt officials has entertained many for centuries. After all, who can resist a bloody tale with mayhem, murder, arson, cannibalism, slaughter, and thievery? And the villains are even less well-behaved! The stories entered Japan in the early 18th century when a translator named Okajima Kanzan published the first ten chapters in Japanese. Later other chapters were translated and published, and other works inspired by it were also written in Japanese. In the 19th century, **Bakin** (AC vol. 1, p. 8) and the famous printmaker Katsushika Hokusai collaborated on an illustrated edition of the work, entitled *Shinpen Suikogaden*. The work took thirty-three years to complete because Bakin had disagreements with Hokusai and was removed from the project, and some twenty-one years elapsed before the next chapter was done by another writer. Ⓐ The anime adaptation of *Giant Robo* incorporates many of the characters from the *Suikoden*, such as the black whirlwind Tetsugyu. • *Suikoden Demon Century* is a tale of the reincarnation of some of the characters into a post-holocaust Japan. • Elements of the *Suikoden* were used by Bakin in his *Nansō Satomi Hakkenden*, which is available as an anime under the title of *The Legend of the Dog Warriors The Hakkenden*.

## 隅田川
## SUMIDAGAWA

A major river flowing through the Shitamachi district of **Tokyo.** The river cuts through so much of Tokyo that it is spanned by more than twenty-five bridges. Much of the Sumidagawa is lined with commercial buildings. In anime and manga, the river is usually associated with the summer **hanabi** (AC vol. 1, p. 39) shows, which date back over 250 years. The wards that it flows next to as it heads to **Tōkyō Wan** are Itabashi and Kita wards, **Adachiku, Arakawa-ku,** Sumida Ward, **Taitō-ku,** Chūō Ward, and **Kōtō-ku.**

🅐 The Sumidagawa is mentioned in *Patlabor Original Series* (ep. 1) and in *Rurouni Kenshin* (TV ep. 17). • The destructive power of the flooding river is seen in *Lone Wolf and Cub* (vol. 22).

## スナック
## SUNAKKU (BAR)

Japan law says that bars must close at 11 P.M. However, if food is served they can remain open. Running a full restaurant is not cheap, so many places started serving simple foods that would qualify them to stay open later. These "bars with snacks" will often have a sign that includes the English word "snack" out front. There is also a daytime version of the sunakku. These are not bars but actual restaurants with a limited menu of easy-to-prepare items. The daytime sunakku are popular with mothers and their children.

Ⓜ The most famous sunakku in anime and manga is the Chachamaru. We see the word "snack" on the street sign in *Maison Ikkoku* (ep. 27)

Ⓜ Night time sunakku are also seen in *Futaba-Kun Change* (vol. 8) and *Rumic Theater: One or Double* (p. 212).

*This **suntetsu** in* Rurouni Kenshin *is one of several concealed weapons used in traditional **jūjutsu** (AC vol. 1, p. 56).*

## 寸鉄 OLD FORM 寸鐵
## SUNTETSU

A short bar, usually metal or wood, used as a weapon in hand-to-hand combat. Usually it has a ring attached so it can be held hidden in the hand, with a finger through the ring, until it is used. The suntetsu is one of the weapons used in several **ryū** of **jūjutsu** (AC vol. 1, p. 56). It was used to defend against weapons, disarm opponents, or injure.

Ⓜ Suntetsu is rather poorly translated as dagger in the *Rurouni Kenshin* TV series (ep. 4), but wisely left as suntetsu in the manga (vol. 1, p. 135).

## すっぽん OR 鼈
## SUPPON (SNAPPING TURTLE)

The snapping turtle is imported, caught in the wild, or farmed in Japan. As a food, it is prepared in a variety of ways, including **sashimi,** deep-fried, and as a base for soup stock. There are even restaurants that specialize in meals in which everything is made with suppon. Sometimes the turtle blood is mixed with **sake** (AC vol. 1, p. 109) to make a fortifying drink. Both the suppon flesh and the blood are thought to be aphrodisiacs.

🅐 As a child, Ataru is compared to a suppon for

his ability to latch onto a girl and not let go in the *Urusei Yatsura* TV series (ep. 28, st. 51). • As a food, the snapping turtle of Koshien in **Kōbe** is mentioned in *Urusei Yatsura* (ep. 55, st. 78). • Megumi gives Akito a drink containing snapping turtle and pit viper blood as well as cow liver, energy drink, **dokudami, sanshō, shiitake,** burdock (**gobō**), and lotus root (**renkon**) in *Martian Successor Nadesico* (ep. 10).

Ⓜ The blood of a snapping turtle becomes a key ingredient in a meal in *Iron Wok Jan* (vol. 9, ch. 78).

薄
## SUSUKI (PAMPAS GRASS)

Usually translated as pampas grass, this reed-like plant is found throughout Japan and East Asia. In the late summer the flower spikes form giving the susuki its distinctive wispy silhouette. The stems are used for making thatched roofs and for a variety of woven items. Some varieties are also used in gardens. The susuki is a seasonal symbol for autumn.

Ⓐ Very early on, we see susuki by moonlight in *Samurai X: Trust and Betrayal,* and as Shino and Hamaji run away in *The Legend of the Dog Warriors The Hakkenden* (ep. 10). • They are also seen in *Patlabor the TV Series* (ep. 2) and *Neon Genesis Evangelion* (ep. 4).

*Dried **susuki** and a dragonfly. This beautiful autumn scene is in* Patlabor.

諏訪湖
## SUWAKO (LAKE SUWA)

Also known as Ga-ko, Lake Suwa is located in Nagano Prefecture. The Chūō Expressway and the Chūō Rail Line pass on opposite sides of this mountain lake. In the **Sengoku jidai** (AC vol. 1, p. 113), the Takeda clan had a small fleet of ships on this lake. Suwako is known for its large number of fish. In the winter ice skating is popular; there are also hot springs in the area.

Ⓐ The aragami Nozuchi is seen in Suwako in the *Blue Seed* TV series (ep. 18). • We hear mention of the Lake Suwa horse market in the *Priest of Mt. Kouya.*

たい OR 鯛
## TAI (SEA BREAM)

Several kinds of fish can be called tai but the term is usually used to refer to the red *madai*. Another kind that is also red is the *chidai*. The distinctive red color makes it easy to spot in anime, and because red is a celebratory color the tai is often used as a food for special occasions. The eating of tai in Japan goes back to prehistory, with bones being found in Jōmon-period archaeological sites. Poems mentioning tai are found in the classic **Man'yōshū** (AC vol. 1, p. 80).

Ⓐ When Tomoe and Kenshin shop, we see a tai hanging by its tail in a fishmonger's shop in *Sam-*

*That big **tai** in the middle looks perfect for a feast. This one is seen in Samurai X Trust and Betrayal.*

urai X: Trust and Betrayal. • A red tai is seen at a meal in *The Legend of the Dog Warriors The Hakkenden* (ep 8). • Kasumi brings tai to a party in ***Ranma 1/2*** (ep. 14). • An entire tai cut as **sashimi** is in *801 TTS Airbats* (ep. 5).

## 平将門 OLD FORM 平將門
## TAIRA NO MASAKADO

d. 940. A warrior of the **Taira** (AC vol. 1, p. 130) family who led the first rebellion by **bushi** against the government, setting up his own state in the **Kantō chihō** (AC vol. 1, p. 61). Legend has it that after his defeat, his head flew to Shibasaki, a village at the end of the **Hibiya** inlet in what is now the Ōtemachi area in **Chiyoda-ku** in central Tokyo. Locals who saw Taira no Masakado as a hero raised the **Masakado-zuka** over the head. They also placed a stone marker in front of the mound and worshipped him as the principle deity of Kanda Myōjin. (The story of his rebellion is told in the *Shōmonki*, which is available in an English translation from Sophia University in Tokyo.)

🅐 In *Doomed Megalopolis*, attempts are made to raise the spirit of Taira no Masakado to destroy Tokyo. • Taira Masakato is mentioned in *Samurai Deeper Kyo* (ep. 6).

## 大正時代
## TAISHŌ JIDAI (TAISHŌ PERIOD)

1912–26. A period of Japanese history in which both democratic and military movements made advances. During World War I, Japan sided with the Allies against Germany and there was a great expansion of industry and trade. An increased labor force also meant demands for workers' rights, as well as broader democratic rights including the right to vote. Frustrated over failures to secure universal suffrage, the left in Japan moved toward extremism, becoming more like the radical movements in the United States and Europe. For example, in 1922 the **Nihon Kyōsantō** (AC vol. 1, p. 95) was founded. The **Kokkai** (AC vol. 1, p. 72) passed laws protecting labor and tenants, established a minimum wage, and, in 1925, passed a law that granted the right to vote to all males over the age of twenty-five. At the same time as the left gained influence in the cities, the right began to gain power in rural areas. The Kokkai also passed laws restricting freedom of the press and political action. In the 1920s, special political police units came into existence.

🅐 The first *Sakura Wars* OVA series begins in Taishō 8 and ends in Taishō 12. The period is mentioned in *Fushigi Yūgi* (ep. 29). • The *Doomed Megalopolis* series ends during Taishō jidai.

## 台東区 OLD FORM 臺東區
## TAITŌ-KU

The smallest of the wards of **Tokyo,** Taitō Ward includes the districts of **Ueno** (AC vol. 1, p. 142) and **Asakusa** (AC vol. 1, p. 6). The ward is located on the west bank of the **Sumidagawa.** It is bordered by **Arakawa-ku** on the north, Sumida Ward on the east, **Chiyoda-ku** on the south, and Bunkyō Ward on the west. Famous landmarks include **Ueno Dōbutsuen** (AC vol. 1, p. 142), **Ueno Kōen** (AC vol. 1, p. 143), **Kokuritsu Kagaku Hakubutsukan, Uguisudani,** and **Asakusa Jinja** (AC vol. 1, p. 7). Train stations include **Ueno Eki** (AC vol. 1, p. 143), and **Uguisudani Eki.**

**WHAT THE HECK IS A TOTORO?**

A few times a year I get an email asking me pretty much the same question. Is a Totoro from Japanese folklore and, if not, what exactly is it? Well, in a sense the big fuzzy creature in *My Neighbor Totoro* is from Japanese folklore, but only indirectly. Japanese tradition has a wide variety of spirits large and small. Some are helpful and benevolent, like our friendly Totoro. If you recall when the father and girls go to the tree there is a small **torii** (AC vol. 1, p. 139) in front of it. The tree is considered a sacred object. As for the name Totoro, well, little Mei is still quite young and has trouble pronouncing some words. What she is trying to say when she says totoro is actually the English word "troll" since, to her, he looks like some pictures she's seen in a book. Watch the movie in Japanese and listen to her words and you'll see what I mean.

🅐 Mitsuru's family runs the fictional Kōryūji temple in Taitō Ward in *Here Is Greenwood* (ep. 2), and it is also mentioned in *You're Under Arrest!: The Motion Picture.*

🅜 Asuma uses a map of Taitō Ward to aid in an explanation in *Mobile Police Patlabor* (vol. 1, p. 136).

### 高杉晋作 FORMAL 高杉晋作
**TAKASUGI SHINSAKU**

1839–67. A **Chōshū Han** retainer who became a major opponent of the Tokugawa **shōgun** (AC vol. 1, p. 123). He was a student of **Yoshida Shōin,** and in 1862 when he was in his early twenties he traveled to Shanghai, where he witnessed the results of European domination and the brutal suppression of the T'ai-p'ing rebellion. This convinced him of the importance of Japan becoming strong enough to oppose the foreigners who could easily reduce Japan to the

subservient status China was in. After his return from China, he founded the **Kiheitai** in 1863. In late 1864, he played a major role in the coup against pro-**bakufu** elements in the Chōshū domain as the leader of the Kiheitai. He then shared control of the clan domain with **Kido Takayoshi** until his death from **kekkaku** shortly before the downfall of the bakufu.

🅐 Takasugi Shinsaku is shown in his role as the leader of the Kiheitai in *Samurai X: Trust and Betrayal.*

### たけのこ OR 竹の子 OR 筍
**TAKENOKO (BAMBOO SHOOT)**

Harvested just as they poke through the ground in the spring or, for some varieties, in the fall, the shoots of only a few bamboo species that were introduced from China are eaten in Japan. The bamboo shoots are boiled in preparation for cooking and used in a variety of dishes. The **Kyoto** (AC vol. 1, p. 77) area has a reputation for takenoko of very high quality.

🅐 We get to see bamboo shoot digging, with Lime digging up one that is far too old, in *Saber Marionette J Again* (ep. 4).

🅜 Bamboo shoots are clearly visible on the ground in a market in *The Legend of Kamui: Perfect Collection* (vol. 1, p. 10).

### 沢庵宗彭 FORMAL 澤庵宗彭
**TAKUAN SŌHŌ**

1573–1645. A famous **Zen** Buddhist monk who entered monastic life at the age of ten. He was at the Daitokuji in **Kyoto** (AC vol. 1, p. 77) from 1594, and in 1608 he gained the position of *dai-sōjo* (head priest) after having lived at other temples in Japan. He left in 1629, having been sent into exile to Kaminoyama after conflicts with local **bakufu** authorities. Takuan later moved to **Edo,** where he took control of Tōkaiji in **Shinagawa-ku** at the request of **shōgun** (AC vol. 1, p. 123) **Tokugawa Iemitsu** in 1638. He was known for his accomplishment in painting, calligraphy, poetry, and **cha-no-yu** (AC vol. 1, p. 17). He is also commonly known for having developed *takuan zuke*, pickled **daikon** (AC vol. 1, p. 21).

🅰 Cherry is Master Takuan in the *Urusei Yatsura* TV series (ep. 55, st. 78) parody of **Yoshikawa Eiji**'s novel of the life of **Miyamoto Musashi** (AC vol. 1, p. 86).

🅼 Takuan shows up to play a major role in *Vagabond* (vol. 2, ch. 12).

## 多摩地区
## TAMA CHIKU (TAMA AREA)

Also called the Tama District, this area is located in the far western part of **Tokyo**. Until recently, it referred to the area not included in the twenty-three wards of Tokyo. Before 1967, Tama was a farming region. Today it is partly a heavily populated residential area as a result of the expansion of the metropolitan portion of Tokyo. There is also a town in the area called Tama, as well as the Tamagawa river and the Tama hills.

🅰 Saito shows up disguised as a medicine seller from Tama in the *Rurouni Kenshin* TV series (ep. 28).

🅼 The Tama DMV office is seen in *Voyeur* (p. 34) and mentioned in *Cannon God Exaxxion* (v. 1 p. 127).

## 多摩ニュータウン
## TAMA NYŪ TAUN (TAMA NEW TOWN)

Starting in 1967, the construction of the massive Tama Nyū Taun project converted rural land from four cities: Tama, **Hachiōji**, Machida, and Inagi into a residential area. Occupants started moving into their homes in 1971. Today it is home to over 300,000 people. It is usually not found on maps because it is not actually a separate town but newly developed portions of the four original cities.

🅰 Studio Ghibli's *Heisei Tanuki Gassen Pompoko* (aka *Pom Poko*) depicts the opposition to the development of Tama New Town by a group of **tanuki** (AC vol. 1, p. 133).

## 卵 OR たまご
## TAMAGO (EGG)

Specifically, bird eggs, usually hen's eggs but sometimes quail eggs. Japanese foods that use eggs are almost always easy to identify. Some **donburi** (AC vol. 1, p. 24) include an egg laid over the top of the other ingredients; **tenpura** or other batters are usually made with egg as an ingredient, as are minced meat foods. Eggs are also eaten raw, hard-boiled (*katayude tamago*), and soft-boiled (*hanjuku tamago*).

🅰 In the song for the closing credits in *Dragon Half,* Mink claims the egg as hers. • At a noodle stand in **Tomakomai,** Asuma orders an egg, which the cook cracks right into his bowl of noodles (**men rui**) in episode 5 of *Patlabor Original Series.*

## 卵酒
## TAMAGO-ZAKE (EGG YOLK IN SAKE)

Hot **sake** (AC vol. 1, p. 109) with the addition of an egg yolk. This traditional cold cure calls for the sake to be heated until much of the alcohol evaporates, that is to a temperature much higher than one would typically use for drinking warmed sake.

🅰 Kasumi makes "egg and sake soup" for Akane when she has a cold in *Ranma 1/2 Hard Battle* (ep. 3), and Manami offers Kyosuke some in *Kimagure Orange Road* (TV ep. 4). • In *Tenchi Universe* (ep. 9), we see a very failed attempt to make this remedy.

## 箪笥 FORMAL 箪笥
## TANSU (WOODEN CHEST)

Tansu were a common item in older Japanese homes and businesses. Used for storing a variety of items, they came in a variety of shapes and sizes. Tansu not only had drawers, but at times also cupboard doors. Usually they are of dark wood, often *kiri* wood, with

*This **kaidan dansu** from Ai Yori Aoshi shows both functionality and beauty in a practical object.*

dark metal fittings. There is even a style of tansu called **kaidan dansu** that doubles as a staircase.

🅰 We see a tansu in Kamaji's place in *Spirited Away*. • In: *Samurai X: Trust and Betrayal,* we see a tansu in the farmhouse where Kenshin and Tomoe live. • In *Grave of the Fireflies,* we see a tansu in Setsuko and Seita's room, and in Otaru's **nagaya** in *Saber Marionette J* (ep. 2). • We also get to see a good example of a tansu in *Millennium Actress.*

Ⓜ In *Black Jack* (vol. 1, p. 114), at Taku's mother's home we see a tansu in the background.

## 盥舟 OR 盥船
## TARAIBUNE (TUB BOAT)

A round wooden boat. These are used on Sado Island to gather seaweed and shellfish in the shallow waters off the rocky coast. They are powered by a single oar, as were most small traditional boats in Japan.

🅰 The best representation of a taraibune in currently available anime is in *Spirited Away*.

## 他流試合
## TARYŪ-JIAI (DUEL)

A duel between two fighters, normally followers of two different **ryū**, as a test of their respective techniques. Perhaps the

swordsman best known for this practice is **Miyamoto Musashi** (AC vol. 1, p. 86).

Ⓜ In *Vagabond* (vol. 2, ch. 15), we see the combat between the young Takezō and **Arima Kihei.** As the story progresses we see many such combats.

## 帝国ホテル OLD FORM 帝國ホテル
## TEIKOKU HOTERU (IMPERIAL HOTEL)

Located in **Tokyo** near the Imperial Palace and **Hibiya** Park. The first building was destroyed by fire. The second building, designed by Frank Lloyd Wright, took six years to complete and partially opened on July 4, 1922. It fully opened on August 31, 1923. The brown stone used in the construction of the building came from the area of **Utsunomiya.** The building survived the **Kantō Daishinsai** and played a crucial role in disaster relief. It also survived the bombings of WWII to become the home of many of General MacArthur's staff during the Occupation. Annexes were added in 1954 and 1956, but they were not enough to accommodate the increase in guests, so the hotel was demolished in 1967 and replaced by the seventeen-story building currently in use. The Meiji Mura Museum in Inuyama, **Aichi Ken** (AC vol. 1, p. 3,) has the original lobby on display. Even the new building was not enough, and the older annexes were replaced by a thirty-one-story tower that opened in 1983.

🅰 A girl meets Ota in the Imperial Hotel in *Patlabor the TV Series* (ep. 12).

## ていしょく OR 定食
## TEISHOKU (SET MEAL)

A pre-planned meal with a set group of foods. Often these are designated by the letters of the alphabet: A, B, C, etc.

🅰 A *yakiniku* teishoku is mentioned in the closing song of *Dragon Half* (pt. 1). • For some reason the "A" set seems popular. In *GTO* (ep. 5) Onizuka offers ten fake combo-A lunch tickets to Kikuchi. • In *Magical Shopping Arcade Abenobashi* (ep. 2), Sashi mentions an "A meal" then wonders if it is possible to order set meals in the strange place they are in. • In the first episode of *You're Under Arrest,* Miyuki tells Natsumi that the "A Lunch" is full of oysters.

## てんぷら OR 天婦羅 OR 天麩羅
## TENPURA

 It is believed that tenpura (usually spelled "tempura" in English) was introduced into Japan by the Portuguese in the 16th century. In the 19th century it became quite popular and was sold from **yatai** (AC vol. 1, p. 147). Today is it mainly sold in restaurants. Tenpura is seafood and/or vegetables coated with a light batter made from flour, water, and egg, and then deep-fried. Usually it is served with a dip (*tentsuyu*) made of **shōyu** (AC vol. 1, p. 124), *mirin,* and **dashi.**

🅐 Botchan enjoys tenpura after a bath in *Botchan* (pt. 1). • Koji eats tenpura shrimp in *Metal Skin Panic—MADOX-01.* • Tenpura is one of the foods for the feast when Kenji shows up in *Student Days,* and Sasami cooks tenpura in *Tenchi The Movie 2: The Daughter of Darkness.*

## 天ぷらそば
## TENPURA SOBA (TENPURA NOODLES)

 **Soba** in **dashi** with one or two **tenpura** shrimp on top served in a large bowl. Occasionally, spinach is included next to the shrimp.

🅐 "Tenpura noodle" is delivered to Onsen Mark in the teachers' office in *Urusei Yatsura* (TV ep. 56, st. 79) and to the Tendo home in *Ranma 1/2 Anything Goes Martial Arts* (ep. 20).

🅜 Twenty orders of "tenpura noodles" are delivered to the Tendo household in *Ranma 1/2* (vol. 6, p. 81).

## てんどん OR 天丼
## TENDON (TENPURA AND RICE)

Tenpura donburi, that is, a **donburi** (AC vol. 1, p. 24) dish made by placing one or two **tenpura**-fried shrimp on rice and then pouring on a **shōyu**-based (AC vol. 1, p. 124) sauce. The shrimp are not as crispy because the batter soaks in the sauce. There are variants of this dish made with other types of seafood.

🅐 Tendon is extorted from Godai by Yotsuya in *Maison Ikkoku* (ep. 38).

🅜 One of the detectives orders "tenpura and rice" in *Domu: A Child's Dream.*

## てっぱん OR 鉄板 OLD FORM 鐵板
## TEPPAN (IRON PLATE)

An iron plate. When it comes to cooking, any flat metal surface that can be heated can serve as a teppan. These are used in some restaurants that serve grilled foods like **okonomiyaki** (AC vol. 1, p. 100). Many such places have a teppan in each table for the customers to cook their own food. They are also used in **yakiniku-ya** and Korean BBQ restaurants, where the customers also cook their own food.

🅐 A teppan built into the table is seen in *Patlabor the TV Series* (ep. 30).

🅜 A teppan is used to cook okonomiyaki by Ukyo in *Ranma 1/2* (vol. 8, p. 16).

## テレビ
## TEREBI (TELEVISION)

Regular TV broadcasting began in Japan in 1953. Given the mountainous geography of Japan, TV reception would be difficult or impossible in most areas without the system of satellite broadcasting that now exists. Not only are TVs found in homes but even in cheap restaurants and some taxi cabs (**Takushi,** AC vol. 1, p. 133). Most towns only get a few channels but **Tokyo** has several. **Nippon Hōsō Kyōkai** (NHK AC vol. 1, p. 96), what would be called public television in the United States, has two channels, 1 and 3 in Tokyo, and charges an annual fee. Very popular are the fifteen-minute dramas based on novels that are broadcast twice each week on Channel 1.

🅐 The news broadcasts on Channel 5 in *Patlabor New Files* (ep. 3) play a significant role in the story, and in *Patlabor the TV Series* (ep. 9) Asuma watches TV in an inn until the coin operated meter runs out. • In *Blue Seed* (ep. 2), Momiji is delighted with the large number of channels in Tokyo.

## 手燭
## TESHOKU (PORTABLE CANDLE HOLDER)

A type of **rōsoku** (candle) holder or stick. Made from metal, the teshoku consists of a round plate with a spike in the center to hold the rōsoku; attached are three legs, one longer than the others that functions as a handle. Teshoku are not very tall and are often seen placed on furniture.

◪ Tomoe uses a teshoku in *Samurai X: Trust and Betrayal*.

## 鉄道 OLD FORM 鐵道
## TETSUDŌ (RAILWAYS)

Early railways date from the 1870s and were all government funded and operated. The first line opened in 1872 and ran from **Tokyo** to **Yokohama,** a distance of 28 kilometers (17.4 miles). Starting in the 1880s, privately funded railways came into existence. In 1874 a rail line between **Osaka** (AC vol. 1, p. 102) and **Kyoto** (AC vol. 1, p. 77) opened. In 1886, a line was begun on the **Tōkaidō** and was completed in 1893. Other lines were constructed on the major islands, and when nationalization took place in 1906–7 most were connected. Other important dates for developments in rail traffic are:

- 1893, the first Japanese-made steam locomotive begins service;
- 1895, the first electric rail line in Kyoto begins service;
- 1927, the first subway opens in Tokyo;
- 1964, the first **Shinkansen** (AC vol. 1, p. 120) trains begin service;
- 1987, denationalization begins.

◪ The Kenshin-gumi takes the train Yokohama for sightseeing trip in *Rurouni Kenshin* TV series (ep. 22).

## 鳥羽伏見の戦い OLD FORM 鳥羽伏見の戰い
## TOBA-FUSHIMI NO TATAKAI (BATTLE OF TOBA-FUSHIMI)

A battle fought on January 27, 1868, at Toba and Fushimi south of **Kyoto** (AC vol. 1, p. 77). This battle between **bakufu** forces and combined forces from the **Satsuma Han** and **Chōshū Han** resulted in a victory for the pro-imperial forces. This is considered the first battle of the **Boshin Sensō.**

◪ It is mentioned in the *Rurouni Kenshin* TV series (ep. 29) that the last time Kenshin and Saito fought each other was at this battle. • The battle of Toba-Fushimi is mentioned toward the end of *Dagger of Kamui.*

## 栃木県 OLD FORM 栃木縣
## TOCHIGI KEN

A prefecture in Central **Honshu** (AC vol. 1, p. 47) bordered by **Gunma Ken, Fukushima Ken, Ibaraki Ken** (AC vol. 1, p. 48), and Saitama Prefecture. The center of Tochigi Prefecture is a plain with mountains on the east and west. The economy is largely agricultural, mainly rice growing along with other grains and vegetables. There is some manufacturing of machinery and textiles.

Ⓜ Toshihiko is from Tochigi Prefecture in *Love Song* (p. 12), as is Uchiyamada in *GTO* (vol. 5, ch. 37).

## とうふ OR 豆腐
## TŌFU

Soybean curd. Soybeans are mashed and boiled to make soybean milk, which is then mixed with a coagulant that makes the tōfu harden. Tōfu came to Japan from China, where it had been developed 2,000 years before, and today plays a major role in **shōjin ryōri** and other forms of Japanese cooking. Tōfu is actually higher in protein than meat. Japanese tōfu is different from the Chinese style and should be sought out for Japanese recipes.

🅰 A **tōfu-ya** makes deliveries in *Urusei Yatsura: Always My Darling.*

Ⓜ In *Ai Yori Aoshi* (vol. 2, p. 33), we can see an eight-sided plate with a block of tofu on it.

## 豆腐屋
## TŌFU-YA (TŌFU SELLER)

A tōfu seller or store. In Japan, one still occasionally sees a tōfu vendor on a bicycle. Tōfu sellers ride around residential areas with a box filled with water and tōfu making direct sales of fresh tōfu to local housewives.

🅰 In *Zenki* (ep. 6) we see one of these tōfu sellers on a back street, one is seen from a distance in *Maison Ikkoku* (ep. 1), and one is blowing his horn in *Ranma 1/2* (TV ep. 23). • In the first episode of *FLCL*, a tōfu-ya horn is heard as Naota is on the phone.

## 戸隠 OLD FORM 戶隱
## TOGAKUSHI

A one-road village located in Nagano Prefecture. Income is still largely obtained from farming and craftsmaking, mainly basketry, for which the area is famous. The area also produces traditional **kasa** (AC vol. 1, p. 62). This village is also known for the **Togakushi Jinja.**

Ⓜ Mai and her father travel to Togakushi in *Mai the Psychic Girl* (Perfect Collection vol. 1, p. 76).

## 戸隠神社 OLD FORM 戶隱神社
## TOGAKUSHI JINJA

A famous **Shintō** (AC vol. 1, p. 121) **jinja** (AC vol. 1, p. 54) located outside the village of **Togakushi** in Nagano Prefecture. Actually it is three separate but interrelated shrines known as Hokosha (outer) Jinja, Chusha (middle) Jinja, and Okusha (inner) Jinja. Hokosha Jinja is in town and Okusha Jinja is much more isolated farther up the slope of Togakushiyama. In fact the road near it is closed in winter. This shrine is accessed by a path through a large **torii** (AC

vol. 1, p. 139) and formal gate, as well as being lined with large **sugi.** The shrine is also the location of the *Togakushi Legend Murders,* a famous crime novel by Yasuo Uchida, which is available in English.

Ⓜ Part of the Okusha Jinja is seen in *Mai the Psychic Girl* (Perfect Collection vol. 1, p. 87–89, 96).

## 東海地方 OLD FORM 東海地方
## TŌKAI CHIHŌ (TŌKAI REGION)

Located on the Pacific coast in central **Honshu** (AC vol. 1, p. 47) between **Kantō chihō** (AC vol. 1, p. 61) and Kinki chihō. **Shizuoka Ken, Aichi Ken** (AC vol. 1, p. 3), **Gifu Ken,** and **Mie Ken** make up this region.

Ⓜ The Tōkai district is mentioned in an announcement at the beginning of *Neon Genesis Evangelion* (ep. 1 and vol. 1).

🅰 When Japan is hit by a **tsunami,** Shizuoka Prefecture in Tōkai chihō in *Blue Seed* (ep. 24) is at the center of the damage. • In *Neon Genesis Evangelion* (ep. 19), the Tōkai chihō is where the NERV HQ is located. • Shishio took a village in the Tōkai chihō as his HQ in *Rurouni Kenshin* (ep. 36). • Tōkai is mentioned by Yuya in *Samurai Deeper Kyo* (ep. 1).

## 東海道 OLD FORM 東海道
## TŌKAIDŌ

Eastern Sea Road. The main road between **Edo** and **Kyoto** (AC vol. 1, p. 77). The route mostly follows the Pacific coast and is approximately 488 kilometers (303 miles) long. The route is an old one, predating written history in Japan. During the **Edo period** (AC vol. 1, p. 25), the Tōkaidō was improved to better handle traffic. There were fifty-three **shukuba machi** along the route. Much of the road is now covered by the modern Tōkaidō highway, but parts of the old road remain. The **Shinkansen** (AC vol. 1, p. 120) line runs roughly parallel to the old route.

🅰 Kenshin walks the Tōkaidō in the *Rurouni Kenshin* TV series (ep. 33).

## OTAKU QUIZ

Which character shares a name with a warship?

Many of the characters in *Neon Genesis Evengelion* are said to have been named after WWII warships. But do you know which ones? From this list of major characters, choose who is named after a ship. For bonus points, find the two who actually share names with two ships.

Asuka Langley Sohryu
Gendo Ikari
Hikari Horaki
Kaworu Nagisa
Kensuke Aida
Kouzou Fuyutsuki
Makoto Hyuga
Maya Ibuki
Misato Katsuragi
Rei Ayanami
Ritsuko Akagi
Ryoji Kaji
Shigeru Aoba
Shinji Ikari
Toji Suzuhara

ANSWERS

Asuka Langley Sohryu—Langley, U.S. aircraft carrier, *Sohryu*, aircraft carrier
Kouzou Fuyutsuki—*Fuyutsuki*, destroyer
Makoto Hyuga—*Hyuga*, battleship
Maya Ibuki—*Maya* and *Ibuki*, both cruisers
Misato Katsuragi—*Katsuragi*, aircraft carrier
Rei Ayanami—*Ayanami*, destroyer
Ritsuko Akagi—*Akagi*, aircraft carrier
Shigeru Aoba—*Aoba*, cruiser

Ⓜ The Tōkaidō is mentioned in *Blade of the Immortal: Dark Shadows* (p. 147) and in *Lone Wolf and Cub* (vol. 1, p. 68).

## 徳川家光
## TOKUGAWA IEMITSU

1604–51. The third Tokugawa **shōgun** (AC vol. 1, p. 123), who ruled from 1623–51. He is known for tightening control over Japan by instituting the **sankin kōtai,** banning all foreign trade except for certain Chinese and Dutch merchants in **Nagasaki** (AC vol. 1, p. 90), and intensifying the persecution of Christianity (**Kirisutokyō,** AC vol. 1, p. 69), policies that existed until the end of the Tokugawa **bakufu.** The Christian revolt that led to the **Shimabara no Ran** took place during his rule.

Ⓐ Tokugawa Iemitsu is seen ordering the suppression of the Shimabara no Ran in *Ninja Resurrection* (ep. 1).

Ⓜ Iemitsu's mother visiting the emperor is mentioned in *Samurai Legend* (p. 52).

## 徳川家康
## TOKUGAWA IEYASU

1543–1616. Tokugawa Ieyasu was born in Mikawa Province, which is now part of **Aichi Ken** (AC vol. 1, p. 3). Born as Matsudaira Takechiyo, he spent his childhood as a political hostage to the Oda and later the Imagawa clans.

After taking control of his father's territory, he aligned himself with **Oda Nobunaga** and attacked his former allies, the Imagawa. At this time, he also obtained imperial permission to take the older name of Tokugawa and chose Ieyasu as his personal name. After the death of Oda Nobunaga, he strengthened his control of his territories.

For a period of time, he was in conflict with **Toyotomi Hideyoshi** (AC vol. 1, p. 140). To end the fighting, however, they formed an alliance, with Ieyasu's son being adopted by Hideyoshi and the sister of Hideyoshi marrying Ieyasu. At one point, he was ordered to abandon his lands and take control of new territories. He set up his headquarters in the small fishing village of **Edo,** which later became the administrative capital of the **bakufu** and was eventually renamed **Tokyo.** In

1600, two years after the death of Hideyoshi, war broke out between the **Tokugawa** (AC vol. 1, p. 137) and the Toyotomi clans. By 1603, Ieyasu was granted the title of **shōgun** (AC vol. 1, p. 123).

🅐 In *Saber Marionette J*, we see a Tokugawa Ieyasu of the future colony nation of Japoness. • Tokugawa Ieyasu at the **Sekigahara no Tatakai** is seen in the beginning of *Samurai Deeper Kyo* (ep. 1). • Tokugawa Ieyasu and the use of **kasō** (AC vol. 1, p. 64) in building Edo are mentioned in *Rurouni Kenshin* (TV ep. 91).

## 徳川光圀
## TOKUGAWA MITSUKUNI

1628–1700. The historical Tokugawa Mitsukuni, also referred to as Mito Kōmon, was the grandson of **Tokugawa Ieyasu** and the lord of the **Mito Han.** He played a major role in promoting intellectual activities, especially the beginning of the writing of the *Dai Nihon Shi* (History of Great Japan), which took until 1906 to complete. His reputation as a ruler inspired an **Edo period** (AC vol. 1, p. 25) fictional account of his travels around Japan. This work inspired other tales, including a twenty-eight-year-long TV series entitled *Mito Kōmon* that aired beginning in 1969. In the TV show, Mito Kōmon traveled in disguise as a retired merchant and fought evil wherever he found it. In the show his identity would be dramatically revealed by a retainer showing his **mon** (AC vol. 1, p. 89).

🅐 Ataru tells Ten he is not Mito Kōmon when he holds out a packet of plant food in *Urusei Yatsura* (TV ep. 29, st. 52). • In *You're Under Arrest* (ep. 1), there is a pun on the name of Mito Boulevard and Mito Kōmon.

## 徳川頼宣 OLD FORM 徳川頼宣
## TOKUGAWA YORINOBU

1602–71. Eighth son of **Tokugawa Ieyasu.** In 1603, he was granted Mito Castle until 1606, when he took control of the Fuchū domain. In 1619 he was granted the more valuable Kii domain, also known as the Wakayama domain. His descendants controlled this domain as the Kii branch of the Tokugawa family until the fall of the **bakufu** in the 19th century.

🅐 In *Ninja Resurrection* (ep. 2) we hear of a strange order by Tokugawa Yorinobu to have all daughters between the ages of fifteen and twenty-two of all the clans brought to him.

Ⓜ Possible treason against the bakufu by Tokugawa Yorinobu is discussed in *Samurai Legend* (ch. 6).

## 徳川吉宗
## TOKUGAWA YOSHIMUNE

1684–1751. The 8th **Tokugawa** (AC vol. 1, p. 137) **shōgun** (AC vol. 1, p. 123). He was a son of the head of the Kii branch of the Tokugawa family, Tokugawa Mitsusada, and great-grandson of **Tokugawa Ieyasu.** In 1697 Yoshimune was made **daimyō** of Sabae. His older brothers died, and in 1705 he became daimyō of the Kii domain. In 1716 the shōgun Tokugawa Ietsugu died as a child leaving no heir. Yoshimune was chosen for the post of shōgun. Unlike some of the previous shōguns who had been raised in the **Edojō,** his experience as a daimyō enabled him to take a very active role in governing. One unusual measure he took was to order the setting up of a box, the *meyasubako,* into which anyone could place suggestions and complaints for the shōgun to read. He also instituted several reforms to deal with financial matters, reduce extravagance, promote science, and encourage traditional **samurai** (AC vol. 1, p. 110) martial arts.

Ⓜ While cramming for a special exam, Onizuka is asked who the 8th Tokugawa shōgun was. He guesses Matsudaira Ken in *GTO* (ep. 14 and vol. 6, ch. 45).

🅐 Yoshimune is one of the historical characters that briefly appear in *Haunted Junction* (ep. 5).

## 徳川慶喜
## TOKUGAWA YOSHINOBU

1837–1913. The 15th and last **Tokugawa** (AC vol. 1, p. 137) **shōgun** (AC vol. 1, p. 123). Born in **Edo,** he was the seventh son of Tokugawa Nariaki, **daimyō** of the **Mito Han.** In fact, his infant name, Shichirōmaro, means "seventh son. " He later was called Keiki. He spent his early childhood in the Mito castle town because his father had obtained special permission for him to grow up there rather in Edo, as was required under the **sankin kōtai.** When he was ten, he was adopted (**yōshi,** AC vol. 1, p. 148) into the prestigious Hitotsubashi family, which needed an heir. It was this adoption that enabled him to qualify as a candidate for shōgun. During the conflicts of the late Tokugawa period, both sides looked to Hitotsubashi Keiki as a potential ally, as he was not only related to the Tokugawa family but was from the Mito domain, a known source of pro-imperial sentiment. It is probably for this reason that **Ii Naosuke** and others backed Tokugawa Iemochi as the 14th shōgun. Instead, Keiki held several important offices in Edo and later **Kyoto** (AC vol. 1, p. 77). In 1867, Hitotsubashi Keiki became head of the Tokugawa family and the 15th shōgun, changing his name to Tokugawa Yoshinobu. Interestingly, both Keiki and Yoshinobu are written with the same **kanji** (AC vol. 1, p. 61) but pronounced differently. In November 1867, Yoshinobu resigned as shōgun, turning over political authority to the emperor. In 1868, the leaders of the **Chōshū Han** and **Satsuma Han** ordered Yoshinobu to surrender the Tokugawa lands. This led to the outbreak of the **Boshin Sensō.** After this conflict, he retired from public life and lived quietly for the rest of his life.

**A** Tokugawa Yoshinobu's fooling his own allies in his retreat to Edo by way of **Osaka** (AC vol. 1, p. 102) is mentioned by Kenshin in *Rurouni Kenshin* (TV ep. 45).

**M** Yoshinobu's granting special powers to **Katsu Kaishū** is mentioned in *Samurai Legend* (ch. 1).

## 東京
## TOKYO

In 1868, during the early **Meiji period** (AC vol. 1, p. 81), the city of **Edo** was renamed Tōkyō (Eastern Capital) and became the official capital of Japan. A major center for the arts, finance, industry, and trade, Tokyo is a modern city built on a site inhabited since prehistoric times. Much of older Tokyo was destroyed in WWII by fire bombings, but the city was rebuilt first as the headquarters of the Occupation forces and later as the capital. The governing structure of Tokyo is complex. It includes the twenty-three wards (*ku*) of the city proper, plus an additional twenty-seven cities (*shi*), one county (*gun*), four island administrations (*shichō*), as well as fourteen towns and villages (*chō, son*) within the prefecture of Tōkyō-to.

**M** Many anime and manga are set in Tokyo, usually in the part of the city that comprises the twenty-three wards. • Kome Sawaguchi in *Blue Seed* is a native of Tokyo.

**A** Most of the *Rurouni Kenshin* TV series takes place in Tokyo of the Meiji period.

## 東京ディズニーランド
## TOKYO DIZUNĪRANDO (TOKYO DISNEYLAND)

Located in **Urayasu, Chiba Ken** (AC vol. 1, p. 18), this amusement park is sometimes referred to as the Magic Kingdom. It opened in 1983 and occupies 204.1 acres of land, about half of which is devoted to parking. This was the first Disneyland outside the United States and is closely modeled on the California park.

**A** Tokyo Disneyland is mentioned in *Patlabor New Files* (ep. 3).

## 東京国立博物館
## TOKYO KOKURITSU HAKUBUTSUKAN (TOKYO NATIONAL MUSEUM)

 The museum has been located in **Ueno Kōen** (AC vol. 1, p. 143) since 1881; the main hall (the Honkan) dates from 1937. Today there are three main buildings, but the museum has expanded to other buildings in the area as its collection has grown. The objects in its holdings date from ancient times to relatively recent works and make up the largest collection of Japanese art in the world. The museum also contains art from other parts of Asia.

🅰 Terrorists attempt to use a rocket to hold the museum hostage in *Patlabor Original Series* (ep. 1).

## 東京証券取引所
## TOKYO SHŌKEN TORIHIKIJO (TOKYO STOCK EXCHANGE)

 Sometimes referred to in English as the Kabuto Stock Exchange, as it is located in Kabutochō. It was founded as a corporate membership non-profit in April 1949, with membership limited to securities companies. While the present market is a mid-20th-century institution, there was an earlier market in the same area that opened in 1878, during the **Meiji period** (AC vol. 1, p. 81); the hours that this market was open were determined by the slow smoldering of a specific length of rope.

🅰 The Kabuto Stock Exchange is mentioned in *Patlabor Original Series* (ep. 5). • The Tokyo Stock Exchange is mentioned on the radio in *Witch Hunter Robin* (ep. 1).

## 東京湾 OLD FORM 東京灣
## TŌKYŌ WAN (TOKYO BAY)

 A bay off the Pacific Ocean bordered by **Chiba Ken** (AC vol. 1, p. 18), **Kanagawa Ken** (AC vol. 1, p. 60), and **Tokyo.** Major ports on this bay include Chiba, Kawasaki, **Yokohama, Yokosuka,** and Tokyo. Until it was heavily polluted by industrialization in the early **Shōwa jidai,** Tōkyō Wan also provided seafood for the area.

🅰 An industrial complex in Tōkyō Wan plays a major role in the first *Patlabor* movie and of course the SV2's facilities are on the edge of the bay. • Aerial views of the bay often turn up in anime. Examples include *Otaku no Video* (pt. 2, 6th anim. seq.) and the third *Patlabor* movie.

## 苫小牧 [市]
## TOMAKOMAI

A city in **Hokkaido** (AC vol. 1, p. 46) located on the southwestern Pacific coast. Tomakomai was founded by colonists in the **Meiji period** (AC vol. 1, p. 81) and is a major ferry terminus for people traveling between **Honshu** (AC vol. 1, p. 47) and Hokkaido. Industry consists of oil refining, aluminum processing, and lumber. The city is also a major manufacturer of paper in Japan.

🅰 We learn that Noa is from Tomakomai in *Patlabor Original Series* (ep. 5) and in *Patlabor the TV Series* (ep. 14).

## 玉蜀黍 OR とうもろこし
## TŌMOROKOSHI (CORN ON THE COB)

Sweet corn. The Japanese do not prepare corn on the cob by boiling it. Instead, they grill the cobs and brush on **shōyu** (AC vol. 1, p. 124).

🅰 Goto is handed some tōmorokoshi in *Patlabor the TV Series* (ep. 40). • Ranma treats Miss Hinako to some tōmorokoshi bought from a cart in a park in *Ranma 1/2* (OVA 4).

Ⓜ Ranma-kun enjoys some himself in *Ranma 1/2* (vol. 8, p. 172).

## トンファ
## TONFA

A weapon from **Okinawa Ken** (AC vol. 1, p. 99), usually used in pairs. Tonfa are made of a length of wood usually 45–60

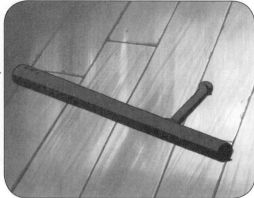

*It looks like a stick with a handle in most people's hands, but don't mess with someone who knows how to use a **tonfa**. This one lays in wait in RUROUNI KENSHIN.*

cm long. A handle at a right angle is set about a quarter of the way down its length. The handle allows the tonfa to be used both to block attacks and to be swung at an opponent. Originally, tonfa were devices used for milling rice. They were first used as weapons in the 17th century when the **Satsuma Han** invaded Okinawa.

🅐 Tonfa are used against swords in the *Rurouni Kenshin* TV series (ep. 42).

## とんカツ OR 豚カツ
## TONKATSU (PORK CUTLET)

A piece of breaded pork that has been deep-fried. Generally this is served on a plate with a thick sauce and shredded cabbage, potato salad, or macaroni salad. Tonkatsu is part of the **donburi** (AC vol. 1, p. 24) dish **katsudon.** In many places you can even specify which cut of pork you would prefer.

🅐 Pork cutlet is one of the earth foods mentioned by Ataru in the *Urusei Yatsura* TV series (ep. 29, st. 52). • Pork cutlets are delivered to the Tendo home in *Ranma 1/2 Anything Goes Martial Arts* (ep. 20).

## 酉の市
## TORI NO ICHI (BIRD FAIR)

Festival of the Rooster. Sometimes also called *tori no machi* or *otorisama*, it is held in November, according to the old lunar calendar, on the days of the rooster at Ōtori shrines. Most years only have two such days in the month, but some have three. During these festivals, vendors sell various items and charms for good luck, especially the **kumade.**

🅐 Shigure says "tori no ichi" when he meets Kenshin at a shrine during the festival in *Samurai X: The Motion Picture.*

## 土佐藩
## TOSA HAN

A domain that, during the **Edo period** (AC vol. 1, p. 25), covered all of Tosa Province, what is now known as **Kōchi Ken.** In 1603, this domain was granted to Yamauchi (sometimes called Yamanouchi) Kazutoyo for supporting **Tokugawa Ieyasu.** In the 19th century, the domain first was aligned with the *kōbu gattai* (union of court and bakufu) movement. Later it would side with the anti-shogunate forces.

Ⓜ **Sakamoto Ryōma** mentions being from Tosa in *Vanity Angel* (issue 5). • Tosa warriors guard the retired emperor in *Samurai Legend* (ch. 7). • Tosa's role in the **bakumatsu** is mentioned in *Rurouni Kenshin* (vol. 1, p. 70).

## 年越しそば
## TOSHIKOSHI SOBA (NEW YEAR'S SOBA)

**Soba** eaten on New Year's Eve. Toshikoshi means "seeing out the old year and seeing in the new." This custom began in the **Edo period** (AC vol. 1, p. 25), because long noodles symbolize long life and soba dough can absorb silver or gold dust, which symbolizes gaining wealth.

🅐 Ayukawa makes toshikoshi soba for Kyosuke on New Year's Eve in the *Kimagure Orange Road* TV series (ep. 39). • Godai brings home lacquer boxes of toshikoshi soba for dinner with Kyoko in *Maison Ikkoku* (ep. 19).

Ⓜ New Year's soba is served in *Ranma 1/2* (vol. 10, p. 44).

## 外様大名 OLD FORM 外樣大名
## TOZAMA DAIMYŌ

 Outside vassals, those who did not have a kin relation or hereditary vassal status. In the **Edo period** (AC vol. 1, p. 25), the tozama daimyō were **daimyō** whose families had attained their status under **Oda Nobunaga** or **Toyotomi Hideyoshi** (AC vol. 1, p. 140) and later swore to serve the **Tokugawa** (AC vol. 1, p. 137). Some tozama daimyō had even aligned themselves with the Tokugawa after the **Sekigahara no Tatakai.** To encourage their loyalty, they were often given higher rank and larger domains than the **fudai daimyō.** At the beginning of the Edo period, there were about 180 tozama daimyō, but infractions on their parts were severely punished and many had their clans abolished, so only ninety-eight existed by the time of the **bakumatsu.** Many at this time sided against the **bakufu.** The two most powerful of these were **Chōshū Han** and the **Satsuma Han.**

Ⓜ In *Lone Wolf and Cub* (vol. 18, p. 11), the New Year's visit of the tozama daimyō to the **Edojō** is mentioned.

## 鍔 OR 鐔
## TSUBA (SWORD GUARD)

 The guard between the cutting edge and **tsuka** of a **nihontō** (AC vol. 1, p. 95). This protects one's hands by blocking the edge of an opponent's blade sliding down one's own blade. Tsuba range in design from very simple to so ornate that they would break if used in battle.

Ⓐ We see tsuba in many anime or manga in which swords are used. • Early in *Samurai X: Trust and Betrayal,* we actually see Kenshin dramatically block a blade with the tsuba of a sheathed nihontō.

*This **tsubaki** from Rurouni Kenshin looks ready to fall. In the autumn the whole flower drops, not just each petal.*

## 椿
## TSUBAKI (CAMELLIA)

These flowering trees occur in the wild in Japan. Several varieties are also grown as ornamentals in a wide range of colors. Tsubaki are often planted in **jinja** (AC vol. 1, p. 54) or **jiin** (AC vol. 1, p. 53) gardens. They are sensitive to the cold so are not found in the northern parts of the country.

Ⓐ Camellias are seen several times in the first street fight in *Samurai X: Trust and Betrayal.* • Falling camellia blossoms have dramatic significance, as we see when Kyoko picks up her purse and leaves in *Maison Ikkoku* (ep. 12), after Tenchi and Haruna make love in *Tenchi Forever,* in Kaoru's fantasy of Kenshin in *Rurouni Kenshin* (ep. 66), and when one falls in Kubo's sick fantasy of Ranma-kun abusing Ranma-chan in *Ranma 1/2* (ep. 4).

## 燕
## TSUBAME (SWALLOW)

Several species migrate to Japan, often nesting on buildings in the spring and summer. A common species is the barn swallow, which is also found in other parts of Asia, Europe, and North America. Because they return as a pair to their nesting areas year after year, they have became a symbol of good luck in

*A **tsuitate** for privacy in* SAMURAI X TRUST AND BETRAYAL.

Japan. There is even a tradition of allowing the birds to build nests in homes or shops. A shelf is placed under the nest to catch their droppings.

Ⓜ Feeding swallow chicks alien snacks has unfortunate side effects in *Urusei Yatsura* (*Return of Lum: Creature Features,* p. 22–, and TV ep. 2, st. 2).

Ⓐ A swallow is seen while Ayukawa plays the sax in *Kimagure Orange Road* TV series (ep. 12).

## 衝立
## TSUITATE (STANDING SCREEN)

A standing screen consisting of a single unit supported on two feet. These are used to separate a corner of a room or are placed in front of an open doorway to gain a little privacy or block a direct breeze.

Ⓐ In *Samurai X: Trust and Betrayal,* we see a tsuitate in one of the rooms, and later Tomoe has placed one so she can write in her diary at night by the light of a candle without the light disturbing Kenshin. • You can also see one in the opening animation for *Ai Yori Aoshi.*

## 柄
## TSUKA (SWORD HILT)

The hilt or handle of a **nihontō** (AC vol. 1, p. 95). These are made of wood wrapped in the skin of a ray, then wrapped again

with cloth or leather. The tsuka is fairly long; the proper grip is with the left hand covering the **kashira** to allow greater control of the blade.

Ⓐ We see tsuka in many anime or manga in which swords are used. In *Samurai X: Trust and Betrayal* we see the proper grip used to hold the tsuka in several scenes.

## 塚原卜伝 OLD FORM 塚原卜傳
## TSUKAHARA BOKUDEN

1490–1571. A 15th-century swordsman who, legend says, was born in Kashima in Hitachi Province in 1490. Legend also says he was trained by his father, a **Shintō** (AC vol. 1, p. 121) priest who also practiced **kenjutsu**. He was adopted by a swordsman of the Shintō Ryū who was impressed by his skill. His adopted father gave him permission to go on a **musha shugyō** at the age of seventeen. As he lived during the **Sengoku jidai** (AC vol. 1, p. 113), he used his skills on the battlefield several times in his life. At the age of thirty-seven, he formed his own **ryū,** also called Shintō Ryū but written with different **kanji** (AC vol. 1, p. 61) that mean "new school." A famous story tells of Tsukahara's encounter with a **samurai** (AC vol. 1, p. 110) on a ferryboat. When the samurai demands to know his school of fighting, his response is the Mutekatsu Ryū, the swordless style. The challenger demands a **taryū-jiai,** so

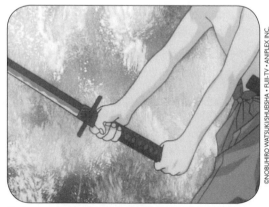

*Notice how the base of the **tsuka** in* SAMURAI X TRUST AND BETRAYAL *is held in traditional **kenjutsu**.*

the ferryman changes course for an island. After the samurai jumps off the boat, Tsukahara grabs the oar and pushes the boat away from the shore, stranding his infuriated opponent. He died at the age of eighty-one, leaving his secret techniques to his **daimyō,** a trusted student, and his son. There is a woodblock print of Tsukahara training **Miyamoto Musashi** (AC vol. 1, p. 86) and using a wooden lid to block the blows of a **bokken** (AC vol. 1, p. 12). This print shows an event that never happened, as Tsukahara died years before Musashi was born.

🅰 Kuno refers to Tsukahara Bokuden using a stew pot lid to block an attack in *Ranma 1/2: Hard Battle* (ep. 12).

Ⓜ Tsukahara Bokuden is mentioned as one of the supreme master swordsmen in *Vagabond* (vol. 11, ch. 107).

## 築地市場
## TSUKIJI SHIJŌ (TSUKIJI FISH MARKET)

 Established in 1935 in Chūō Ward, Tsukiji is the major wholesale fish market for all of Japan. Its full name is Tokyo Chūō Oroshiuri Shijō. Daily, the amount of fish sold is in the thousands of tons with millions of dollars changing hands. This makes this fish market the largest in the world. The facility is managed by the metropolitan government. Each workday begins at around 2 A.M., with early auctions starting at 5 A.M.

🅰 The Tsukiji fish market is attacked by a hungry **Kaiju** in the *Kimagure Orange Road* TV series(ep. 40).

## 佃島
## TSUKUDAJIMA

An area of **Tokyo** in Chūō Ward built on reclaimed land during the **Edo period** (AC vol. 1, p. 25), mainly from an island. This area was originally populated by fishermen who had been relocated from the **Osaka** (AC vol. 1, p. 102) area and who were under orders to sup-

ply the **shōgun** (AC vol. 1, p. 123) with fish and keep an eye on activities on the bay. Many of the homes in the area have an old-fashioned air because they date from the 1920s, having escaped the devastation of both the **Kantō Daishinsai** and the air raids of WWII. Many residents work in the nearby **Tsukiji Shijō.**

🅰 The black labor is spotted in Tsukudajima in the 2nd precinct in *Patlabor New Files* (ep. 1).

Ⓜ Tsukuda Island is seen on a map in *Lone Wolf and Cub* (vol. 22, p. 185).

## つくね
## TSUKUNE (MEATBALLS)

 Meatballs made from minced meat, fish, or fowl mixed with egg. They can be simmered, deep-fried, or grilled.

🅰 Mrs. Ichinose orders **bīru** (AC vol. 1, p. 10), cuttlefish, and chicken tsukune in *Maison Ikkoku* (ep. 4). • Oji orders tsukune fish balls at a **yatai** (AC vol. 1, p. 147) in *The Legend of Black Heaven* (ep. 12).

## 綱
## TSUNA (ROPE)

In general, just a rope. In **sumō** (AC vol. 1, p. 127), tsuna look like a coil of rope with large loops tied around the wrestler's body. They are made of white cotton wrapped around copper wire and are only worn by sumō wrestlers who have been granted the rank of *yokozuna* ("yoko/tsuna," or horizontal hawser) The sumō tsuna is a symbol of great strength and of purity.

🅰 Bloodberry in *Saber Marionette J* wears a tsuna.

## 津波
## TSUNAMI (TIDAL WAVE)

Tidal waves caused by underwater earthquakes. These can cause extensive damage along coastlines. As Japan's coastline tends to be heavily populated, some tsunami have killed thousands. The Japanese Meteorological

Agency monitors earthquakes and issues tsunami warnings.

⚔ Shizuoka is at the center of damage when it is hit by tsunami in the *Blue Seed* TV series (ep. 24).

## 通称 FORMAL 通稱
## TSŪSHŌ

❋ A name given to male children upon reaching a certain age. In the past, among nobles and **samurai** (AC vol. 1, p. 110) families in Japan there was a tradition of male children having their childhood name (**yōmyō**) replaced by a tsūshō, which they would use for the rest of their lives. This normally happened at age fifteen. Another kind of name that could be granted was the *jitsumyō* or *nanori*, a very formal adult name that included the clan name. This name was very rarely used to refer to the person; the tsūshō would be used instead.

⚔ Shinta is renamed Kenshin in *Samurai X: Trust and Betrayal*.

## うどん OR 饂飩
## UDON

♨ A type of noodle (**men rui**). Udon are thick wheat noodles served in a broth, usually with additional ingredients such as **tenpura** on top.

⚔ Hikaru makes udon for Madoka in *Kimagure*

*Orange Road* (ep. 27). • A good view of udon in a dark brown stock is seen in *Patlabor 3*.

Ⓜ At the beginning of *Blade of the Immortal: Beasts,* Shinriji brings Hyakurin some udon.

## 鶯谷駅 OLD FORM 鶯谷驛
## UGUISUDANI EKI (UGUISUDANI STATION)

🌏 A train station on the **Yamanote sen** between **Ueno Kōen** (AC vol. 1, p. 143) and Negishi, and east of the Kan-eiji cemetery.

⚔ Uguisudani Eki is seen in *Here Is Greenwood* (ep. 6), "Uguisudani Sta" is on a street sign in *Patlabor Original Series* (ep. 1), and Uguisudani Station is mentioned by Natsumi in *You're Under Arrest* (ep. 37).

Ⓜ Yamazaki reports that he dropped off Ota at Uguisudani Station in *Mobile Police Patlabor* (vol. 1, p. 150).

## 鶯谷
## UGUISUDANI (VALLEY OF THE BUSH WARBLERS)

🌏 In the **Edo period** (AC vol. 1, p. 25), a flock of bush warblers (uguisu) was released in this part of **Edo**. They nested in the trees and gave the area its present name. At that time, the area was at the edge of the city. Today it is well within the developed part of Tokyo, in **Taitō-ku** northeast of **Ueno Kōen** (AC vol. 1, p. 143).

⚔ Shinshi is assigned to cover Uguisudani in the first episode of the *Patlabor Original Series.* • In *Here Is Greenwood* (ep. 1), we learn that Mitsuru is from Uguisudani.

## 鰻丼 OR うなぎどんぶり
## UNAGI DONBURI

♨ Grilled **unagi** (AC vol. 1, p. 144) over rice in a **donburi** (AC vol. 1, p. 24). While there is no special season for eating unagi, it is popular in the hottest part of summer. This dish is also known as *unadon*.

 Maho serves unagi donburi in *Mahoromatic* (ep. 7).

## 浦安 [市]
## URAYASU

 A city in **Chiba Ken** (AC vol. 1, p. 18) on **Tōkyō Wan** (Tokyo Bay) across the Kyūedogawa river from **Edogawa-ku.** It was a fishing village during the **Edo period** (AC vol. 1, p. 25). Today this is an industrial area and the location of **Tokyo Dizunīrando.**

 We see the Urayasu of the future in *Otaku no Video* (pt. 2. 6th anim. seq.). • Urayasu is mentioned in *Patlabor New Files.* (ep. 3).

## 丑の刻参り OLD FORM 丑の刻参り
## USHI NO KOKU MAIRI (NAILING A DOLL TO A TREE)

"Visiting the shrine at the hour of the cow," roughly 2 A.M. A practice originating during the **Edo period** (AC vol. 1, p. 25). Also known as *ushi no toki mairi*, it involves nailing an image, usually made of straw or paper, of a person to a tree, or occasionally to a **torii** (AC vol. 1, p. 139) at a **jinja** (AC vol. 1, p. 54). The purpose of this ritual is to place a curse on someone. Traditionally, the person doing this dressed all in white and wore a crown—more like an inverted trivet—with lit candles. While nailing the doll, he would ask the **kami** (AC vol. 1, p. 59) to curse the person. After seven days of doing this each night the curse takes effect. Now in anime and manga the ritual is used as a comedic way to indicate vengeful anger, and the location of the tree is usually not a shrine but any nearby tree. In some cases, the nailing of the doll is not even part of the scene, but the candles still are.

 Nailing of a doll is at the end of the first scene in *Dragon Half* (pt. 1)

## 宇都宮 [市] FORMAL 宇都宮
## UTSUNOMIYA

 The capital of **Tochigi Ken.** In the **Kamakura period** (AC vol. 1, p. 59) and the **Muromachi period** (AC vol. 1, p. 90), it was under the control of the Utsunomiya family. In the **Edo period** (AC vol. 1, p. 25), it was both a castle town and **shukuba machi.** During this time, it was under the control of various clans; in 1774 the Toda were granted it as part of their domain. The brown stone used to build the **Teikoku Hoteru** in **Tokyo** came from this area.

 In *Patlabor the TV Series* (ep. 9), we hear that while on his way to **Sakata,** Inubashiri dumped the taxi (**takushi** AC vol. 1, p. 133) he hijacked in Utsunomiya when it ran out of gas. • We find out that Oji's boss commutes from Utsunomiya in *The Legend of Black Heaven* (ep. 1).

Ⓜ Utsunomiya is mentioned in *Lone Wolf and Cub* (vol. 6, p. 183).

# V

## バージンロード OR ヴァージン・ロード
## VIRGIN ROAD

 A poetic term used to describe the center aisle in a wedding chapel that the bride walks down. Often these are covered with a special white carpet.

Ⓜ "Virgin Road" is a story title in the *Countdown* series and is seen at the end of that tale.

Bloodberry refers to the parade route as her and Otaru's virgin road in *Saber Marionette J* (OVA ep. 13).

*See the **Wakō Clock Tower**? You know the scene is set in the Ginza as seen here in* PATLABOR.

© 1990 HEADGEAR / EMOTION / TFC / NTV

### わかめ OR 若布 OR 和布
## WAKAME

*Undaria pinnitifida.* A type of seaweed often used in **misoshiru** (AC vol. 1, p. 85), often in short lengths. It is the dark green stuff that tastes so good. It is also used in *sunomono* (a type of salad) and *nuta* (a cooked salad containing fish). Wakame is found all over Japan and harvested in May and June. Wakame found off the coast of Tokushima is considered to be superior to that from other places. Wakame is sold either salted or dried, but both have to be soaked before use. The salted variety expands to about three times and the dried to about ten times its previous size.

 Hanako has an unwanted, and visible only to her, visitor push her hand so a whole package of wakame goes into a soup pot in *Rumic Theater* (p. 183). The visitor is a **zashiki warashi** (AC vol. 1, p. 150), but in the Viz translation it is referred to as a gremlin.

### 和光の時計台 OR 和光の時計塔
## WAKŌ CLOCK TOWER

The clock tower on the Wakō Department Store building has been a major landmark in the **Ginza** (AC vol. 1, p. 35) district of **Tokyo** since 1932. The building served as a PX during the American Occupation after WWII; before 1947 it was called the Hattori Building.

 The Wakō Clock Tower opens episode 10 of *Patlabor the TV Series.* • It is seen in *Jin-Roh*, and destroyed in *Lupin the 3rd Dragon of Doom.*

 It is seen at night as part of a Ginza street scene in *Club 9* (vol. 1, ch. 6).

### 藁人形
## WARA NINGYŌ (STRAW DOLL)

Often made for a ritual purpose, to protect or harm, then destroyed. In anime and manga, it is usually seen in relation to the **ushi no koku mairi.**

 We see a straw doll when Haruto complains that the chairman is collecting occult junk in *Haunted Junction* (ep. 1). • A straw doll of Lum falls from Ran's bag in the *Urusei Yatsura* OVA "Inaba the Dreammaker."

## わらび OR 蕨
## WARABI (BRACKEN)

*Pteridium aquilinum*. A type of **sansai** mixed with rice and used in soups and stews. It is gathered in the wild and also commercially grown. It can be quite bitter, so it is boiled and the water discarded to make it more palatable.

Ⓜ Rin orders warabi sweet cake and barley tea (**mugicha**) at a roadside tea house in *Blade of the Immortal: Cry of the Worm.*

## わさび OR 山葵
## WASABI

*Wasabia japonica*. Grated wasabi (oroshi-wasabi) is used in **sushi** (AC vol. 1, p. 128) and is also served with **sashimi,** along with **shōyu** (AC vol. 1, p. 124) and with cold **soba.** Why use wasabi with sushi and sashimi? Well, it cuts the fish odor, tastes good with raw fish, and has some antibacterial action. Wasabi is similar to horseradish in effect, but is milder and has a different flavor. It is not a cheap condiment but is expensive even in Japan. Cheaper restaurants use a substitute made from horseradish and mustard (**karashi**). This kind is most common in the United States. In Japanese markets you can get both the faux wasabi or the real thing as powder (*kona wasabi*), or in tubes, or as roots. Real wasabi has a short shelf life so you have to use it quickly.

Ⓐ Wasabi is mentioned in *Maison Ikkoku* (ep. 6).

*This simple water-grown **wasabi** root can now be found in Asian markets. Just use a very fine grater.*

## 柳生十兵衛三厳 FORMAL 柳生十兵衛三嚴
## YAGYŪ JŪBEI MITSUYOSHI

Head of the **Edo** branch of the Yagyū Shinkage Ryū school of armed and unarmed combat. His family had become the sword instructors of the **Tokugawa** (AC vol. 1, p. 137) clan in 1594 after a dramatic defeat of **Tokugawa Ieyasu** in a practice bout with **bokken** (AC vol. 1, p. 12) against Jūbei's grandfather. Jūbei was fired from his position after a drunken incident and reinstated twelve years later. Many believed this incident never happened and was a fiction created to allow him to freely travel as a spy for the **shōgun** (AC vol. 1, p. 123) **Tokugawa Iemitsu.** Such speculations were partly fueled by the fact that his family came from an area famous for its practitioners of **ninjutsu** (AC vol. 1, p. 95). Many stories have been written about this part of his life and made into movies and anime.

**A** Jūbei is the main character of *Ninja Resurrection,* and also plays a major role in *Jūbei-Chan.* • The Jūbei in *Ninja Scroll* is not Yagyū Jūbei but Kibagami Jūbei.

**M** Yagyū Jūbei is also a major character in *Samurai Legend.*

## やきめし OR 焼き飯 OLD FORM 燒き飯
## YAKIMESHI (FRIED RICE)

Also known as *chāhan*. This Chinese dish, commonly found in Japan, is made with bits of egg, pork, green onion, peas, or other green vegetables mixed together in a pan. It is a handy way to use leftover rice. In fact, some say the best rice to use for this dish is that which has sat overnight.

**A** Notice that Noa uses a **renge** to eat her yakimeshi in *Patlabor the TV Series* (ep. 12), an example of the Japanese view that foods should be eaten with the utensils of their country of origin.

**M** Yakimeshi is also eaten with a renge by Shiina and Hiro in *Shadow Star: Shadows of the Past.*

## やきにくや OR 焼き肉屋 OR 焼肉屋
## YAKINIKU-YA (KOREAN BBQ RESTAURANTS)

These can be spotted by their signs in Korean, as well as by the smell of cooking meat. The food, meat and vegetables, is cooked by the customers on a griddle (**teppan**) mounted to the table or counter in front of them.

**M** The coach treats Kosaku to Korean BBQ in the *One Pound Gospel* anime and manga (vol. 1, p. 39).

**A** A yakiniku **teishoku** is mentioned in the closing song of *Dragon Half* (pt. 1). • Korean BBQ is mentioned by Sakamoto in *Maison Ikkoku* (ep. 5).

**M** In the "Paranoiya Diary by Chief Assistant Kyochan" in *Futaba-kun Change* (vol. 4), the assistants pig out on Korean BBQ while their boss eats cup **rāmen** (AC vol. 1, p. 105) at home. • At the end of volume 6 of *Silent Möbius* (p. 191), several members of the AMP go out to a yakiniku-ya, but you don't see them. All you see is the food, the griddle, and their comments.

## 薬師寺 OLD FORM 藥師寺
## YAKUSHIJI

The Yakushi Temple, completed in 697 in Nishinokyō, a suburb to the west of the city of **Nara,** to fulfill a promise made by Emperor Tenmu while his consort was ill. In the 8th century, the temple was moved to Nara. The temple is one of the two main temples of the Hossō Buddhist sect. The main hall is flanked by two pagodas and contains a statue of Yakushi Nyorai, the Buddha of healing.

**A** The Yakushi Temple near the intersection of roads 9 and 122 is mentioned in *Blue Seed* (ep. 14).

## 山県有朋 OLD FORM 山縣有朋
## YAMAGATA ARITOMO

1838–1922. A major figure of the **Meiji period** (AC vol. 1, p. 81) and **Taishō jidai.** Born in **Hagi** in the **Chōshū Han.** In 1870–82, he played a major role in military affairs. During that time, he restructured the military along Prussian lines and played a major role in combating the **Seinan Sensō.** In 1882, his position changed to president of the Board of Legislation. Sixteen months later he became home minister, an office he held for seven years. He reorganized the **Naimushō** and the police system, including restricting political activity by parties. He was promoted to general and became prime minister for the first time from December 1889 to May 1891. His second term as prime minister was from November 1898 to October 1900. During the **Nichiro Sensō** (AC vol. 1, p. 93), he was chief of the General Staff. In recognition for his service, he was granted the title of *kōshaku* (prince) in 1907. For the rest of his life he had a powerful influence on the Japanese government.

🅰 We see Yamagata Aritomo in the *Rurouni Kenshin* TV series, first appearing in the third episode.

## 山口県 OLD FORM 山口縣
## YAMAGUCHI KEN

 A prefecture in the far west of **Honshu** (AC vol. 1, p. 47) bordered by **Shimane** (AC vol. 1, p. 118) and Hiroshima prefectures, the **Nihonkai,** and the Hibiki Sea. Yamaguchi Prefecture is connected to **Kyushu** (AC vol. 1, p. 78) by a bridge and tunnel at the city of **Shimonoseki.** Agricultural products include rice and citrus fruit. During the **Edo period** (AC vol. 1, p. 25) this area was the **Chōshū Han.**

Ⓜ At end of *Ogenki Clinic* (vol. 1), Inui notes in his resume that he was born in Yamaguchi Prefecture. • That Yamaguchi Prefecture was a Chōshū domain before the **Meiji period** (AC vol. 1, p. 81) is noted in *Rurouni Kenshin* (vol. 1, p. 70).

## やまのいも OR 山の芋
## YAMANOIMO

The yam, also known as the *yamaimo.* Many varieties of yam are grown in Japan, including an unusual one shaped like the leaf of the **ginkgo** (AC vol. 1, p. 35).

🅰 Eating a yam and then farting is mentioned by Sashi in *Magical Shopping Arcade Abenobashi* (ep. 1).

Ⓜ In *Rumic Theater: One or Double* (p. 102), the school gardening club is harvesting yams.

## 山手線
## YAMANOTE SEN (YAMANOTE LINE)

A major commuter train line in **Tokyo** that makes a loop around a large portion of the center of the city. The Yamanote Line is 34.5 kilometers (22 miles) long and passes through twenty-nine stations, including major ones like **Tokyo Eki** (AC vol. 1, p. 138), **Ueno Eki**

**HOW I GOT TO YAOICON**

I was a guest at YaoiCon2001 in San Francisco. It all started when a woman approached me at another convention and asked me to be a guest. My response was swift: "Well, I know what **YAOI** and *shōnenai* are, but I really have no interest in those genres. I'm honored to be invited and willing to be a guest. But honestly, what could I do? Have a panel in which I sit up front and ask the audience questions about their interests?" At that point we both knew we had a panel.

For those who don't know about YAOI and *shōnenai*, the con is devoted to stories involving male-male romances that are created by women for women.

The con went well. When asked by an attendee if I was having fun, I smiled and said, "Lots. But I can't find a single thing in the dealer's room."

Indeed, I did have a blast. It was unusual to be at a con that was mainly attended by women. I learned a lot from listening to the panels, which had Japanese guests. Even Yonezawa Yoshihiro, one of the founders of the famous Tokyo Comic Market (**Komiketto** AC vol. 1, p. 73), was there. It was also a sign that women have made it into American fandom in a significant way. When women organize successful cons around their interests it shows the fan scene has a strength that is not to be underestimated.

If you are interested in this branch of entertainment I recommend YaoiCon as worth checking out. I know several women who attend each year and always seem to have a good time. The con does have an eighteen-or-older policy due to the explicit nature of some of the material. Visit www.yaoicon.com for more information.

(AC vol. 1, p. 143), **Akihabara Eki,** and **Shinjuku Eki.** A full circuit around the loop takes about one hour and passes through the more affluent parts of the city.

🅰 Kazuya accompanies Miya as she goes home on the Yamanote line in *Here Is Greenwood* (ep. 5). • Eiri's body was found on the tracks of the Yamanote train line in *Serial Experiments Lain* (ep. 9). • In *Tenchi The Movie: Tenchi Muyo in Love*, Ryoko takes the Yamanote line as everyone divides up to carry out their missions.

## 山科 [区]
## YAMASHINA

 A town midway between **Kyoto** (AC vol. 1, p. 77) and **Ōtsu** in Kyōto-fu. After the Ōnin War, the Ikkō built a fortress here. **A** We hear a concerned man tell a young woman to return to her home in Yamashina, in *Samurai X: Trust and Betrayal*.

## 大和
## YAMATO

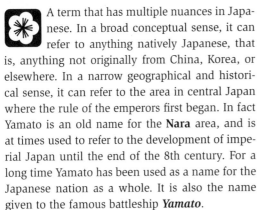 A term that has multiple nuances in Japanese. In a broad conceptual sense, it can refer to anything natively Japanese, that is, anything not originally from China, Korea, or elsewhere. In a narrow geographical and historical sense, it can refer to the area in central Japan where the rule of the emperors first began. In fact Yamato is an old name for the **Nara** area, and is at times used to refer to the development of imperial Japan until the end of the 8th century. For a long time Yamato has been used as a name for the Japanese nation as a whole. It is also the name given to the famous battleship *Yamato*. **A** Early in *Princess Mononoke*, at the meeting in the village shrine, it is noted by one of the elders that 500 years have passed since the Yamato, translated as Mikado in the subtitles and as Emperor in the re-dub, drove the **Emishi**, a word used only in the re-dub in this scene, into the land they are in. **M** In *Lone Wolf and Cub* (vol. 13, p. 34), Yamato is used as a place name.

## 大和
## YAMATO (BATTLESHIP)

 The largest battleship in WWII, with a crew of around 2,500. Launched in December 1941, it participated in the battles

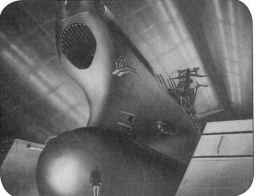

*In* FAREWELL TO SPACE BATTLESHIP YAMATO IN THE NAME OF LOVE, *the sunken battleship* **Yamato** *is resurrected for space travel.*

of Midway (June 1942), the Philippine Sea (June 1944), and Leyte Gulf (October 1944). Under U.S. attack it sank along with several other ships on its way to **Okinawa** (AC vol. 1, p. 99) in April 1945 near Bōnomisaki, spelling the end of the Japanese Imperial Navy. **A** We see the remains of the *Yamato* in *Moldiver* (ep. 4) • Happosai brings a model of the *Yamato* to the **sentō** (AC vol. 1, p. 115) in *Ranma 1/2 Anything Goes Martial Arts* (ep. 22).

## 山吉盛典
## YAMAYOSHI MORISUKE

A governor of **Fukushima Ken** in the **Meiji period** (AC vol. 1, p. 81). He was one of the last people to speak to **Ōkubo Toshimichi,** who told him of his expectations for Japan. **A** Yamayoshi from the Fukushima Prefecture Association is introduced to Himura in *Rurouni Kenshin* (ep. 31).

## やおい
## YAOI

An abbreviation for "Yama-nashi, Ochi-nashi, Imi-nashi" (no climax, no punch line, no meaning). This term is used for a genre of **dōjinshi** (AC vol. 1, p. 23) that usually, but not always, consists of amusing stores of male characters from commercial manga and anime in gay situations. The genre is mainly produced by and for female fans.

## 八ツ橋
## YATSUHASHI

 A type of pastry made from rice flour in the shape of a bridge. This pastry is from **Kyoto** (AC vol. 1, p. 77) and is one of several kinds that can be used in **cha-no-yu** (AC vol. 1, p. 17). Legend has it that these represented a bridge made by a mother whose son had drowned in a place because there was no bridge.

🅰 Sojiro offers some yatsuhashi to Usui in *Rurouni Kenshin* (ep. 44).

## ようかん OR 羊羹
## YŌKAN

A sweet jelly originally made mainly from *azuki* beans that have been ground up. Other ingredients can include wheat flour, *an*, **kanten,** *kuzu,* or sugar. Common flavorings include *matcha* and **kaki.** The mixture is placed in molds to give it a definite shape. This sweet is one of several that may be served as part of the ceremonies of **cha-no-yu** (AC vol. 1, p. 17).

🅼 Yōkan is among the foods distributed to the guests of the shōgun at the celebration of Kajō-no-Shukujitsu in *Lone Wolf and Cub* (vol. 20, p. 23).

## 横浜 OLD FORM 横濱
## YOKOHAMA

The capital of **Kanagawa Ken** (AC vol. 1, p. 60). Until the end of the **Edo period** (AC vol. 1, p. 25) it was a fishing village. With the signing of the **Nichibei Shūkō Tsūshō Jōyaku** in 1858, it was opened as an international trade port. In 1872, the first rail line (**tetsudō**) in Japan was opened between **Tokyo** and Yokohama. By the early 20th century, thousands of non-Japa-nese, mostly Chinese, lived in this thriving seaport. Today, Yokohama is the largest port, and part of the largest industrial zone, in Japan.

🅰 Nina and Irene go shopping in Yokohama Chinatown in *Bubblegum Crisis* OVA series (ep. 2). • Kyoko and Mitaka go to Yokohama for a romantic dinner in *Maison Ikkoku* (ep. 12). • The Kanzaki home is in Yokohama in *Sakura Wars* (OVA 2)

🅼 Dr. Kisaragi arrives in Yokohama by ship in *Black Jack* (vol. 1, p. 76).

## 横浜ベイブリッジ
## YOKOHAMA BEI BURIJI (YOKOHAMA BAY BRIDGE)

A cable-stayed bridge with a length of 860 meters (2,822 feet). This bridge opened in September 1989 and is a major landmark of the area. It is easy to recognize because of its distinctive H-shaped towers. The road that runs over it is the **Shuto Kōsoku Wangan Sen** (Bayshore Expressway).

🅼 In *GTO* (ep. 8 and vol. 4, ch. 27), Onizuka intimidates some of his students into bungee jumping from the Yokohama Bay Bridge. Don't try this on your trip to Japan.

🅰 Shinobu is taking the Bayshore Expressway on her way to the Yokohama Bay Bridge early in *Patlabor 2* when she gets stopped in traffic. • The Yokohama Bay Bridge is in the background of Nakajima's and Natsumi's romantic fantasies in *You're Under Arrest* (ep. 11).

## 横須賀 [市] OLD FORM 横須賀
## YOKOSUKA

A city southwest of **Tokyo** on the Miura Peninsula at the mouth of **Tōkyō Wan** in **Kanagawa Ken** (AC vol. 1, p. 60). In the **Meiji period** (AC vol. 1, p. 81), modern shipyards were built on the location of the old **bakufu** shipyards. Yokosuka was the location of a major Japanese naval base until the end of WWII. Today, it is the Japanese base for the U.S. 7th Fleet, as well as a base for the Kaijō **Jieitai** (AC vol. 1, p. 53). It is also a major shipping port, has automobile factories, and supports a strong fishing industry.

**A** Yokosuka is seen on a highway sign, as is the U.S. base, in *Shonan Bakusozoku*. • Kensuke is said to have gone to New Yokosuka to see a new battleship in *Neon Genesis Evangelion* (ep. 17).

**M** The UN Fleet is off the coast of New Yokosuka in *Neon Genesis Evangelion* (Special Collector's Edition vol. 4, p. 8).

## 横田空軍基地
## YOKOTA AIR BASE

A major base of the U.S. Air Force, specifically the Fifth Air Force, located in the **Tama** area of **Tokyo** at the junction of Fussa-shi, Mizuho-machi, and Musashimura-yama-shi.

**A** Yokota Air Base is the location of most of the story of *Blood the Last Vampire*. • This is where Clancy arrives in the *Patlabor Original Series* (ep. 2). • In *Gasaraki* (ep. 21, "Run"), Mihara was taken to the Yokota Air Base.

## 幼名
## YŌMYŌ (MALE CHILD'S NAME)

A name traditionally given to a boy child, often with a **maru** ending. Usually this is done at an event called **shichiya** not too long after the child is born. When the boy was old enough, usually at around age fifteen, he was given a **tsūshō** to replace his yōmyō.

**A** Shinta is renamed Kenshin in *Samurai X: Trust and Betrayal*.

## 吉田松蔭
## YOSHIDA SHŌIN

1830–59. Real name: Yoshida Norikata. A **Chōshū Han** teacher of pro-imperial views who had a great influence on the forces opposing the **bakufu**; his teachings are thus partially responsible for the emergence of the **Meiji period** (AC vol. 1, p. 81). He was known as

a scholar, author, and military expert. As a young man he attempted to stow away on the flagship of Commodore **Perry** to learn more about the West. For this he was imprisoned and later placed under house arrest. He had a private school in his home and many of his students became **shishi** leaders. His role in a failed plot to assassinate Manabe Akikatsu, a high-ranking official, led to his execution during the **Ansei no Taigoku.**

**A** The funeral of Yoshida Shōin is seen in *Samurai X: Trust and Betrayal*.

## 吉田東洋
## YOSHIDA TŌYŌ

1816–62. A **samurai** (AC vol. 1, p. 110) from **Tosa Han** who sought to reform domain policies, including building a navy and giving priority to ability rather than family status in promotions. His plans were opposed by both traditional conservatives and **shishi**. He died on a rainy night in May 1862 at the hands of assassins sent by Takechi Zuizan.

**M** **Sakamoto Ryōma** mentions being falsely accused of being part of the assassination in issue 5 of *Vanity Angel.*

## 吉川英治
## YOSHIKAWA EIJI

1892–1962. A novelist whose real name was Yoshikawa Hidetsugu. He was born in **Kanagawa Ken** (AC vol. 1, p. 60) in a former **samurai** (AC vol. 1, p. 110) family. Yoshikawa starting working at eleven and attended night schools. He became an employee of the *Maiyū Shinbun* (newspaper) in 1921 but lost that job in 1923 due to the **Kantō Daishinsai**. In 1925, he began publishing successful adventure stories, often set in the **Edo period** (AC vol. 1, p. 25). These tales were serialized in newspapers before being collected into books. From 1935 to 1939 what would become his most famous work *Musashi*, was serialized. *Musashi* is a fictional version of the life of the famous swordsman **Miyamoto Musashi**

(AC vol. 1, p. 86). In 1981 it was translated into English in a heavily edited version that included only about one-quarter of the text. The novel has also been made into several movies, the major ones being *Miyamoto Musashi* (1940–42), *Samurai* (1955–57, the famous trilogy), and a five-part series also titled *Miyamoto Musashi* (1961–65). *Musashi* was the NHK (**Nippon Hōsō Kyōkai,** AC vol. 1, p. 96) Taiga Drama in the year 2003.

Ⓜ *Vagabond* is the manga adaptation of Yoshikawa's *Musashi*. • The *Urusei Yatsura* TV series (ep. 55, st. 78) has a parody of *Musashi*.

## 吉野家
## YOSHINOYA

A chain of **gyūdon** (AC vol. 1, p. 37) restaurants that originated in the late 19th century. In the 1970s, Yoshinoya overexpanded, and it nearly went bankrupt in 1980. With the help of a large loan from the Saison Group, plus a strategy of using American beef, which is cheaper than Japanese beef, the company recovered. In November 2000, its stock was listed on the **Tokyo Shōken Torihikijo** and is now doing very well. The company has expanded its outlets overseas, including the United States.

Ⓐ Lum has gyūdon in a "Yochinoya" in *Urusei Yatsura Movie 1 Only You.*

Ⓜ At his class's lunch break, Onizuka requests a special big portion of **kare raisu** (AC vol. 1, p. 62) like they serve at Yoshinoya, in the Kodansha Bilingual Comics edition of *GTO* (vol. 3, p. 65 and 68). • The Tokyopop edition removed the name of the chain in this section. However, we do see Yoshinoya on a bag later in the Tokyopop translation of the manga (vol. 19, ch. 156).

## 葭簀
## YOSHIZU (REED SCREEN)

Screens made of marsh reeds, often stood or hung vertically. These are strongly associated with hot weather, as they are used to block the sun at doorways and windows

*Botchan in* BOTCHAN *[from the Animated Classics of Japanese Fiction series] enjoys a cool snack while shaded by* **yoshizu***.*

of homes, as well as at food stalls, restaurants, desert shops, beer gardens, and all sorts of other shops. They are also used as partitions. In stories, they are often seen at beaches.

Ⓐ A yoshizu is seen against a wall at the shaved ice place in *Botchan* (pt. 1), and we see one at the filming of the ferry scene in *Here Is Greenwood* (ep. 3). • One is leaning against the outside of the building providing privacy as Ryunosuke takes a bath in a barrel outdoors in the *Urusei Yatsura* OVA "Nagisa's Fiance."

Ⓜ A yoshizu is seen leaning on the **yatai** (AC vol. 1, p. 147) that serves **oden** (AC vol. 1, p. 98) under the tracks in *Maison Ikkoku* (vol. 7, p. 70).

## 四谷
## YOTSUYA

A district of **Tokyo** now located in **Shinjuku-ku** (AC vol. 1, p. 120) near **Chiyoda-ku.** The name is written with **kanji** (AC vol. 1, p. 61) that mean "four valleys" but may have originally been "four shops." In the **Edo period** (AC vol. 1, p. 25), this was the area near the Yotsuya gate near the **Edojō** and included the homes of some **daimyō.** This was also the location of the murders that inspired the famous **kabuki** play *Tōkaidō Yotsuya Kaidan* (The Ghost

Stories at Yotsuya on the **Tōkaidō**). In the **Meiji period** (AC vol. 1, p. 81), Yotsuya was the location of some of the worst slums of Tokyo.

Ⓜ The Don is taken to the Shimokura Hospital in Yotsuya in *Sanctuary* (anime and manga vol. 2, p. 36).

Ⓜ The battle early on in chapter 4 of *Silent Möbius* (vol. 2, p. 43) takes place in "what used to be called Yotsuya." • The bell in Yotsuya for tolling the hours is mentioned in *Lone Wolf and Cub* (vol. 4, p. 12).

## 雪女
## YUKI ONNA (SNOW WOMAN)

In folklore, a wraithlike woman seen on snowy nights dressed in white and often described as having a child in her arms. Some stores say she is a woman who died while giving birth. Unusual events during the snowy season are often attributed to her.

Ⓜ Takahashi Rumiko has her own take on the snow woman with her character Oyuki in *Urusei Yatsura* (TV ep. 8, st. 15 and *Lum Urusei Yatsura Perfect Collection,* p. 200, where it is translated as "snow fairy").

Ⓜ The story "Wasted Minds" in *Rumic World Trilogy* (vol. 2, p. 160) also uses the unconventional translation of "snow fairy."

## 湯沸かし器
## YUWAKASHIKI (WALL-MOUNTED WATER HEATER)

These hot water heaters conserve energy by not turning on until they are needed.

Ⓐ In anime, these heaters usually occupy the background in kitchen scenes; some examples include *Kimagure Orange Road* (ep. 1), *Ranma 1/2* (OVA 3), *Urusei Yatsura* (TV ep. 15, st. 29), *Zenki* (ep. 6), and *GTO* (ep. 1).

## 在日米軍
## ZAINICHI BEIGUN (UNITED STATES ARMED FORCES IN JAPAN)

A controversial legacy of the Occupation is the presence of U.S. military bases in Japan. Originally, the forces of the Occupation took over existing Japanese bases at the end of WWII. With the signing of the San Francisco Peace Treaty in 1951, and many agreements after that period, U.S. troops continue to have facilities in Japan, with the Japanese government picking up a portion of the expenses. The U.S. military has jurisdiction over its own on-duty personnel when it comes to crimes, accidents, and other incidents. The Japanese government has jurisdiction if something happens when the service person is off-duty, though there have been cases of U.S. personnel being sent back to the United States by U.S. authorities before prosecution could take place. Major bases currently exist at: **Yokota Air Base,** Sasebo, **Yokosuka,** Zama, and various parts of **Okinawa Ken** (AC vol. 1, p. 99).

Ⓐ Yokosuka is seen in *Shonan Bakusozoku.* • Yokota is in *Blood the Last Vampire,* the *Patlabor Original Series* (ep. 2), and in *Gasaraki* (ep. 21, "Run").

## 座椅子 OLD FORM 坐椅子
## ZAISU (LEGLESS CHAIR)

Legless chairs used in rooms with **tatami** (AC vol. 1, p. 134) floors. They consist of a cushioned base with a back and occasionally an armrest to lean on. These provide the back support of a European-style chair in a traditional Japanese setting.

🅐 Misato uses a zaisu in *Neon Genesis Evangelion* (ep. 12). We also see them in *Zenki* (ep. 8) and *Martian Successor Nadesico* (ep. 16).

🅜 An excellent view of zaisu is in *Sanctuary* (vol. 4, p. 246). • Kyoko uses one in *Maison Ikkoku* (vol. 2, p. 19).

## 石榴 or 柘榴
## ZAKURO (POMEGRANATE)

This plant is grown both for the fruit and as an ornamental. Zakuro also have a religious significance. It is associated with Kishimojin, the Buddhist protector of children, who is often depicted holding a zakuro.

🅐 Zakuro are mentioned and seen in *Samurai X: Trust and Betrayal*.

🅜 In *Lone Wolf and Cub* (vol. 16, p. 175), we see ripe zakuro as Ōgami rides a horse beneath a tree.

## 坐禅 or 座禅 OLD FORM 坐禪
## ZAZEN (ZEN MEDITATION)

A form of Buddhist (**bukkyō** AC vol. 1, p. 15) meditation done while sitting in a lotus position, that is, with the legs crossed in front of you. This form of meditation is more highly emphasized in the Sōtō school of **Zen** than it is in the Rinzai school of Zen. Scenes where zazen is taking place may also have someone standing or walking holding a stick known as a **keisaku or kyōsaku** depending on the school of Zen Buddhism.

🅐 Yurika does zazen in *Martian Successor Nadesico* (ep. 5) as do Smith, Saeko, and Ryo in *City Hunter* (ep. 21).

🅜 In *Vagabond* (vol. 11, ch. 104), it is mentioned that **samurai** (AC vol. 1, p. 110) outnumbered monks in the meditation halls of Sangen'in Temple.

## 筮竹
## ZEICHIKU

A type of plant stalk that is used in bundles of fifty in a Chinese traditional method of divination. The stalks are divided into small bundles by a set procedure that involves discarding parts of the bundles until, by a process of counting the remaining ones, an odd or even number is reached. This is done six times, and each number produces a solid or divided line. **Sangi** (AC vol. 1, p. 111) are used to keep track of each result. A copy of the *I Ching*, an ancient Chinese book known in Japan as the *Eki-kyō*, is consulted to obtain the divination.

🅐 Zeichiku can be seen in the background in the first visit to the medium's office in the *Phantom Quest Corps* (ep. 1). • Zeichiku and sangi are used by a fortuneteller at a shrine in *Doomed Megalopolis* (ep. 2). • Zeichiku are used by Goemon in *Lupin*

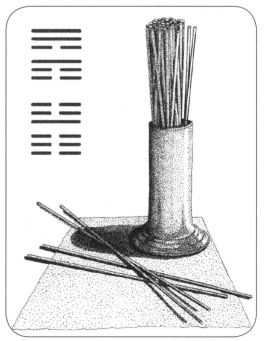

*Yarrow or bamboo, either can be used to make* **zeichiku**.

the 3rd Royal Scramble (ep. "But Your Brother Was Such a Nice Guy"). The result of this particular divination was "A wise man never courts danger."
• In *Millennium Actress,* we see a fortuneteller with these on the street in Manchuria.

## 禅 FORMAL 禪
## ZEN (BUDDHISM)

A school of Buddhism (**bukkyō,** AC vol. 1, p. 15) that places meditation (**zazen**) at the core of its teachings. Originating in China, where it is called Ch'an, Zen entered Japan in 1191 when Eisai founded the Rinzai branch and later when **Dōgen** (AC vol. 1, p. 23) founded the Sōtō branch in 1227. These became the major two branches of Zen Buddhism in Japan. Zen became a significant movement in the **Kamakura period** (AC vol. 1, p. 59), growing in popularity among **bushi** and intellectuals. Later, it would greatly influence arts such as gardening, painting, and **cha-no-yu** (AC vol. 1, p. 17; tea ceremony), and would also influence **bushidō.**

🅰 Yurika practices zazen in *Martian Successor Nadesico* (ep. 5).

🅼 The famous Zen monk **Takuan Sōhō** shows up to play a major role in *Vagabond* (vol. 2, ch. 12).

## ぜん OR 膳
## ZEN (SMALL INDIVIDUAL TABLE FOR FOOD)

Not to be confused with the Buddhist sect. As the Japanese traditionally ate while sitting on the floor, each person would have one or more zen for their food. At home, one zen was usual for meals; more than one was for special feasts. The zen continued to be a major household item until the end of the 19th century, when the **chabudai** (AC vol. 1, p. 17) came into use. Poorer folks usually did not use zen. Rather, they simply ate around the kitchen fire using a low tray called an **oshiki.**

🅰 We see a zen in front of Otomi's father as he eats in *Sanshiro the Judoist* (pt. 2). • In *Samurai*

*One **zen** for each person. Here in SAMURAI X TRUST AND BETRAYAL the small tables are better than one large table that takes up space even when no one is using it.*

*Deeper Kyo* (ep. 26), we get a good view of a zen. In *Spirited Away,* we see them stacked in a hall.

🅼 Meals are eaten from zen in *Rurouni Kenshin* (vol. 1, p. 91) and *Vagabond* (vol. 3, ch. 23).

## ゼロ戦 OR 零戦 (REISEN) OLD FORM 零戰
## ZEROSEN (ZERO FIGHTER)

The Zero Fighter. A **Mitsubishi**-designed fighter plane that was designed to be launched from an aircraft carrier. Until the United States was finally able to develop better fighters, this plane, with its long range and 20mm guns, provided the Japanese with a tactical advantage early in WWII. The designation Zero comes from it being a Type 0 plane, that is, a plane put into service in the year 2,600, according to the old Japanese calendar. The official U.S. military code name assigned to the Zero was Zeke, but most soldiers used the Japanese designation.

🅰 In *The Cockpit* story 2, "Mach Thunder Force," the pilot of a U.S. scout plane identifies Zero escorts and **Betty**s. • Archer remembers being shot down by a Zero in *Lupin the 3rd: The Pursuit of Harimao's Treasure.*

🅼 Zero fighters are mentioned in *Wild 7* (vol. 5, p. 16) and seen in the *Fist of the Blue Sky* (vol. 1, ch. 1).

蔵面 OR 造面 OR 雑面 OLD FORM 藏面 OR 雜面
## ZŌMEN (WHITE SQUARE MASK)

 A simple mask made originally of paper and later of cloth, often silk, with abstract patterns painted on the front. These are used in some **bugaku** dance performances.

▲ Early in *Spirited Away,* we see several red-robed figures leave a ferry wearing zōmen.

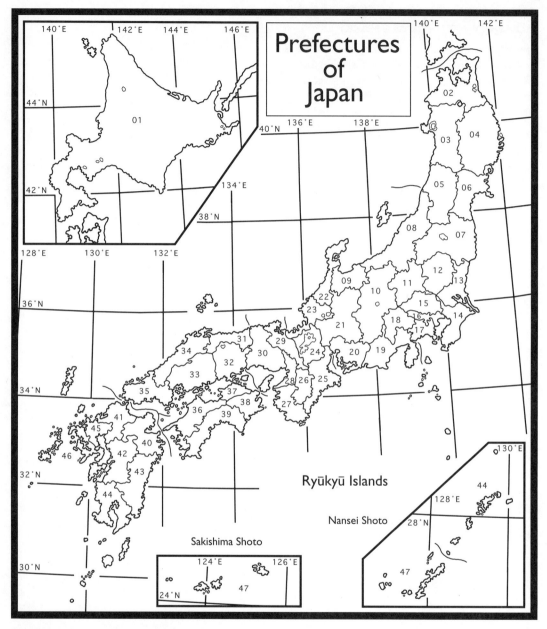

Prefectures
of
Japan

Ryūkyū Islands

Nansei Shoto

Sakishima Shoto

## PREFECTURES OF JAPAN

In the Meiji period, the older administrative divisions were restructured into the forty-seven prefectures of present-day Japan. In many cases the name of the prefecture and the name of its capital are the same. This can make it difficult to determine which is being referred to. If you listen carefully to the Japanese dialogue and hear the suffix -shi after the name, you will know it is the city being talked about. The prefecture names set in boldface have a corresponding entry in *The Anime Companion*.

## Prefectures by Map Number

| | | |
|---|---|---|
| 1 | **Hokkaidō** 兵庫県 | *(AC vol. 1, p. 46)* |
| 2 | Aomori Ken 青森県 | |
| 3 | Akita Ken 秋田県 | |
| 4 | **Iwate Ken** 岩手県 | |
| 5 | Yamagata Ken 山形県 | |
| 6 | **Miyagi Ken** 宮城県 | *(AC vol. 1, p. 86)* |
| 7 | **Fukushima Ken** 福島県 | |
| 8 | Niigata Ken 新潟県 | |
| 9 | Toyama Ken 富山県 | |
| 10 | Nagano Ken 長野県 | |
| 11 | **Gunma Ken** 群馬県 | |
| 12 | **Tochigi Ken** 栃木県 | |
| 13 | **Ibaraki Ken** 茨城県 | *(AC vol. 1, p. 48)* |
| 14 | **Chiba Ken** 千葉県 | *(AC vol. 1, p. 18)* |
| 15 | Saitama Ken 埼玉県 | |
| 16 | **Tōkyō-to** 東京都 | |
| 17 | **Kanagawa Ken** 神奈川県 | |
| 18 | Yamanashi Ken 山梨県 | |
| 19 | **Shizuoka Ken** 静岡県 | |
| 20 | **Aichi Ken** 愛知県 | *(AC vol. 1, p. 3)* |
| 21 | **Gifu Ken** 岐阜県 | |
| 22 | Ishikawa Ken 石川県 | |
| 23 | Fukui Ken 福井県 | |
| 24 | Shiga Ken 滋賀県 | |
| 25 | **Mie Ken** 三重県 | |
| 26 | Nara Ken 奈良県 | |
| 27 | Wakayama Ken 和歌山県 | |
| 28 | Ōsaka-fu 大阪府 | |
| 29 | Kyôto-fu 京都府 | |
| 30 | **Hyōgo Ken** 兵庫県 | |
| 31 | Tottori Ken 鳥取県 | |
| 32 | **Okayama Ken** 岡山県 | |
| 33 | Hiroshima Ken 広島県 | |
| 34 | **Shimane Ken** 島根県 | *(AC vol. 1, p. 118)* |
| 35 | **Yamaguchi Ken** 山口県 | |
| 36 | Ehime Ken 愛媛県 | |
| 37 | Kagawa Ken 香川県 | |
| 38 | Tokushima Ken 徳島県 | |
| 39 | **Kōchi Ken** 高知県 | |
| 40 | Ōita Ken 大分県 | |
| 41 | Fukuoka Ken 福岡県 | |
| 42 | Kumamoto Ken 熊本県 | |
| 43 | Miyazaki Ken 宮崎県 | |
| 44 | Kagoshima Ken 鹿児島県 | |
| 45 | Saga Ken 佐賀県 | |
| 46 | Nagasaki Ken 長崎県 | |
| 47 | **Okinawa Ken** 沖縄県 | *(AC vol. 1, p. 99)* |

## Prefectures in Alphabetical Order

| | | |
|---|---|---|
| **Aichi Ken** 愛知県 *(AC vol. 1, p. 3)* | | 20 |
| Akita Ken 秋田県 | | 3 |
| Aomori Ken 青森県 | | 2 |
| **Chiba Ken** 千葉県 *(AC vol. 1, p. 18)* | | 14 |
| Ehime Ken 愛媛県 | | 36 |
| Fukui Ken 福井県 | | 23 |
| Fukuoka Ken 福岡県 | | 41 |
| **Fukushima Ken** 福島県 | | 7 |
| **Gifu Ken** 岐阜県 | | 21 |
| **Gunma Ken** 群馬県 | | 11 |
| Hiroshima Ken 広島県 | | 33 |
| **Hokkaidō** 北海道 *(AC vol. 1, p. 46)* | | 1 |
| **Hyōgo Ken** 兵庫県 | | 30 |
| **Ibaraki Ken** 茨城県 *(AC vol. 1, p. 48)* | | 13 |
| Ishikawa Ken 石川県 | | 22 |
| **Iwate Ken** 岩手県 | | 4 |
| Kagawa Ken 香川県 | | 37 |
| Kagoshima Ken 鹿児島県 | | 44 |
| **Kanagawa Ken** 神奈川県 | | 17 |
| **Kōchi Ken** 高知県 | | 39 |
| Kumamoto Ken 熊本県 | | 42 |
| Kyōto-fu 京都府 | | 29 |
| **Mie Ken** 三重県 | | 25 |
| **Miyagi Ken** 宮城県 *(AC vol. 1, p. 86)* | | 6 |
| Miyazaki Ken 宮崎県 | | 43 |
| Nagano Ken 長野県 | | 10 |
| Nagasaki Ken 長崎県 | | 46 |
| Nara Ken 奈良県 | | 26 |
| Niigata Ken 新潟県 | | 8 |
| Ōita Ken 大分県 | | 40 |
| **Okayama Ken** 岡山県 | | 32 |
| **Okinawa Ken** 沖縄県 *(AC vol. 1, p. 99)* | | 47 |
| Ōsaka-fu 大阪府 | | 28 |
| Saga Ken 佐賀県 | | 45 |
| Saitama Ken 埼玉県 | | 15 |
| Shiga Ken 滋賀県 | | 24 |
| **Shimane Ken** 島根県 *(AC vol. 1, p. 118)* | | 34 |
| **Shizuoka Ken** 静岡県 | | 19 |
| **Tochigi Ken** 栃木県 | | 12 |
| Tokushima Ken 徳島県 | | 38 |
| **Tōkyō-to** 東京都 | | 16 |
| Tottori Ken 鳥取県 | | 31 |
| Toyama Ken 富山県 | | 9 |
| Wakayama Ken 和歌山県 | | 27 |
| Yamagata Ken 山形県 | | 5 |
| **Yamaguchi Ken** 山口県 | | 35 |
| Yamanashi Ken 山梨県 | | 18 |

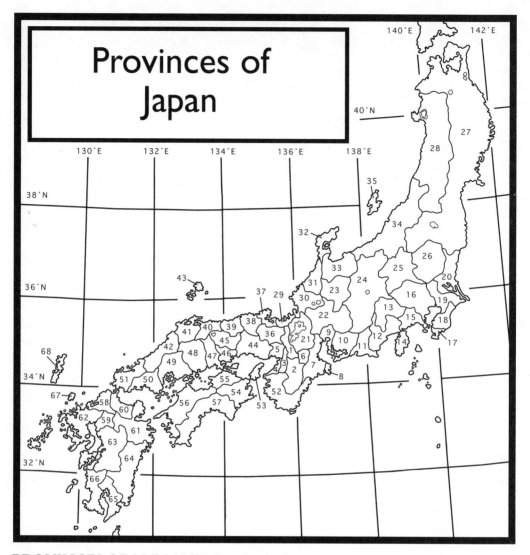

## PROVINCES OF JAPAN FROM 824 TO 1868

The A.D. 824 administrative reorganization of the Japanese provinces established borders that lasted until 1868. The provinces were grouped into eight larger administrative regions: Kinai 畿内, Tōkaidō 東海道, Tōzandō 東山道, Hokurikudō 北陸道, San'indō 山陰道, San'yōdō 山陽道, Nankaidō 南海道, and Saikaidō 西海道.

Hokkaidō (Ezochi) and Okinawa Ken (Ryūkyū) were not part of this administrative structure.

The numbers in the three lists below—Provinces by Map Number, Provinces by Map Number and Region, and Provinces in Alphabetical Order—correspond to the numbered locations on the map. Alternative names of the provinces are given in parentheses.

## *Provinces by Map Number*

The old provinces are now part of the following present-day prefectures:

1 Yamashiro 山城 (a part of Kyōto-fu)
2 Yamato 大和 (Nara Ken)
3 Kawachi 河内 (a part of Ōsaka-fu)
4 Izumi 和泉 (a part of Ōsaka-fu)
5 Settsu 摂津 (a part of Ōsaka-fu and a part of Hyōgo Ken)
6 Iga 伊賀 (a part of Mie Ken)
7 Ise 伊勢 (a part of Mie Ken)
8 Shima 志摩 (a part of Mie Ken)
9 Owari 尾張 (a part of Aichi Ken)
10 Mikawa 三河 (a part of Aichi Ken)
11 Tōtōmi 遠江 (a part of Shizuoka Ken)
12 Suruga 駿河 (a part of Shizuoka Ken)
13 Kai 甲斐 (Yamanashi Ken)
14 Izu 伊豆 (a part of Shizuoka Ken and a part of Tōkyō-to. Several islands which had belonged to Izu-no-kuni now belong to Tōkyō-to.)
15 Sagami 相模 (Kanagawa Ken)
16 Musashi 武蔵 (a part of Tōkyō-to, a part of Saitama Ken, and a part of Kanagawa Ken)
17 Awa 安房 (a part of Chiba Ken)
18 Kazusa 上総 (a part of Chiba Ken)
19 Shimōsa 下総 (a part of Chiba Ken, a part of Ibaraki Ken, and a part of Saitama Ken)
20 Hitachi 常陸 (a part of Ibaraki Ken)
21 Ōmi 近江 (Shiga Ken)
22 Mino 美濃 (a part of Gifu Ken)
23 Hida 飛騨 (a part of Gifu Ken)
24 Shinano 信濃 (Nagano Ken)
25 Kōzuke 上野 (Gunma Ken)
26 Shimotsuke 下野 (Tochigi Ken)
27 Mutsu 陸奥 (Fukushima Ken, Miyagi Ken, Iwate Ken, Aomori Ken, and a part of Akita Ken)
28 Dewa 出羽 (Yamagata Ken and a part of Akita Ken)
29 Wakasa 若狭 (a part of Fukui Ken)
30 Echizen 越前 (a part of Fukui Ken)
31 Kaga 加賀 (a part of Ishikawa Ken)
32 Noto 能登 (a part of Ishikawa Ken)
33 Etchū 越中 (Toyama Ken)
34 Echigo 越後 (a part of Nīgata Ken)
35 Sado 佐渡 (a part of Nīgata Ken)
36 Tanba 丹波 (a part of Kyōto-fu and a part of Hyōgo Ken)
37 Tango 丹後 (a part of Kyōto-fu)
38 Tajima 但馬 (a part of Hyōgo Ken)
39 Inaba 因幡 (a part of Tottori Ken)
40 Hōki 伯耆 (a part of Tottori Ken)
41 Izumo 出雲 (a part of Shimane Ken)
42 Iwami 石見 (a part of Shimane Ken)
43 Oki 隠岐 (a part of Shimane Ken)
44 Harima 播磨 (a part of Hyōgo Ken)
45 Mimasaka 美作 (a part of Okayama Ken)
46 Bizen 備前 (a part of Okayama Ken)
47 Bitchū 備中 (a part of Okayama Ken)
48 Bingo 備後 (a part of Hiroshima Ken)
49 Aki 安芸 (a part of Hiroshima Ken)
50 Suō 周防 (a part of Yamaguchi Ken)
51 Nagato 長門 (a part of Yamaguchi Ken)
52 Kii 紀伊 (Wakayama Ken and a part of Mie Ken)
53 Awaji 淡路 (a part of Hyōgo Ken)
54 Awa 阿波 (Tokushima Ken)
55 Sanuki 讃岐 (Kagawa Ken)
56 Iyo 伊予 (Ehime Ken)
57 Tosa 土佐 (Kōchi Ken)
58 Chikuzen 筑前 (a part of Fukuoka Ken)
59 Chikugo 筑後 (a part of Fukuoka Ken)
60 Buzen 豊前 (a part of Fukuoka Ken and a part of Ōita Ken)
61 Bungo 豊後 (a part of Ōitaken)
62 Hizen 肥前 (Saga Ken and a part of Nagasaki Ken)
63 Higo 肥後 (Kumamoto Ken)
64 Hyūga 日向 (Miyazaki Ken and a part of Kagoshima Ken)
65 Ōsumi 大隅 (a part of Kagoshima Ken)
66 Satsuma 薩摩 (a part of Kagoshima Ken)
67 Iki 壱岐 (a part of Nagasaki Ken)
68 Tsushima 対馬 (a part of Nagasaki Ken)

## *Provinces by Map Number and Region*

Kinai 畿内

1 Yamashiro 山城 (Sanshū 山州, Jōshū 城州, Yōshū 雍州)
2 Yamato 大和 (Washū 和州, Washū 倭州)
3 Kawachi 河内 (Kashū 河州)
4 Izumi 和泉 (Senshū 泉州)
5 Settsu 摂津 (Sesshū 摂州)

Tōkaidō 東海道

6 Iga 伊賀 (Ishū 伊州, Gashū 賀州)
7 Ise 伊勢 (Seishū 勢州)
8 Shima 志摩 (Shishū 志州)
9 Owari 尾張 (Bishū 尾州, Chōshū 張州)
10 Mikawa 三河 (Sanshū 三州, Sanshū 参州)
11 Tōtōmi 遠江 (Enshū 遠州)
12 Suruga 駿河 (Sunshū 駿州)
13 Kai 甲斐 (Kōshū 甲州)
14 Izu 伊豆 (Zushū 豆州)
15 Sagami 相模 (Sōshū 相州)
16 Musashi 武蔵 (Bushū 武州)
17 Awa 安房 (Bōshū 房州)
18 Kazusa 上総 (Sōshū 総州)
19 Shimōsa 下総 (Sōshū 総州)
20 Hitachi 常陸 (Jōshū 常州)

Tōzandō 東山道

21 Ōmi 近江 (Gōshū 江州)
22 Mino 美濃 (Nōshū 濃州)
23 Hida 飛騨 (Hishū 飛州)
24 Shinano 信濃 (Shinshū 信州)
25 Kōzuke 上野 (Jōshū 上州)
26 Shimotsuke 下野 (Yashū 野州)
27 Mutsu 陸奥 (Ōshū 奥州)
28 Dewa 出羽 (Ushū 羽州)

Hokurikudō 北陸道

29 Wakasa 若狭 (Jakushū 若州)
30 Echizen 越前 (Esshū 越州)
31 Kaga 加賀 (Kashū 加州, Gashū 賀州)
32 Noto 能登 (Nōshū 能州)
33 Etchū 越中 (Esshū 越州)
34 Echigo 越後 (Esshū 越州)
35 Sado 佐渡 (Sashū 佐州)

San'indō 山陰道

36 Tanba 丹波 (Tanshū 丹州)
37 Tango 丹後 (Tanshū 丹州)
38 Tajima 但馬 (Tanshū 但州)
39 Inaba 因幡 (Inshū 因州)

40 Hōki 伯耆 (Hakushū 伯州)
41 Izumo 出雲 (Unshū 雲州)
42 Iwami 石見 (Sekishū 石州)
43 Oki 隠岐 (Inshū 隠州)

San'yōdō 山陽道

44 Harima 播磨 (Banshū 播州)
45 Mimasaka 美作 (Sakushū 作州)
46 Bizen 備前 (Bishū 備州)
47 Bitchū 備中 (Bishū 備州)
48 Bingo 備後 (Bishū 備州)
49 Aki 安芸 (Geishū 芸州)
50 Suō 周防 (Bōshū 防州)
51 Nagato 長門 (Chōshū 長州)

Nankaidō 南海道

52 Kii 紀伊 (Kishū 紀州)
53 Awaji 淡路 (Tanshū 淡州)
54 Awa 阿波 (Ashū 阿州)
55 Sanuki 讃岐 (Sanshū 讃州)
56 Iyo 伊予 (Yoshū 予州)
57 Tosa 土佐 (Doshū 土州)

Saikaidō 西海道

58 Chikuzen 筑前 (Chikushū 筑州)
59 Chikugo 筑後 (Chikushū 筑州)
60 Buzen 豊前 (Hōshū 豊州)
61 Bungo 豊後 (Hōshū 豊州)
62 Hizen 肥前 (Hishū 肥州)
63 Higo 肥後 (Hishū 肥州)
64 Hyūga 日向 (Nisshū 日州)
65 Ōsumi 大隅 (Gūshū 隅州)
66 Satsuma 薩摩 (Sasshū 薩州)
67 Iki 壱岐 (Isshū 壱州)
68 Tsushima 対馬 (Taishū 対州)

## Provinces in Alphabetical Order

| | |
|---|---|
| Aki 安芸 (Geishū 芸州) | 49 |
| Awa 阿波 (Ashū 阿州) | 54 |
| Awa 安房 (Bōshū 房州) | 17 |
| Awaji 淡路 (Tanshū 淡州) | 53 |
| Bingo 備後 (Bishū 備州) | 48 |
| Bitchū 備中 (Bishū 備州) | 47 |
| Bizen 備前 (Bishū 備州) | 46 |
| Bungo 豊後 (Hōshū 豊州) | 61 |
| Buzen 豊前 (Hōshū 豊州) | 60 |
| Chikugo 筑後 (Chikushū 筑州) | 59 |
| Chikuzen 筑前 (Chikushū 筑州) | 58 |
| Dewa 出羽 (Ushū 羽州) | 28 |
| Echigo 越後 (Esshū 越州) | 34 |
| Echizen 越前 (Esshū 越州) | 30 |
| Etchū 越中 (Esshū 越州) | 33 |
| Harima 播磨 (Banshū 播州) | 44 |
| Hida 飛騨 (Hishū 飛州) | 23 |
| Higo 肥後 (Hishū 肥州) | 63 |
| Hitachi 常陸 (Jōshū 常州) | 20 |
| Hizen 肥前 (Hishū 肥州) | 62 |
| Hōki 伯耆 (Hakushū 伯州) | 40 |
| Hyūga 日向 (Nisshū 日州) | 64 |
| Iga 伊賀 (Ishū 伊州, Gashū 賀州) | 6 |
| Iki 壱岐 (Isshū 壱州) | 67 |
| Inaba 因幡 (Inshū 因州) | 39 |
| Ise 伊勢 (Seishū 勢州) | 7 |
| Iwami 石見 (Sekishū 石州) | 42 |
| Iyo 伊予 (Yoshū 予州) | 56 |
| Izu 伊豆 (Zushū 豆州) | 14 |
| Izumi 和泉 (Senshū 泉州) | 4 |
| Izumo 出雲 (Unshū 雲州) | 41 |
| Kaga 加賀 (Kashū 加州, Gashū 賀州) | 31 |
| Kai 甲斐 (Kōshū 甲州) | 13 |
| Kawachi 河内 (Kashū 河州) | 3 |
| Kazusa 上総 (Sōshū 総州) | 18 |
| Kii 紀伊 (Kishū 紀州) | 52 |
| Kōzuke 上野 (Jōshū 上州) | 25 |
| Mikawa 三河 (Sanshū 三州, Sanshū 参州) | 10 |
| Mimasaka 美作 (Sakushū 作州) | 45 |
| Mino 美濃 (Nōshū 濃州) | 22 |
| Musashi 武蔵 (Bushū 武州) | 16 |
| Mutsu 陸奥 (Ōshū 奥州) | 27 |
| Nagato 長門 (Chōshū 長州) | 51 |
| Noto 能登 (Nōshū 能州) | 32 |
| Oki 隠岐 (Inshū 隠州) | 43 |
| Ōmi 近江 (Gōshū 江州) | 21 |
| Ōsumi 大隅 (Gūshū 隅州) | 65 |
| Owari 尾張 (Bishū 尾州, Chōshū 張州) | 9 |
| Sado 佐渡 (Sashū 佐州) | 35 |
| Sagami 相模 (Sōshū 相州) | 15 |
| Sanuki 讃岐 (Sanshū 讃州) | 55 |
| Satsuma 薩摩 (Sasshū 薩州) | 66 |
| Settsu 摂津 (Sesshū 摂州) | 5 |
| Shima 志摩 (Shishū 志州) | 8 |
| Shimōsa 下総 (Sōshū 総州) | 19 |
| Shimotsuke 下野 (Yashū 野州) | 26 |
| Shinano 信濃 (Shinshū 信州) | 24 |
| Suō 周防 (Bōshū 防州) | 50 |
| Suruga 駿河 (Sunshū 駿州) | 12 |
| Tajima 但馬 (Tanshū 但州) | 38 |
| Tanba 丹波 (Tanshū 丹州) | 36 |
| Tango 丹後 (Tanshū 丹州) | 37 |
| Tosa 土佐 (Doshū 土州) | 57 |
| Tōtōmi 遠江 (Enshū 遠州) | 11 |
| Tsushima 対馬 (Taishū 対州) | 68 |
| Wakasa 若狭 (Jakushū 若州) | 29 |
| Yamashiro 山城 (Sanshū 山州, Jōshū 城州, Yōshū 雍州) | 1 |
| Yamato 大和 (Washū 和州, Washū 倭州) | 2 |

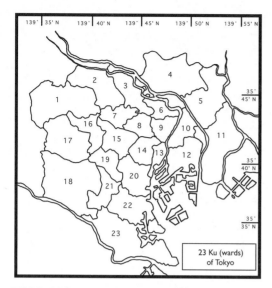

23 Ku (wards) of Tokyo

13 Chūō-ku 中央区
14 **Chiyoda-ku** 千代田区
15 **Shinjuku-ku** 新宿区 *(AC vol. 1, p. 120)*
16 **Nakano-ku** 中野区
17 Suginami-ku 杉並区
18 Setagaya-ku 世田谷区
19 **Shibuya-ku** 渋谷区
20 **Minato-ku** 港区
21 Meguro-ku 目黒区
22 **Shinagawa-ku** 品川区
23 Ōta-ku 大田区

# THE WARDS OF TOKYO

The highly developed urban part of Tokyo is divided into twenty-three special administrative districts or wards, called *ku* in Japanese. This urban area is what we often associate with Tokyo, even though it takes up only about one-third of the total metropolitan area. The present divisions were established following the overthrow of the shōgun in 1868 and thus do not appear in stories set in earlier periods. Almost all anime or manga set in modern Tokyo take place in the twenty-three *ku*. The *ku* listed in boldface below have a corresponding entry in *The Anime Companion*.

## *Tokyo Wards by Map Number*

1 **Nerima-ku** 練馬区
2 Itabashi-ku 板橋区
3 Kita-ku 北区
4 **Adachi-ku** 足立区
5 Katsushika-ku 葛飾区
6 **Arakawa-ku** 荒川区
7 Toshima-ku 豊島区
8 Bunkyō-ku 文京区
9 **Taitō-ku** 台東区
10 Sumida-ku 墨田区
11 **Edogawa-ku** 江戸川区
12 **Kōtō-ku** 江東区

## *Tokyo Wards in Alphabetical Order*

| | |
|---|---|
| **Adachi-ku** 足立区 | 4 |
| **Arakawa-ku** 荒川区 | 6 |
| Bunkyō-ku 文京区 | 8 |
| **Chiyoda-ku** 千代田区 | 14 |
| Chūō-ku 中央区 | 13 |
| **Edogawa-ku** 江戸川区 | 11 |
| Itabashi-ku 板橋区 | 2 |
| Katsushika-ku 葛飾区 | 5 |
| Kita-ku 北区 | 3 |
| **Kōtō-ku** 江東区 | 12 |
| Meguro-ku 目黒区 | 21 |
| **Minato-ku** 港区 | 20 |
| **Nakano-ku** 中野区 | 16 |
| **Nerima-ku** 練馬区 | 1 |
| Ōta-ku 大田区 | 23 |
| Setagaya-ku 世田谷区 | 18 |
| **Shibuya-ku** 渋谷区 | 19 |
| **Shinagawa-ku** 品川区 | 22 |
| **Shinjuku-ku** 新宿区 *(AC vol. 1, p. 120)* | 15 |
| Suginami-ku 杉並区 | 17 |
| Sumida-ku 墨田区 | 10 |
| **Taitō-ku** 台東区 | 9 |
| Toshima-ku 豊島区 | 7 |

# ENGLISH–JAPANESE REVERSE LOOKUP GLOSSARY

This glossary contains entries from both Volume 1 and Volume 2 of *The Anime Companion*. Entries in this volume are marked by a bullet.

- abacus: **soroban**
- abstinence: **tachimono**
- acupuncture: **hari**
- Adachi Ward: **Adachi-ku**
- address: **atena**
- administrative representatives: **daikan**
- adoption: **yōshi**
- Air Self Defense Force: **jieitai**
- Aizu Basin: **Aizu Bonchi**
- Akihabara Station: **Akihabara Eki**
- alcove: **tokonoma**
- altar on wall: **kamidana**
- altar, family, Buddhist: **butsudan**
- altar, family, Shintō: **kamidana**
- altar, memorial, Buddhist: **butsudan**
- alternative attendance: **sankin kōtai**
- amulet: **ofuda, omamori**
- anglerfish: **ankō**
- anniversary of death: **meinichi**
- annual events: **matsuri to nenchū gyōji**
- Ansei Crackdown: **Ansei no Taigoku**
- Ansei Purge: **Ansei no Taigoku**
- Aoyama Cemetery: **Aoyama Reien**
- apartment, edo period: **nagaya**
- apparition: **bakemono**
- apprentice geisha: **maiko**
- apricot: **ume, umeboshi**
- apron: **kappōgi**
- Arakawa Ward: **Arakawa-ku**
- archery: **kyūdō**
- Army, Imperial Japanese: **Dai Nippon Teikoku Rikugun**
- arranged marriage meeting: **omiai**
- arranged marriage: **kon'in**
- arrowroot cake: **kuzu mochi**
- arrows, New Year's: **hamaya**

- art, erotic: **shunga**
- Asakusa Shrine: **Asakusa Jinja**
- ascetic practice: **Shugendō, tachimono, yama-bushi**
- Awa Dance: **Awa Odori**
- Awaji Island: **Awajishima**

- badger: **tanuki**
- baka bomb: **Ōka**
- ball of food: **dango**
- balls of floating fire: **hitodama**
- bamboo flute: **shakuhachi**
- bamboo or wood food steamer: **seirō**
- bamboo pipe (garden decoration): **shishiodoshi**
- bamboo sheath: **takenokawa**
- bamboo shoot: **takenoko**
- bamboo sword: **shinai**
- banner knight: **hatamoto**
- bannermen: **hatamoto**
- banners and standards: **hata, fū-rin-ka-zan, koinobori, matoi, nobori**
- banquet: **enkai**
- bar girl: **hosutesu**
- bar: **sunakku**
- barley tea: **mugicha**
- baseball, high school: **kōkō yakyū**
- Bashō Matsuo: **Bashō**
- basin at Shintō shrine: **temizuya**
- bath in home: **furo**
- bath, public, at hot spring: **onsen**
- bath, public: **sentō**
- Battle of Dannoura: **Dannoura no Tatakai**
- Battle of Goryōkaku: **Goryōkaku no Tatakai**
- Battle of Sekigahara: **Sekigahara no Tatakai**
- Battle of Toba-Fushimi: **Toba-Fushimi no Tatakai**

- battledore market: **hagoita ichi**
- battledore: **hagoita**
- Bayshore Expressway: **Shuto Kōsoku Wangan Sen**
- beads: **magatama**
- beckoning cat: **manekineko**
- beckoning
- bedding: **futon**
- "beef bowl": **gyūdon**
- beef hot pot: **gyūnabe**
- beeper: **poke-beru**
- beer: **bīru**
- bell on rope at shrine: **suzu**
- bell ringing at New Year's: **Joya no kane**
- bell used in Buddhist service: **kei**
- bell: **bonshō, kei, suzu**
- belly: **hara**
- belt: **obi**
- betrothal gift: **yuinō**
- bikers: **bōsōzoku**
- bird fair: **tori no ichi**
- black ships: **Perry, Matthew Calbraith**
- blanquillo: **amadai**
- blinds: **sudare**
- blood type: **ketsueki-gata**
- bloomers: **burūmā**
- boar: **inoshishi**
- bobbing cow toy: **akabeko**
- bobbing ox toy: **akabeko**
- bodhisattva: **bosatsu, Jizō**
- Bon dance: **Bon Odori**
- bonfire: **okuribi**
- bonito, dried shaved: **kezuribushi**
- bonito, dried: **katsuobushi**
- bonus: **shōyo**
- Boshin Civil War: **Boshin Sensō**
- botan mochi: **ohagi**
- bow: **ojigi**
- bowl: **chawan, donburi**
- box lunch: **bentō**

Boys' Day: **Kodomo no Hi**
Boys' Festival: **Kodomo no Hi**
- bracken: **warabi**
brain death: **zōki ishioku**
brazier: **shichirin**
- bread crumbs: **panko**
breakfast: **chōshoku**
bride's headdress: **tsunokakushi**
bronze mirror: **seidōkyō**
Buddhism: **bukkyō**
Buddhist family altar: **butsudan**
Buddhist memorial altar:
   **butsudan**
Buddhist practice: **en no gyōja**
Buddhist prayer: **nenbutsu**
Buddhist rosary: **juzu**
Buddhist temple bell: **bonshō**
Buddhist temple: **jiin**
Bullet Train: **Shinkansen**
- burdock: **gobō**
- bureau or wooden chest: **tansu**
business card: **meishi**
business crest: **mon**
buying gifts on vacation: **miyage**

cabaret girl: **hosutesu**
calling card: **meishi**
- camellia: **tsubaki**
- candle holder, portable: **teshoku**
- candle: **rōsoku**
card games: **hanafuda, uta
   karuta**
carp streamer: **koinobori**
carp: **koi**
- carrot: **ninjin**
carrying cloth: **furoshiki**
castle: **shiro**
cat: **neko**
- cedar: **sugi**
censorship: **ken'etsu**
- ceramic pot for cooking: **donabe**
- chain and sickle: **kusarigama**
- chain-mail vest: **kusari-katabira**
- chain with weights: **kusarifundo**
- changing child's name: **tsūshō**
cha-no-yu sweets: **yōkan**
characters, Chinese: **kanji**
charm, Shintō: **ofuda, omamori**

cherry blossom viewing: **hanami**
cherry blossom: **sakura**
chess: **shōgi**; see also **go**
- chest, wooden: **tansu**
- chidai: **tai**
- child name (male): **yōmyō**
- child's plate: **okosama-ranchi**
Children's Day: **Kodomo no Hi**
- chili spice mix: **shichimi
   tōgarashi**
- Chinese restaurant: **chūka ryōri-
   ya**
- Chinese spoon: **renge**
- Chinese-lantern plant market:
   **hōzuki ichi**
- Chinese-lantern plant: **hōzuki**
- chirirenge: **renge**
- Chiyodajō: **Edojō**
chop: **hanko**
chopsticks: **hashi**
Christianity: **Kirisutokyō**
Christmas: **Kurisumasu**
chrysanthemum: **kiku**
- chūka sierō: **seirō**
cicada sound: **semi**
clapping hands: **kashiwade**
class number, homeroom: **homurūmu**
cleaning classroom: **school
   students cleaning classroom
   and grounds**
- closets for storing futon: **oshiire**
clothing. See "Clothing" in
   section "Entries Arranged by
   Category"
- cloud shelves: **chigai-dana**
- cock fair: **tori no ichi**
coffee shop: **kissaten**
coffeehouse: **kissaten**
colored cords on envelope or gift:
   **mizuhiki**
comb: **kushi**
comic books: **manga**
comic market: **Komiketto**
- Coming of Age ceremony:
   **genpuku**
- Coming-of-Age Day: **Seijin no
   Hi**

- Commodore Perry: **Perry,
   Matthew Calbraith**
Communist Party of Japan: **Nihon
   Kyōsantō**
commuting: **tsūkin**
company housing: **shataku**
- condom: **kondomu**
Confucianism: **Jukyō**
Constitution: **Nihonkoku Kenpō**
cooking apron: **kappōgi**
- cooking pot: **nabe, kama**
- corn on the cob: **tōmorokoshi**
- cosplay: **kosupure**
- costume play: **kosupure**
cowherd and weaver story:
   **Tanabata**
crab with face pattern: **heikegani**
cracker, rice: **senbei**
cram school: **yobikō**
crane: **tsuru**
cranes, a thousand: **senbazuru**
cremation: **kasō**
crest: **mon**
- croquette: **korokke**
- crossdressing "hostesses": **nyū
   hāfu**
crow: **karasu**
- cryptomeria: **sugi**
cucumber: **kyūri**
cup and ball toy: **kendama**
curry rice: **karē raisu**
- curry: **karē**
curtain: **noren**
cushion for sitting: **zabuton**
cuttlefish: **ika**

- daimyō domain: **han**
- dance with basket: **dojōsukui**
- dance with coin on nose:
   **dojōsukui**
dance: **Awa Odori, Bon Odori**
- dart: **shuriken**
death anniversary: **meinichi**
death fire: **hitodama**
death, legal definition of: **zōki
   ishi-oku**
- decorated bamboo rake: **kumade**
decorative alcove: **tokonoma**

deer: **shika**
- delivery of prepared food: **demae**
Democratic Socialist Party: **Minshatō**
demon: **oni, tengu**
- Demoness of Adachi: **Adachigahara**
- demon-faced edge tile: **onigawara**
department store: **depāto**
devil's tongue jelly: **konnyaku**
dice: **saikoro**
Diet or Parliament: **Kokkai**
- dim sum: **shūmai**
directions to addresses: **atena**
divination: **sangi, mikuji, zeichiku**
divination: **zeichiku**
doll display: **Hina Matsuri**
Doll Festival: **Hina Matsuri**
- doll, nailing to tree: **ushi no koku mairi**
- domain: **han**
- dōmyō: **yōmyō**
door: **fusuma, shōji**
- dosō: **dozō**
dowry: **yuinō**
- dragon: **ryū**
dream eater: **baku**
- dressing up in costume: **kosupure**
- dried bonito shaved: **kezuribushi**
- dried bonito: **katsuobushi**
drink. See "Food and Drink" in section "Entries Arranged by Category"
- drink: **tamago-zake**
drinks, mixing Japanese and Western: **chanpon**
- drop lid: **otoshibuta**
drum: **taiko**
drunkard: **yopparai**
DSP: **Minshatō**
- duel: **taryū-jiai**
- dumpling: **dango**
dumpling: **manjū**
duster: **hataki**

ear cleaning tool: **mimikaki**
ear scoop: **mimikaki**
- Earthquake of 1923: **Kantō Daishinsai**
earthquake: **jishin**
- Ebisu (people): **Emishi**
- ecchi: **hentai**
Economic Planning Agency: **Keizai Kikaku Chō**
- Edo Bay: **Tōkyō Wan**
- Edo Castle: **Edojō**
- Edogawa Ward: **Edogawa-ku**
eel: **unagi**
- egg yolk in sake: **tamago-zake**
- egg: **tamago**
eggplant: **nasu**
electric rice cooker: **denki-gama**
emissary, imperial: **Tenshō Ken'ō Shisetsu**
- encouraging stick: **keisaku**
- edge tile with demon face: **onigawara**
engagement gift: **yuinō**
entryway where you remove shoes: **genkan**
EPA: **Keizai Kikaku Chō**
- equinox bean cake: **ohagi**
- erotic art: **shunga**
- esoteric buddhism: **mikkyō**
- esoteric teachings, buddhist: **mikkyō**
etiquette: **noodle slurping**
European mission: **Tenshō Ken'ō Shisetsu**
examination hell: **shiken jigoku**
exorcism: **tsukimono otoshi**
- Expressway Bayshore Line: **Shuto Kōsoku Wangan Sen**
- expressway: **kōsoku dōro**
- Ezo (people): **Emishi**

- faggot (derogatory): **okama**
fair day: **ennichi**
fairy: **tennyo**
family altar, Shintō: **kamidana**
family crest: **mon**
fan: **ōgi** (folding), **uchiwa** (non-folding)

fanzine: **dōjinshi**
fart: **he**
feast day: **ennichi**
feng shui: **kasō**
ferryboat: **renraku-sen**
- Festival of the Rooster: **tori no ichi**
festival: **Bon, Hina Matsuri, Kodomo no Hi, matsuri to nenchū gyōji**
field trip: **shūgaku ryokō**
fire brigade standard: **matoi**
fire pit: **irori**
fire: **okuribi**
firearm: **teppō**
firefly: **hotaru**
fireworks: **firecrackers in the sky, hanabi**
fish cake: **tai-yaki**
fish ornaments on roof: **shachihoko**
- fish paste cake: **hanpen**
fish paste swirl: **naruto**
- fish sausage: **chikuwa**
fish, goby: **haze**
- fish, raw: **sashimi**
fish-shaped percussion instrument: **mokugyo**
flag: **fū-rin-ka-zan, koinobori, matoi, nobori**
- flat tray for serving food: **oshiki**
flint and steel: **hiuchi-ishi**
floating balls of fire: **hitodama**
floor covering: **tatami**
floor cushion: **zabuton**
- flower arranging: **ikebana**
flower viewing: **hanami**
flute, bamboo: **shakuhachi**
- folded paper objects: **origami**
- folding screen: **byōbu**
food cart/mobile stall: **yatai**
food container: **donburi**
food model: **shokuhin sanpuru**
- food steamer, bamboo or wood: **seirō**
food. See "Food and Drink" in section "Entries Arranged by Category"

foods to not be eaten together: **mismatched foods**
- foot soldiers: **ashigaru**
football, Japanese: **kemari**
foreigner: **gaijin**
form: **kata**
formal banquet: **enkai**
fortune stick: **mikuji**
- fortune telling: **zeichiku**
fortunetelling: **mikuji, sangi, zeichiku**
- four legged standing lantern: **kaku andon**
fox: **Inari, kitsune**
fried noodles: **yakisoba**
- fried pork filet: **hirekatsu**
- fried rice: **yakimeshi**
- fritters: **tenpura**
- Fuji Five Lakes: **Fuji Goko**
- Fukushima Prefecture: **Fukushima Ken**
funeral tablet, name on: **kaimyō**
- futon storage closets: **oshiire**

- Ga-ko: **Suwako**
game, Othello: **Osero**
- game: **ohajiki**
games and sports. See "Entertainment/Game" and "Sport/Activity" in section "Entries Arranged by Category"
gangster: **yakuza**
garden decoration: **shishiodoshi**
- garden guard: **niwaban**
gate pine: **kadomatsu**
gate: **torii**
geisha, apprentice: **maiko**
Genji family: **Minamoto**
geomancy: **kasō**
gesture: **inzō**
ghost fire: **hitodama**
ghost: **yūrei**
giant lantern float: **Nebuta Matsuri**
- giant monster: **kaiju**
- Gion Festival: **Gion Matsuri**
Gion temple bell: **Heike Monogatari**
- girl: **shōjo**

Girls' Day: **Hina Matsuri**
globe fish: **fugu**
goby: **haze**
god of happiness, wealth, long life: **Jurōjin Fukurokuju**
god of thunder: **Raijin**
god vehicle: **shintai**
god: **kami**
goddess of the river: **Benten**
Goemon: **Ishikawa Goemon**
Golden Pavilion: **Kinkakuji**
goldfish dipping: **kingyo-sukui**
goldfish: **kingyo**
- Goryōkaku, Battle of: **Goryōkaku no Tatakai**
gourd: **hisago**
gravesite visit: **hakamairi**
graveyard, wooden stake in: **sotoba**
- Great Ansei Crackdown: **Ansei no Taigoku**
- Great Kanto Earthquake: **Kantō Daishinsai**
Great Wisdom Kings: **Fudō-Myōō**
- ground cherry market: **hōzuki ichi**
- ground cherry: **hōzuki**
Ground Self Defense Force: **Jieitai**
- guard for sword: **tsuba**
guardian gods: **jūni jinshō**
- guji: **amadai**
- Gunma Prefecture: **Gunma Ken**
gun: **teppō**
gym shorts: **burūmā**

- H: **hentai**
hairpin: **hana-kanzashi**
halberd: **naginata**
- Hamaguri Gomon Incident: **Hamaguri Gomon no Hen**
- han lord: **daimyō**
hand gesture: **inzō, kuji**
- hand guard: **tsuba**
handkerchief: **hankachi**
Haneda Airport: **Tōkyō Kokusai Kūkō**
hanging scroll: **kakemono**
- hard liquor: **shōchū**
- Harris Treaty: **Nichibei Shūkō**

**Tsūshō Jōyaku**
hat: **sando-gasa**
haunting: **goryō**
- hawser: **tsuna**
- headband with candles: **ushi no koku mairi**
headband: **hachimaki**
Health and Welfare Ministry: **Kōseishō**
health drink: **eiyō drink**
Hearn, Lafcadio: **Koizumi Yakumo**
hearth: **irori**
heavenly maiden: **tennyo**
Heike family: **Taira**
- hettsui: **kamado**
Hida Mountains: **Hida Sanmyaku**
high school baseball: **kōkō yakyū**
- Highest Joy: **Gokuraku**
- hilt, sword hilt: **tsuka**
- Himeji Castle: **Himejijō**
- Hirohito (Shōwa Emperor): **Shōwa Tennō**
historical period: **jidai**
- Hitotsubashi Keiki: **Tokugawa Yoshinobu**
- hoe: **kuwagara**
holiday: **bon, ennichi, hina matsuri, kurismasu, Kodomo no Hi, nebuta matsuri, setsubun**
- home delivery of prepared food: **demae**
- Home Ministry: **Naimushō**
homeroom: **homurūmu**
- homosexual (male, derogatory): **okama**
- honor the emperor, expel the barbarians: **sonnō jōi**
horse's leg: **uma-yaku**
hostess: **hosutesu**
- hot pot dish: **chirinabe**
- hot pot dishes: **nabemono**
- hot pot: **gyūnabe**
hot rodders: **bōsōzoku**
hot spring, Azabu Number Ten: **Azabu Jūban**
hot spring: **onsen**
hot tea over rice: **chazuke**

- hot water heater, wall mounted: **yuwakashiki**
  housecleaning: **susu-harai**
  housing, company: **shataku**
  hydrangea: **ajisai**
- Hyōgo Prefecture: **Hyōgo Ken**
- Hyōgo: **Kōbe**

- iai-jutsu: **battō-jutsu**
  Ibaraki Prefecture: **Ibaraki Ken**
  "idol" singer: **aidoru**
- Imperial Hotel: **Teikoku Hoteru**
- Imperial Japanese Army: **Dai Nippon Teikoku Rikugun**
- Imperial Meiji Army: **Dai Nippon Teikoku Rikugun**
- imperial reverence barbarian expulsion movement: **sonnō jōi**
  Imperial University: **Teikoku Daigaku**
  indigenous Japanese: **Ainu**
- individual small table for food: **zen**
  inebriation: **yopparai**
- infantry: **ashigaru**
  ink on face: **hanetsuki**
  ink: **sumi**
- Inland Sea: **Seto Naikai**
  inn: **ryokan**
  instrument: **biwa, shamisen**
- intendants: **daikan**
- Interior Ministry: **Naimushō**
- International Military Tribunal for the Far East: **Sensō Hanzai ni Kansuru Saiban**
  Iris Festival: **Kodomo no Hi**
- irises: **ayame**
- iron pot: **nabe**
- Issa: **Kobayashi Issa**
- itinerant training in martial arts: **musha shugyō**
- Iwate Prefecture: **Iwate Ken**
  Izumo Province: **Izumo no kuni**
  Izumo Shrine: **Izumo Taisha**

  jacket worn over kimono: **haori**
  Japan Broadcasting Corporation: **Nippon Hōsō Kyōkai**
  Japan Communist Party: **Nihon Kyōsantō**
  Japan Railways: **Jē Āru**
  Japanese chess: **shōgi**
  Japanese Industrial Standards: **Nihon Kōgyō Kikaku**
  Japanese inn: **ryokan**
- Japanese pepper: **sanshō**
  Japanese sword: **nihontō**
  Japanese-style banquet: **enkai**
- Japan-U.S. Friendship and Commerce Treaty: **Nichibei Shūkō Tsūshō Jōyaku**
- Japan-U.S. Trade and Commerce Treaty: **Nichibei Shūkō Tsūshō Jōyaku**
- Japan-U.S. Treaty of Amity and Commerce: **Nichibei Shūkō Tsūshō Jōyaku**
  jelly fish: **kurage**
  JIS: **Nihon Kōgyō Kikaku**
- *Journey to the West*: **Saiyūki**
- Jubei: **Yagyū Jūbei Mitsuyoshi**
  juvenile delinquent: **yankī**

- Kabuto Stock Exchange: **Tokyo Shōken Torihikijo**
- Kagoshima Han: **Satsuma Han**
- Kahaku: **onigawara**
- kaku sierō: **seirō**
  Kamakura shogunate: **Kamakura period**
- kamikaze pilots: **Kamikaze Tokubetsu Kōgekitai**
- Kamikaze Special Attack Force: **Kamikaze Tokubetsu Kōgekitai**
- Kanagawa treaty: **Nichibei Washin Jōyaku**
- Kanto quake: **Kantō Daishinsai**
  Kantō region: **Kantō chihō**
- Katsu Awa: **Katsu Kaishū**
- Katsu Rintarō: **Katsu Kaishū**
- Katsu Yasuyoshi: **Katsu Kaishū**
- Katsura Kogorō: **Kido Takayoshi**
- Kawanishi flying boat: **Emily (aircraft)**
- kazari kumade: **kumade**
  Keio Plaza Hotel: **Keio Puraza Hoteru**

- kelp: **konbu**
- Kido Kōin: **Kido Takayoshi**
- Kinmon Incident: **Hamaguri Gomon no Hen**
  kindergarten: **shūgakuzen kyōiku**
- kirazu: **o-kara**
- Kiso Kaidō: **Nakasendō**
  kiss: **kisu**
  kitchen robe: **kappōgi**
  kite flying: **tako-age**
  Kiyomizu Temple: **Kiyomizudera**
  knots, decorative: **mizuhiki**
- Kōan War: **Kōan no Eki**
- Kōchi Han: **Tosa Han**
- Kōchi Prefecture: **Kōchi Ken**
- kogomi: **kusasotetsu**
- korean bbq restaurants: **yakiniku-ya**
- Kosoji: **Nakasendō**
- ku: **Adachi-ku, Arakawa-ku, Chiyoda-ku, Edogawa-ku, Kita-ku, Kōtō-ku, Minato-ku, Nakano-ku, Nerima-ku, Shibuya-ku, Shinagawa-ku, Taitō-ku**
- kudo: **kamado**
- Kugisho Navy Special Attacker Ōka: **Ōka**
- kura: **dozō**
- kusari: **kusarifundo**
- kyōsaku: **keisaku**
- Kyoto Deputy: **Kyōto shoshidai**
- Kyōto Military Commissioner: **Kyōto Shugoshoku**

- Lake Biwa: **Biwako**
- Lake Suwa: **Suwako**
  lance: **naginata**
  lantern festival: **Bon**
- lantern with shoji covering, standing: **kaku andon**
- lantern, four legged standing: **kaku andon**
  lantern, red: **aka-chōchin**
  lantern, stone: **ishi-dōrō**
  lanterns, hanging: **chōchin, tsuri dōrō**
  laver: **nori**

LDP: **Jiyū Minshutō**
- leek: **negi**
  legislature: **Kokkai**
- legless chair: **zaisu**
- lesbian: **rezubian**
  Liberal Democratic Party:
  **JuyūMinshutō**
- lid that fits inside pot:
  **otoshibuta**
  life force: **ki**
  lightweight kimono: **yukata**
  little finger
- lizard's tail: **dokudami**
  loanword: **gairaigo**
  loincloth: **fundoshi**
  Lolita complex: **rorikon**
- lord: **daimyō**
- lotus root: **renkon**
  lovers's suicide: **shinjū**
- lucky rake fair: **tori no ichi**
  lunch box: **bentō, ekiben**
  lute priest: **biwa hōshi**
- lute, round: **gekkin**
  lute: **biwa**

- madai: **tai**
  magic syllables: **kuji**
  mah-jongg: **mājan**
- male child's name: **yōmyō**
- male homosexual (derogatory):
  **okama**
  mandarin orange: **mikan**
  maple: **kaede to momiji**
- marathon monks: **kaihōgyō**
- marbles, flat: **ohajiki**
  Maritime Self Defense Force:
  **Jieitai**
  marriage ceremony: **shinzen**
  **kekkon**
  marriage: **kon'in**
- marsh reed screen: **yoshizu**
  martial art: **judō, jūjutsu, kendō,**
  **kyūdō, ninjutsu**
  martial arts training hall: **dōjō**
- mask, white square: **zōmen**
  mask: **okame, surgical masks**
  **worn in public**
  massage parlor: **sōpurando**
  master: **sensei**

- Masuda Shirō Tokisada:
  **Amakusa Shirō**
  mattress: **futon**
  McDonald's: **Makudonarudo**
- meatballs: **tsukune**
  Meiji Shrine: **Meiji Jingū**
  memorial altar, Buddhist:
  **butsudan**
  men in black: **kurogo**
- men of high purpose: **shishi**
  mermaid: **ningyo**
- Michi no Miya: **Shōwa Tennō**
- Mie Prefecture: **Mie Ken**
  military art of the ninja: **ninjutsu**
- Military Commissioner for Kyōto:
  Kyōto Shugoshoku
- military government: **bakufu**
- Minato Ward: **Minato-Ku**
  miniature tree: **bonsai**
  Ministry of Health and Welfare:
  **Kōseishō**
  Ministry of International Trade
  and Industry: **Tsūshō Sangyō**
  **Shō**
- Ministry of the Interior:
  **Naimushō**
  mirror: **seidōkyō**
  miso soup: **misoshiru**
- mister lady: **nyū hāfu**
- misutā redii: **nyū hāfu**
- Mito Kōmon: **Tokugawa**
  **Mitsukuni**
- Mitsubishi Navy type-1 plane:
  **Betty (aircraft)**
- Mitsubishi Zero-type carrier-
  based fighter: **Zerosen**
  Miyagi Prefecture: **Miyagi Ken**
- mochi: **sakura mochi, ohagi**
  money offering: **saisen**
  monk hat: **sando-gasa**
- Monkey King: **Son Goku**
  monkey show: **saru mawashi**
  monkey: **saru**
- monster, giant: **kaiju**
  monster: **bakemono**
- moon lute or moon guitar:
  **gekkin**
  morning glory: **asagao**
  motorcycle gang: **bōsōzoku**

- Mount Hiei: **Hieizan**
  mountain spirit: **tengu**
- mountain vegetables: **sansai**
  moxa treatment: **kyū**
  moxibustion: **kyū**
  Mt. Aso: **Asosan**
  Mt. Fuji: **Fujisan**
  Mt. Kōya: **Kōya-san**
  Mt. Kurama: **Kuramayama**
  mudra: **inzō**
- mushroom, type of: **shiitake**
  musical instrument: **biwa,**
  **koto, mokugyo, shakuhachi,**
  **shamisen**
  musician: **chindonya**
- mustard: **karashi**

- nabe, meals cooked in:
  **chirinabe, nabemono**
- nailing doll to tree: **ushi no**
  **koku mairi**
- Nakano Ward: **Nakano-Ku**
  name card: **meishi**
- name of male child: **yōmyō**
  name on funeral tablet: **kaimyō**
- name, changing child's: **tsūshō**
- naming a baby: **shichiya**
- nanairo tōgarashi: **shichimi**
  **tōgarashi**
  Narita Airport: **Shin Tōkyō**
  **Kokusai Kūkō**
- National Science Museum:
  **Kokuritsu Kagaku**
  **Hakubutsukan**
  neighborhood association:
  **chōnaikai**
- Nerima Ward: **Nerima-Ku**
- new half: **nyū hāfu**
  new religions: **shinkō shūkyō**
  New Tokyo International Airport:
  **Shin Tōkyō Kokusai Kūkō**
  New Year's arrow: **hamaya**
  New Year's bell ringing: **joya no**
  **kane**
  New Year's card: **nengajō**
  New Year's food: **osechi-ryōri**
  New Year's ornament: **kadomatsu**
  New Year's pine: **kadomatsu**
  New Year's shrine or temple visit:

hatsumōde
New Year's soup: **zōni**
New Year's temple bell: **joya no kane**
newspaper: **shinbun**
NHK: **Nippon Hōsō Kyōkai**
nine magic syllables: **kuji**
ninja: **ninjutsu**
Nippon Telegraph and Telephone Corporation: **Nippon Denshin Denwa**
- noh: **nō**
- noodles, thick: **udon**
noodles: **hiyamugi, sōmen; rāmen; yakisoba**
- noodles: **men rui, soba, udon**
Northern Alps: **Hida Sanmyaku**
NRM: **shinkō shūkyō shinkō**
NTT: **Nippon Denshin Denwa**
nymph: **tennyo**

- ocean whitefish: **amadai**
octopus balls or dumplings: **tako-yaki**
octopus: **tako**
- Odaiba Seaside Park: **Odaiba Kaihin Kōen**
offering box at shrine or temple: **saisen**
office lady: **OL**
ogre: **oni**
- Oguri Kōzuke no Suke: **Oguri Tadamasa**
- oil of toad: **gama no abura**
oiled paper umbrella: **kasa**
- Okayama Prefecture: **Okayama Ken**
- omelet rice: **omu-raisu**
*on* and *kun* readings: **kanji**
- one pot meal: **chirinabe, nabemono**
one-man orchestra: **chindonya**
- oniwaban: **niwaban**
orange: **mikan**
organ transplant: **zōki ishioku**
organizational crest: **mon**
origami: **senbazuru**
Osaka Tower: **Tsūtenkaku**
- ostrich fern: **kusasotetsu**

- otorisama: **tori no ichi**
outdoor stall: **yatai**
- *Outlaws of the Marsh*: **Suikoden**
ox-drawn carriage: **gissha**
"out with bad luck, in with good" (*oni wa soto, fuku wa uchi*): **setsu-bun**

pager: **poke-beru**
- painting on walls and screens: **shōheiga**
- paintings, erotic: **shunga**
- Palace Gate Incident: **Hamaguri Gomon no Hen**
palanquin: **kago, koshi, mikoshi**
- pampas grass: **susuki**
pancake: **okonomiyaki**
paper streamer: **gohei**
paper strip: **tanzaku**
paper, umbrella: **kasa**
- Paradise: **Gokuraku**
Parliament: **kokkai**
party: **enkai**
- patriots: **shishi**
pay phone: **denwa**
Peach Boy: **Momotarō**
Peach Festival: **hina matsuri**
- peasant revolt: **ikki**
- peeping tom: **nozoki**
period, historical
- persimmons: **kaki**
pickle: **tsukemono, umeboshi**
pickled apricot: **umeboshi**
pickled plum: **umeboshi**
- picture card shows: **kami-shibai**
- pig thigh: **dokudami**
pilgrimage: **junrei**
pillow: **makura**
pinball: **pachinko**
- pink movies: **pinku eiga**
pipe, tobacco: **kiseru**
pissing in public: **tachishōben**
- pizza: **okonomiyaki**
- playboy: **onnatarashi**
plum: **ume, umeboshi**
pocket door: **tobukuro**
poem card: **uta karuta**
poetry card game: **uta karuta**
police box: **kōban**

police truncheon, Edo period: **jitte**
police, riot: **kidōtai**
Police, Tōkyō Metropolitan: **Keishichō**
- pomegranate: **zakuro**
- pommel at base of sword: **kashira**
pop singer: **aidoru**
- pork cutlet donburi: **katsudon**
- pork cutlet: **tonkatsu**
- pork filet, fried: **hirekatsu**
- pornography: **pinku eiga**
porridge: **kayu**
portable shrine: **mikoshi**
- post station town: **shukuba machi**
posthumous Buddhist name: **kaimyō**
pot hook: **jizaikagi**
- pot over open fire: **nabe**
- pot, ceramic for cooking: **donabe**
- pot, cooking: **nabe, kama**
potstickers: **gyōza**
prayer beads: **juzu**
prayer: **inori, nenbutsu**
- prefecture: **ken**
preschool education: **shūgakuzen kyōku**
priestess, Shintō: **miko**
prime minister: **Okada Keisuke**
- prints, erotic: **shunga**
Prize, Akutagawa: **Akutagawa shō**
puffer fish: **fugu**
puppet play: **bunraku**
- Pure Land: **Gokuraku**

- queer: **okama**

rabu hoteru: **love hotels**
raccoon dog: **tanuki**
- radio calisthenics: **rajio taisō**
radish: **daikon**
- railways: **tetsudō**
rain charm: **teruteru bōzu**
rain doors: **amado**
raincoat made from reeds: **mino**
rainwear: **mino**

- Ranzan: **Arashiyama**
- Rat Boy: **Nezumi Kozo**
- raw fish: **sashimi**
  red and white: **aka to shiro**
  red lantern: **aka-chōchin**
  red sake cups at wedding: **sakazuki**
  reed raincoat: **mino**
- reed screen: **yoshizu**
- Reishiki Kanjō Sentōki: **Zerosen**
- restaurant, Chinese: **chūka ryōri-ya**
- revere the emperor, expel the barbarians: **sonnō jōi**
- rezu: **rezubian**
  rice ball: **nigirimeshi**
  rice bowl: **chawan**
  rice cake: **kashiwa mochi, mochi**
  rice cooker: **denki-gama**
- rice cooking pot: **kama**
  rice cracker: **senbei**
  rice kami: **Inari**
  rice porridge: **kayu**
- rice with red beans: **sekihan**
  rice, cooked: **gohan**
  rickshaw: **jinrikisha**
  rifle: **teppō**
  riot police: **kidōtai**
  ritual suicide: **harakiri, kaishakunin, seppuku**
- River Styx: **Sanzu no Kawa**
- River to the Otherworld: **Sanzu no Kawa**
- roof tile with demon face: **onigawara**
- roof tiles: **kawara**
- Rooster Festival: **tori no ichi**
  rope, sacred: **shimenawa**
  rosary: **juzu**
- Rose of Versailles: **Berusaiya no Bara**
- Rotte: **Lotte Co., Ltd.**
  round bell on rope at shrine: **suzu**
- row house: **nagaya**
  Russo-Japanese War: **Nichiro Sensō**
- ryofundo: **kusarifundo**

sacred rope: **shimenawa**
sacred tree: **shinboku**
sailor suit: **sailor fuku**
sake cup: **choko, masuzake, sakazuki**
sake flask: **tokkuri**
- sake with an egg yolk: **tamago-zake**
sake, spiced: **toso**
salaried man: **sararīman**
- salmon roe: **ikura**
samurai, masterless: **rōnin**
- samurai: **bushi**
sand shaped like stars: **hoshi suna**
sandals: **geta, zōri**
- sandfish: **hatahata**
- Sapporo Snow Festival: **Sapporo Yuki Matsuri**
- saruraceae: **dokudami**
sash: **obi**
- Satchō Rengō: **Satchō Dōmei**
satsuma orange: **mikan**
- Satsuma Rebellion: **Seinan Sensō**
- Satsuma-Chōshū Alliance: **Satchō Dōmei**
- saury: **sanma**
- sausage, fish: **chikuwa**
scabbard: **saya**
scattering soybeans: **setsubun**
- school (martial arts): **ryū (martial arts style)**
school trip: **shūgaku ryokō**
school uniform, girl's: **sailor fuku**
scissors paper stone: **jan-ken**
scraper: **ichimonji**
- screen and wall painting: **shōheiga**
- screen standing: **tsuitate**
- screen, folding: **byōbu**
scroll, hanging: **kakemono**
SDF: **Jieitai**
- sea bream: **tai**
sea goddess: **Benten**
- Sea of Japan: **Nihonkai**
seal: **hanko**
seasonal symbol: **Awa Odori,**

Bon Odori, hotaru, kadomatsu, kiku, matsuri to nenchū gyōji
seaweed: **nori**
- seaweed: **wakame, nori**
- secret buddhism: **mikkyō**
- secret teachings, buddhist: **mikkyō**
Self Defense Forces: **jieitai**
- set meal: **teishoku**
- Seto Inland Sea: **Seto Naikai**
seven deities of good fortune: **Shichifuku-jin**
7-5-3 Festival: **Shichi-go-san**
Seven Lucky Gods: **Shichifuku-jin**
- seven spice mix: **shichimi tōgarashi**
- seven tastes: **shichimi tōgarashi**
- Seventh Night: **shichiya**
- sex films: **pinku eiga**
shaking hands: **akushu-suru**
shaved ice: **kakigōri-ki**
- sheath: **saya**
shell-matching game: **kai-awase**
- she-male: **nyū hāfu**
- shī mēru: **nyū hāfu**
- Shibaguchi: **Shinbashi**
- Shimabara Uprising: **Shimabara no Ran**
- Shinbashi Station: **Shinbashi Eki**
- Shinjuku Station: **Shinjuku Eki**
Shintō charm and talisman: **ofuda, omamori**
Shintō family altar: **kamidana**
Shintō heaven: **Takamagahara**
Shintō religious costume: **saifuku**
Shintō shrine handwashing area: **temizuya**
Shintō shrine: **jinja**
Shintō wedding: **shinzen kekkon**
- shisutā bōi: **nyū hāfu**
- shogunate: **bakufu**
shout: **ki-ai**
- Shōwa Emperor: **Shōwa Tennō**
- Shōwa period: **Shōwa jidai**
shrine card: **senja-fuda**
shrine gate: **torii**

- shukueki: **shukuba machi**
- Shuto Expressway Wangan Line: **Shuto Kōsoku Wangan Sen**
  shutter, box for storing: **tobukuro**
  shuttlecock game: **hanetsuki**
- sickle and chain: **kusarigama**
  signature: **hanko**
- sister boy: **nyū hāfu**
  sitting cushion: **zabuton**
  skiing: **sukī**
  slips of paper pasted to temples and shrines: **senja-fuda**
- small individual table for food: **zen**
- small taverns: **izakaya**
- snack: **sunakku**
- snapping turtle: **suppon**
  sneeze: **kushami**
- Snow Festival, Sapporo: **Sapporo Yuki Matsuri**
- snow woman: **yuki onna**
- snowshoes: **kanjiki**
  soapland: **sōpurando**
- soba for the new year: **toshikoshi soba**
  socks with split toe: **tabi**
  sōmen: **hiyamugi, sōmen**
  song style: **enka**
  sorceress: **miko**
- soup stock: **dashi**
  soup: **misoshiru, zōni**
  souvenir: **miyage**
  soy sauce: **shoyu**
  soybean: **miso, nattō, Setsubun**
  soybean paste: **miso**
- soybeans boiled in the pod: **edamame**
  sparkler: **senkō-hanabi**
  spatula: **ichimonji**
  spiced sake: **toso**
  spirit lights: **hitodama**
- spoon, Chinese: **renge**
  spring onion: **negi**
  spy: **ninjutsu**
  square wooden box for sake: **masu**
  squid: **ika**
  stacked boxes used for holding

  food: **jūbako**
  stage: **yagura**
  stagehand: **kurogo**
  stamina drink: **eiyō drink**
- standard bearer: **hatamoto**
  standards and banners: **fū-rin-ka-zan, koinobori, matoi**
- standing lantern with shoji covering: **kaku andon**
- standing lantern, four legged: **kaku andon**
- standing screen: **tsuitate**
  standing under a waterfall: **mizugori**
  statue of man and dog in park: **Saigō Takamori**
- steamer, bamboo or wood: **seirō**
  stickers in phone booth: **pinkku bira**
  stickers pasted to temples andshrines: **senja-fuda**
- stick-shaped snack: **Pocky**
  stilts, "bamboo horse": **takeuma**
  stone dogs: **koma-inu**
  stone lantern: **ishi-dōrō**
  stone lions: **koma-inu**
- storage closets for futon: **oshiire**
- storehouse, traditional: **dozō**
  storm shutters: **amado, tobukuro**
- stove: **kamado**
- straw doll: **wara ningyō**
- straw figure, large: **sanemori-sama**
  straw raincoat: **mino**
  straw rope: **shimenawa**
  streamers on a stick: **gohei**
  street vendor: **yatai**
- style (martial arts): **ryū (martial arts style)**
- Sugawara Michizane: **Sugawara no Michizane**
  suicide, group: **shinjū**
  suicide: **seppuku, kaishakunin, shinjū**
- Sumida River: **Sumidagawa**
  sun goddess: **Amaterasu Ōmikami**
  supernatural being: **bakemono,**

  **baku, oni, kappa, kami, kitsune, tanuki, tengu**
  supernatural cat: **bakemononeko**
- Suwa, Lake: **Suwako**
- swallow: **tsubame**
  sweet potato: **satsumaimo**
- sweet snack: **yōkan**
- sword guard: **tsuba**
- sword hilt or handle: **tsuka**
- sword sheath or scabbard: **saya**
- sword wearing forbidden by law: **haitōrei**
- swordsmanship: **kenjutsu**
  syllabary: **kana**
- Szechwan pepper: **sanshō**

  table: **chabudai, kotatsu**
  tag: **onigokko**
- Taishō period: **Taishō jidai**
- Taito district: **Taitō-ku**
- Taito Ward: **Taitō-ku**
  Takarazuka Opera Company: **Takarazuka Kagekidan**
  taking off shoes: **genkan**
  talisman, Shintō: **ofuda, omamori**
  tangerine: **mikan**
  Tango Festival: **Kodomo no Hi**
- tanuki donburi: **tendon**
  tapir: **baku**
  tattoo: **irezumi**
- tavern, small: **izakaya**
  taxi: **takushī**
- TB: **kekkaku**
  tea bowl: **chawan**
- tea ceremony sweets: **yōkan**
  tea ceremony: **cha-no-yu**
  tea: **cha**
  teacher: **sensei**
  telephone: **denwa**
- television: **terebi**
- Tenman Tenjin: **Sugawara no Michizane**
  temple bell: **bonshō**
  temple dogs: **koma-inu**
  Temple of the Golden Pavilion: **Kinkakuji**
- tenpura and rice: **tendon**
- tenpura donburi: **tendon**

- tenpura noodles: **tenpura soba**
- Tenjin: **Sugawara no Michizane**
  tennis: **tenisu**
- thick noodles: **udon**
  Third Month Festival: **hina matsuri**
  throwing soybeans: **setsubun**
- throwing stars: **shuriken**
- tidal wave: **tsunami**
- tile fish: **amadai**
- tile, end, with demon face: **onigawara**
- tile, roof: **kawara**
  TMPD: **Keishichō**
- toad oil: **gama no abura**
- Toba-Fushimi, Battle of: **Toba-Fushimi no Tatakai**
- Tochigi Prefecture: Tochigi Ken
- tōfu lees: **o-kara**
- tōfu seller on bicycle: **tōfu-ya**
- Togakushi Shrine: **Togakushi Jinja**
  toilet, Japanese: **benjo**
- Tōkai region: **Tōkai chihō**
- Tokkōtai: **Kamikaze Tokubetsu Kōgekitai**
- Tokugawa Keiki: **Tokugawa Yoshinobu**
- Tokyo Bay: **Tōkyō Wan**
- Tokyo Chūō Oroshiurishijō: **Tsukiji Shijō**
  Tokyo City Hall: **Tōkyō Tochōsha**
- Tokyo Disneyland: **Tokyo Dizunīrando**
  Tokyo Dome: **Tōkyō Dōmu**
- Tokyo Earthquake of 1923: **Kantō Daishinsai**
  Tokyo International Airport: **Tōkyō Kokusai Kūkō**
  Tokyo Metropolitan Government Offices: **Tōkyō Tochōsha**
  Tokyo Metropolitan Police: **Keishichō**
- Tokyo National Museum: **Tokyo Kokuritsu Hakubutsukan**
  Tokyo Station: **Tōkyō Eki**
- Tokyo Stock Exchange: **Tokyo Shōken Torihikijo**

Tokyo Tower: **Tōkyō Tawā**
Tokyo University: **Tōkyō Daigaku**
- Tokyo War Trials: **Sensō Hanzai ni Kansuru Saiban**
- top: **koma**
- tori no machi: **tori no ichi**
  tossing soybeans: **setsubun**
  town committee or council: **chōnaikai**
  toy: **kaishakunin,**
- traditional storehouse: **dozō**
  train: **commuter trains, Shinkansen**
- training (warrior's) pilgrimage or journey: **musha shugyō**
  training hall: **dōjō**
- tray, flat for serving food: **oshiki**
- Treaty of Kanagawa: **Nichibei Washin Jōyaku**
- Treaty of Peace and Amity Between the United States and the Empire of Japan: **Nichibei Washin Jōyaku**
  tree, sacred: **shinboku**
- tsuka-gashira: **kashira**
- Tsukiji fish market: **Tsukiji Shijō**
- tuberculosis: **kekkaku**
- tuifa: **tonfa**
  turkish bath: **sōpurando**
- turtle, snapping: **suppon**
- tv: **terebi**
  twelve guardians of yakushi-nyorai: **jūni-jinshō**
  typhoon: **taifū**

- U.S. Air Force Base at Yokota: **Yokota Air Base**
- U.S.-Japan treaties: **Nichibei Shūkō Tsūshō Jōyaku (1858), Nichibei Washin Jōyaku (1854)**
  Ueno Park: **Ueno Kōen**
  Ueno Zoo: **Ueno Dōbutsuen**
- Uguisudani Station: **Uguisudani Eki**
  umbrella: **kasa**
- unadon: **unagi donburi**
  underwear: **fundoshi**

- United States Armed Forces in Japan: **Zainichi Beigun**
  university: **Teikoku Daigaku**
  unohana: **o-kara**
  urinating in the street: **tachishōben**

Vajra: **kongōshō**
Valentine's Day: **Sei Barentain no Shukujitsu**
- Valley of the Bush Warblers: **Uguisudani**
- vegetables, mountain: **sansai**
- vegetarian cooking: **shōjin ryōri**
  vending machine: **jidō-hanbaiki**
  vengeful ghost: **goryō**
  veranda: **engawa**
- Versailles no Bara: **Berusaiya no Bara**
  visiting grave: **meinichi, hakamairi**
  visiting shrine: **hatsumōde**
  vitamin drink: **eiyō drink**
  volcano: **Asamayama, Aso-san**
  votive card: **senja-fuda**

- wa sierō: **seirō**
- wall and screen painting: **shōheiga**
  wallet: **inrō**
- Wangan Expressway: **Shuto Kōsoku Wangan Sen**
- war literature: **sensō bungaku**
- warning staff: **keisaku**
  Warring States period: **Sengoku jidai**
- warrior pilgrimage or journey: **musha shugyō**
- warrior: **bushi**
  Waseda University: **Waseda Daigaku**
- water heater, wall mounted: **yuwakashiki**
- *Water Margin*: **Suikoden**
  water, used in purification: **misogi, mizugori**
  watermelon smashing with a stick: **suika-wari**

- watermelon: **suika**
  waving
- way of the fist: **kenpō**
  "Way of the Sword": **kendō**
- way of the warrior: **bushidō**
  weapon. See "Weaponry/War"
  in section "Entries Arranged by
  Category"
- wearing headband with candles:
  **ushi no koku mairi**
  wearing surgical mask on the
  street: **surgical masks worn in
  public**
- wearing swords forbidden by
  law: **haitōrei**
  wedding ceremony: **shinzen
  kekkon**
- welsh onion: **negi**
- Western Pure Land: **Gokuraku**
  white costume for religious
  ceremony: **saifuku**
- white square mask: **zōmen**
- White Tiger Brigade: **Byakkotai**
- wild boar: **inoshishi**

- wild greens: **sansai**
  willow: **yanagi**
  wind bell: **fūrin**
  wind, forest, fire, mountain: **fū-
  rin-ka-zan**
- woman deceiver: **onnatarashi**
- woman, young: **shōjo**
- wood or bamboo food steamer:
  **seirō**
- wooden chest: **tansu**
  wooden paddle for game: **hagoita**
  wooden plaques, hanging: **ema**
  wooden sandals: **geta**
  wooden stakes in graveyard:
  **sotoba**
  wooden sword: **bokken**
  word game: **shiritori**
  wrapping cloth: **furoshiki**
  wrestling: **sumō**
  writing: **kanji, kana**

- x-rated films: **pinku eiga**

- Yakushi Temple: **Yakushiji**

- Yamaguchi Prefecture:
  **Yamaguchi Ken**
- yamaimo: **yamanoimo**
- Yamanote line: **Yamanote sen**
  Yankee: **yankī**
  year's end cleaning: **susu-harai**
- yen: **en**
  yin-yang block: **sangi**
- Yokohama Bay Bridge:
  **Yokohama Bei Buriji**
- yolk of an egg in sake: **tamago-
  zake**
- Yoshida Masaaki: **Yoshida Tōyō**
- yoshido: **yoshizu**
- young woman: **shōjo**
- yuki jorō: **yuki onna**

- Zeke fighter: **Zerosen**
- zelkova: **keyaki**
- zen meditation: **zazen**
- zen stick: **keisaku**
- Zero fighter: **Zerosen**
- Zero-type carrier-based fighter:
  **Zerosen**

## ENTRIES ARRANGED BY CATEGORY

This glossary contains entries from both Volume 1 and Volume 2 of *The Anime Companion*. Entries in
this volume are marked by a bullet.

### *Building/Structure/Landmark*

- Akihabara Eki (Akihabara
  Station)
  Aoyama Reien
  Asakusa Jinja
  Budōkan
  depāto (department store)
  dōjō (training hall)
- dozō (traditional storehouse)
- Edojō (Edo Castle)
- Himejijō (Himeji Castle)
  Hōryūji
  Ise Jingū (Ise Shrine)
  Izumo Taisha
  jiin (Buddhist temple)
  jinja (Shintō shrine)
- Kabukiza

Kaminarimon
- Kaneiji
  Keio Puraza Hoteru (Keio Plaza
  Hotel)
  Kinkakuji (Temple of the Golden
  Pavilion)
  kissaten (coffeehouse)
  Kiyomizudera
  kōban (police box)
- Kokuritsu Kagaku Hakubutsukan
  (National Science Museum)
- kōsoku dōro (expressway)
- Masakado-zuka (Masakado's
  mound)
- Masuya
  Meiji Jingū (Meiji shrine)
  My City

- nagaya (row house)
  Nihonbashi
- Odaiba Kaihin Kōen (Odaiba
  Seaside Park)
  rabu hoteru (love hotel)
- Rainbow Bridge
- Ryōgokubashi
  ryokan (Japanese inn)
- Ryōunkaku
  Sensōji
  sentō (public bath)
- Shinbashi Eki (Shinbashi Station)
  Shin Tōkyō Kokusai Kūkō (New
  Tokyo International Airport)
- Shinjuku Eki (Shinjuku Station)
  shiro (castle)
- Shuto Kōsoku Wangan Sen

(Bayshore Expressway)
- Studio ALTA
Teikoku Daigaku (Imperial University)
- Teikoku Hoteru (Imperial Hotel)
- Togakushi Jinja
Tōkyō Daigaku (Tokyo University)
- Tokyo Dizunīrando (Tokyo Disneyland)
Tōkyō Dōmu
Tōkyō Eki (Tokyo Station)
- Tokyo Kokuritsu Hakubutsukan (Tokyo National Museum)
Tōkyō Kokusai Kūkō
- Tokyo Shōken Torihikijo (Tokyo Stock Exchange)
Tōkyō Tawa (Tokyo Tower)
Tōkyō Tochōsha (Tokyo Metropolitan Government Offices)
- Tsukiji Shijō (Tsukiji fish market)
Tsūtenkaku (Osaka Tower)
Ueno Dōbutsuen (Ueno Zoo)
Ueno Eki (Ueno Train Station)
Ueno Kōen (Ueno Park)
- Uguisudani Eki (Uguisudani Station)
- Wakō Clock Tower
- Waseda Daigaku (Waseda University)
- Yakushiji
- Yamanote sen (Yamanote line)
- Yokohama bei buriji (Yokohama Bay Bridge)

## Clothing

burūma (gym shorts worn by girls)
fundoshi (loincloth)
geta (wooden sandals)
hachimaki (headband)
hakama (trousers)
hana-kanzashi (hairpin)
haori (jacket)
happi (coat)
inrō
- kanjiki (snowshoes)

kappōgi (cooking apron)
kimono
kushi (comb)
mino (rainwear)
obi (sash, belt)
sailor fuku (sailor suit)
sando-gasa (hat)
tabi (split-toed sock)
- tsuna (rope)
tsunokakushi (headdress)
yukata (lightweight kimono)
zōri (thonged sandals)

## Culture

aka to shiro (red and white)
akushu suru (shaking hands)
Akutagawa Shō
Awa Odori
bakemono (monster)
bakeneko (monster cat)
baku (dream eater)
banzai
cha-no-yu (tea ceremony)
Crane Wife
dogs and pregnant women
drinks, pouring for another
four things to fear in life
gairaigo (loanword)
- Gion Matsuri (Gion Festival)
goryō (vengeful ghost)
hanami (flower viewing)
hatsumōde
- hentai
Hina Matsuri (Doll Festival)
- hōzuki ichi (Chinese-lantern plant market)
- ikebana (flower arranging)
- iroha
- kabuki mono
kana (syllabary)
kanji (chinese character)
- kekkaku (tuberculosis)
Kintarō
Kodomo no Hi (Children's Day)
koinobori (carp streamer)
kon'in (marriage)
- kondomu (condom)
Kurisumasu (Christmas)

Man'yōshū
matsuri to nenchū gyōji (festivals and annual events)
Nebuta Matsuri (Nebuta Festival)
nengajō (New Year's card)
ningyo (mermaid)
- nomi-ya
- nyū hāfu (she-male)
ojigi(bow)
okuribi (ritual bonfire)
omiai
oni (demon)
- rezubian (lesbian)
- Saiyūki (Journey to the West)
- Sanka (a nomadic people)
- Sapporo Yuki Matsuri (Sapporo Snow Festival)
Sei Barentain no Shukujitsu (Valentine's Day)
- Seijin no Hi (Coming-of-Age Day)
- sensō bungaku (war literature)
Setsubun
Shichi-go-san (7-5-3 Festival)
- shichiya (naming a baby)
shinzen kekkon (Shintō wedding)
- soroban (abacus)
- Suikoden (Outlaws of the Marsh)
taiko (large drum)
Tanabata
tengu (mountain spirit)
- tori no ichi (bird fair)
- tsūshō
- virgin road
White Day
- Yamato
yobikō (cram school)
- yōmyō (male child's name)
- yūrei (ghost)
- zōmen (white square mask)

## Entertainment/Game

aidoru ("idol" singer)
- akabeko (bobbing ox toy)
- Berusaiya no Bara (The Rose of Versailles)
biwa
- bugaku

bunraku
- charumera
chindonya (music maker)
dōjinshi (fanzine)
- dojōsukui
enka (popular song)
enkai (party)
firecrackers in the sky
- gekkin (moon lute)
go
hagoita (paddle)
hanabi (fireworks)
hanafuda
- izakaya (small tavern)
jan-ken
- kabuki
kai-awase (shell-matching game)
- kaiju (giant monster)
- kami-shibai
karaoke
kendama (cup and ball toy)
kingyo-sukui (goldfish dipping)
- koma (spinning top)
Komiketto
- kosupure (costume play)
koto
kurogo (stagehand)
mājan (mah-jongg)
manga (Japanese comic)
- Märchen (magical folk tale)
mokugyo
- Nō
- ohajiki
okame
onigokko (tag)
- origami
Osero ("Othello")
pachinko
- pinku eiga (pink movie, sex films)
- rajio taisō (radio calisthenics)
saikoro (dice)
- Sanmon Gosan no Kiri
saru mawashi (monkey show)
senkō-hanabi (sparkler)
shakuhachi
shamisen
shiritori (word game)
shōgi (Japanese "chess")
- shunga (erotic art)

suika-wari (watermelon game)
- sunakku (bar)
Takarazuka Kagekidan
  (Takarazuka Opera Company)
takeuma (bamboo horse or stilts)
tako-age (kite flying)
- terebi (television)
uma-yaku
uta karuta (poem card)
- yagura (stage)
- YAOI

## Food and Drink

- akagai
- amadai
- ankō
anmitsu
- anpan
bentō (box lunch for one person)
bīru (beer)
Boss Coffee
Calpis
cha (tea)
chanpon
chazuke
- chikuwa (fish sausage)
- chirinabe (hot pot dish)
- Choco Flake
choko (sake cup)
chōshoku (breakfast)
- chūka ryōri-ya (Chinese
  restaurant)
daikon (radish)
- dango (dumpling)
- dashi (soup stock)
- donabe (ceramic pot)
donburi (food bowl)
- edamame
eiyō drink (nutritional
  supplement drink)
ekiben (station) lunch
fugu (puffer fish)
- fugu-chiri
- gobō (burdock)
gohan (cooked rice)
- Green Gum
gyōza (potsticker)
gyūdon (beef bowl)

- gyūnabe (beef hot pot)
- hanpen (fish paste cake)
hashi (chopsticks)
- hatahata (sandfish)
haze (goby)
- hirekatsu (fried pork filet)
hisago (gourd)
hiyamugi, sōmen (noodles)
ika (squid and cuttlefish)
- ikura
- IN Shirīzu
- kaki (persimmon)
kakigōri-ki (shaved ice)
- kama meshi
- kanten
- karashi (mustard)
- karē (curry)
karē raisu (curry rice)
kashiwa mochi
- katsudon (pork cutlet donburi)
- katsuobushi (dried bonito)
kayu (rice porridge)
- kezuribushi (shaved dried bonito)
- kibidango
- kinpira-gobō
- konbu (kelp)
konnyaku (devil's tongue root)
- konpeitō
- korokke (croquette)
- kusasotetsu (ostrich fern)
- kushi-dango
- kuzu mochi (arrowroot cake)
kyūri (cucumber)
manjū (bun, dumpling)
masu (box measure)
- men rui (noodles)
mikan
mismatched foods
miso (soy bean paste)
- miso-rāmen
misoshiru (miso soup)
mochi (rice cake)
- mugicha (barley tea)
- nabemono (one pot meal)
- nabeyaki-udon
naruto
nasu (eggplant)
nattō
- negi (spring onion)

nigirimeshi (rice ball)
- ninjin
noodle slurping
nori (seaweed, laver)
oden
- ohagi (equinox bean cake)
- okara (tōfu lees)
okonomiyaki
- okosama-ranchi (child's plate)
- omuraisu (omelet rice)
osechi-ryōri (New Year's food)
- panko (bread crumbs)
- Pocari Sweat
- Pocky
rāmen (noodles)
- Ramune
- renge (Chinese spoon)
- renkon (lotus root)
sakazuki (sake cup)
sake
- sakura mochi
- sanma
- sansai (mountain vegetables)
- sanshō (Szechwan pepper)
- sashimi (sliced raw meat)
satsumaimo (sweet potato)
- sekihan (rice with red beans)
senbei (rice cracker)
shabu-shabu
- shichimi tōgarashi (seven spice mix)
shichirin (ceramic brazier)
- shiitake
shiruko
- shōchū (hard liquor)
- shōjin ryōri (vegetarian cooking)
shokuhin sanpuru (food model)
shōyu (soy sauce)
- shūmai (dim sum)
- soba
- suika (watermelon)
sukiyaki
- suppon (snapping turtle)
sushi
- tai (sea bream)
tai-yaki
takenokawa (bamboo sheath)
- takenoko (bamboo shoot)

tako (octopus)
takoyaki
- tamago (egg)
- tamago-zake (egg yolk in sake)
- teishoku (set meal)
- tenpura
- tenpura soba (tenpura noodles)
- tendon (tenpura and rice)
- teppan (iron plate)
- tōfu
tokkuri (sake flask)
- tōmorokoshi (corn on the cob)
- tonkatsu (pork cutlet)
- toshikoshi soba (New Year's soba)
toso
- tsukemono (pickle)
- Tsukune (meatballs)
UCC Coffee
- udon
ume
umeboshi (salted Japanese apricot)
umeshu (plum "wine")
unagi (eel)
- unagi donburi
- wakame
- warabi (bracken)
- wasabi
- yakimeshi (fried rice)
- yakiniku-ya (Korean barbeque restaurant)
yakisoba (noodles)
yakitori
- yamanoimo
- yatsuhashi
- yōkan
- zakuro (pomegranate)
- zōni

## General

aka-chōchin (red lantern)
atena (address)
benjo (toilet)
bōsōzoku (gang)
chalk marks and illegally parked cars

chōchin (hanging paper lantern)
commuter train
- daikan
- daimyō (han lord)
- demae (delivery of prepared food)
denwa (telephone)
- en (yen)
- gama no abura (toad oil)
hachikō
hankachi (handkerchief)
hanko (seal)
hara (stomach, belly)
hari (acupuncture)
he (fart)
headlights off
hiuchi-ishi (flint and steel)
homurūmu (homeroom)
irezumi (tattoo)
ishi-dōrō (stone lantern)
Jē Aru (JR)
jidō-hanbaiki (vending machine)
jinrikisha (rickshaw)
kago (sedan chair)
kaishakunin
kappa
kasa (umbrella)
kasō (cremation)
kasō (geomancy)
ketsueki-gata (blood type)
ki (spirit, life force)
ki-ai (shout)
kiseru (tobacco pipe)
kisu (kiss)
- koku (volume measurement)
koshi (palanquin)
kushami (sneeze)
- kuwa (hoe)
kyū (moxibustion)
- Lotte Co., Ltd.
magatama (beads)
Makudonarudo (McDonald's)
manekineko ("beckoning cat")
- maru
meishi (business card)
mimikaki (ear scoop)
- Mitsubishi
miyage (souvenir)
mizuhiki (decorative cords)

mother-in-law
neko (cat)
Nippon Denshin Denwa (Nippon Telegraph and Telephone Corporation)
Nippon Hōsō Kyōkai (Japan Broadcasting Corporation)
noren (split curtains)
- nozoki (peeping Tom)
ōgi (folding fan)
- okama (male homosexual, derogatory)
- onnatarashi (playboy)
otaku
pinkku bira ("pink leaflets")
poke-beru (beeper)
red triangle
renraku-sen (ferryboat)
rorikon ("lolita complex")
sangi (yin-yang divination block)
seidōkyō (bronze mirror)
senbazuru (origami paper cranes)
shiken jigoku (examination hell)
shinbun (newspaper)
shinjū (double or group suicide)
Shinkansen (New Trunk Line, Bullet Train)
shishiodoshi (deer scare)
- shōjo (young woman)
shōyo (bonus)
shūgaku ryokō (school trip)
shūgakuzen kyōiku (preschool education)
sōpurando ("soapland")
students cleaning school
sumi (ink)
surgical masks worn in public
suzu (round bells)
tachishōben (peeing in the street)
takushi (taxi)
tanzaku
- taraibune (tub boat)
- tetsudō (railway)
- tōfu-ya (tōfu seller)
tsūkin (commuting)
tsuri-dōrō (hanging lantern)

uchiwa (non-folding fan)
water holding as punishment
yatai (outdoor stall)
yōshi (adoption)
- Yoshinoya
- yoshizu (reed screen)
yuinō (betrothal gift)
- zōki ishioku (organ transplant)

## Geographical Feature/Location

- Adachi-ku
Aichi Ken
- Aizu Bonchi (Aizu Basin)
- Aizu Han
- Akasaka
Akashi
Akihabara
Aoyama
- Arai-chō
- Arakawa-ku
- Arashiyama
Asakusa
Asamayama
Aso-san (Mt. Aso)
Atami
- Awajishima
- Azabu
Azabu Jūban
- Biwako (Lake Biwa)
Chiba Ken
- Chigasaki
- Chiyoda-ku
- Chōshi
- Chōshū Han
Dotonbori
- Edo
- Edogawa-ku
Enoshima
- Fuji Goko (Fuji Five Lakes)
Fuji-san (Mt. Fuji)
- Fukagawa
- Fukushima Ken
- Gifu Ken
Ginza
Gion
- Gunma Ken
- Hachiōji

- Hagi
- Hakodate
Hakone
Harajuku
Hayama
- Hibiya
Hida Sanmyaku
- Hieizan (Mount Hiei)
Hiroshima
Hokkaido
Honshu
- Hyōgo Ken
Ibaraki Ken
- Inokashira Onshi Kōen
- Iriya
Iruma
Ise
- Iwate Ken
Izumo
- Kabukichō
Kamakura
Kanagawa Ken
- Kanaya
Kantō chihō (Kantō region)
- ken (prefecture)
- Kōbe
- Kōchi Ken
- Kōtō-ku
Kōya-san (Mt. Kōya)
Kuramayama
Kyoto
Kyushu
- Maebashi
- Mie Ken
- Minato-ku
- Mitaka
- Mito Han
Miyagi Ken
- Morioka
Nagasaki
- Nakano-ku
- Nakasendō
- Nara
- Nerima-ku
- Nihonkai (Sea of Japan)
- Okayama Ken
Okinawa Ken
Onomichi


145

Ōsaka
- Ōtsu
Roppongi
- Sakata
Sapporo
- Senju
- Seto Naikai (Seto Inland Sea)
- Shibuya-ku
- Shikoku
Shimane Ken
- Shinbashi
- Shimo Suwa
- Shimoda
- Shimonoseki
- Shinagawa-ku
Shinjuku
- Shizuoka Ken
- Sumidagawa
- Suwako (Lake Suwa)
- Taitō-ku
- Tama Chiku (Tama Area)
- Tama Nyū Taun (Tama New Town)
- Tochigi Ken
- Togakushi
- Tōkai chihō (Tōkai region)
- Tōkaidō
- Tokyo
- Tōkyō Wan (Tokyo Bay)
- Tomakomai
- Tosa Han
- Tsukudajima
- Ueno
- Uguisudani (Valley of the Bush Warblers)
- Urayasu
- Utsunomiya
- Yamaguchi Ken
- Yamashina
- Yokohama
- Yokosuka
- Yokota Air Base
- Yotsuya

## History/Society

- Ansei no Taigoku (Ansei Purge)
- bakufu (shogunate)

- bakumatsu
- Boshin Sensō (Boshin Civil War)
chōnaikai (neighborhood association)
- Dai Nippon Teikoku Rikugun (Imperial Japanese Army)
Edo Period
- Emishi
- Engi Era
February 26, 1936
- fudai daimyō
fū-rin-ka-zan
- genpuku (boy's coming of age ceremony)
gissha (ox cart)
- Goryōkaku no Tatakai (Battle of Goryōkaku)
- Haitōrei
- Hamaguri Gomon no Hen
- han (daimyō domain)
hata (ceremonial banner)
- hatamoto (bannermen)
Heian Period
Heike Monogatari
Heisei Period
- Ikedaya Jiken
- ikki (peasant revolt)
Jiyū Minshutō (Liberal Democratic Party)
Jukyō (Confucianism)
Kamakura Period
- Kantō Daishinsai (Tokyo Earthquake of 1923)
Keishichō (Tōkyō Metropolitan Police Department)
Keizai Kikaku Chō (Economic Planning Agency)
ken'etsu (censorship)
- Kōan no Eki (Kōan War)
Kokkai (Diet)
Kōseishō (Ministry of Health and Welfare)
- Kyōto Shoshidai (Kyoto Deputy)
- Kyōto Shugoshoko (Kyoto Military Commissioner)
matoi (banner, standard)
Meiji Period
Minamoto

Minshatō (Democratic Socialist Party)
mon (family or organizational crest)
Muromachi Period
- Naimushō (Ministry of the Interior)
- Nichibei Shūkō Tsūshō Jōyaku (Japan-U.S. Friendship and Commerce Treaty)
- Nichibei Washin Jōyaku (Treaty of Kanagawa)
Nihon Kōgyō Kikaku (Japanese Industrial Standards)
Nihon Kyōsantō (Japanese Communist Party)
Nihonkoku Kenpō (Constitution of Japan)
ninjutsu
- niwaban
nobori (banner)
- sankin kōtai (alternative attendance)
- Satchō Dōmei (Satsuma-Chōshū Alliance)
- Satsuma Han
- Seinan Sensō (Satsuma Rebellion)
- Sekigahara no Tatakai (Battle of Sekigahara)
Sengoku jidai
- sensō hanzai ni kansuru saiban (Tokyo war trials)
seppuku (ritual suicide)
- Shimabara no Ran (Shimabara Uprising)
- Shinsengumi
- shishi (men of high purpose)
- Shōgitai
- Shōwa jidai (Shōwa period)
- shukuba machi (post station town)
- sonnō jōi (revere the emperor, expel the barbarians)
taira
- Taishō jidai (Taishō period)
tenshō ken'ō shisetsu
- Toba-Fushimi no Tatakai (Battle of Toba-Fushimi)

Tokugawa
tozama daimyō
Tsūshō Sangyō Shō (Ministry
of International Trade and
Industry)

## Home

amado (rain doors)
- byōbu (folding screen)
chabudai
chawan (small bowl)
- chigai-dana (cloud shelves)
denki-gama (electric rice cooker)
engawa (veranda)
fūrin (wind bell)
furo (bath)
furoshiki (carrying cloth)
fusuma
futon
genkan (entryway)
hataki
hibachi (charcoal heater)
ichimonji (spatula)
irori (sunken hearth)
jizaikagi (pot hook)
jūbako (stacking boxes)
kadomatsu (pine gate)
- kaidan tansu
kakemono (hanging scroll)
- kaku andon (four-legged standing
lantern)
- kama (cooking pot)
- kamado (stove)
- kawara (roof tiles)
kotatsu
makura (pillow)
- nabe (iron pot)
- onigawara (demon-faced edge tile)
- oshiire (futon storage closet)
- oshiki (flat serving tray)
- otoshibuta (drop lid)
ranma (transom)
renting
- rōsoku (candle)
- seirō (food steamer)
shachihoko (dolphin roof
ornament)

shataku (company housing)
- shōheiga (screen and wall
painting)
shōji
sudare (hanging blinds)
susu-harai (end-of-year-house-
cleaning)
- tansu (wooden chest)
tatami
- teshoku (portable candle holder)
tobukuro (pocket door)
tokonoma (decorative alcove)
- tsuitate (standing screen)
- yuwakashiki (wall-mounted water
heater)
- zabuton (floor cushion)
- zaisu (legless chair)
- zen (small individual table for
food)

## Nature

ajisai (Japanese hydrangea)
asagao (morning glory)
- ayame (iris)
bonsai
ginkgo
heikegani
hoshi-suna ("star" sand)
hotaru (firefly)
- hōzuki (Chinese-lantern plant)
- inoshishi (wild boar)
jishin (earthquake)
kaede to momoji (maple tree)
karasu (crow)
- keyaki (zelkova)
kiku (chrysanthemum)
kingyo (goldfish)
kitsune (fox)
koi (carp)
kurage (jellyfish)
onsen (hot spring)
sakura (cherry blossom)
saru (monkey)
semi (cicada)
shika (deer)
- sugi (cedar)
- susuki (pampas grass)

taifū (typhoon)
tanuki
- tsubaki (camellia)
- tsubame (swallow)
- tsunami (tidal wave)
tsuru (crane)
- yanagi (willow)

## People

aging population
Ainu
Akagawa Jirō
Akutagawa Ryūnosuke
- Amakusa Shirō
- Arima Kihei
Bakin
- Bando Tamasaburo V
- Bashō
Benkei
biwa hōshi ("lute priest")
Dōgen
- Edogawa Rampo
En no Gyōja
Enomoto Ken'ichi
gaijin (foreigner)
geisha
Genji
Hayashi Fumiko
Hearn, Lafcadio
Higuchi Ichiyō
- Hijikata Toshizō
hosutesu ("hostess")
- Ii Naosuke
- Ikeda Terumasa
- Ikumatsu
- Ishida Mitsunari
Ishihara Shintarō
Ishikawa Goemon
- Ishikawa Takuboku
- Itagaki Taisuke
Izumi Kyōka
- Izumo no Okuni
- Katō Kiyomasa
- Katsu Kaishū
Kawabata Yasunari
- Kido Takayoshi
kidōtai (riot police)

147

- Kobayashi Issa
- Kondō Isami
- Konishi Yukinaga
  Kume Masao
  Kurama Tengu
  maiko (apprentice geisha)
  miko (shrine maiden)
  Minamoto no Yorimitsu
  Minamoto no Yoshitsune
- Miyabe Teizō
  Miyamoto Musashi
  Miyazawa Kenji
  Momotarō (Peach Boy)
  Mori Ōgai
  Murasaki Shikubu
  Mushanokōji Saneatsu
  Natsume Sōseki
- Nezumi Kozō
- Oda Nobunaga
- Oguri Tadamasa
  Okada Keisuke
- Okita Sōji
- Ōkubo Toshimichi
  OL ("office lady")
  Ōtomo no Yakamochi
  Ozaki Shirō
- Perry, Matthew Calbraith
  rōnin
  Saigō Takamori
  Saigyō
- Sakamoto Ryōma
  samurai
  sarariman ("salaried man")
  senpai (senior)
  sensei (teacher, master)
  Shinran
  shōgun
- Shōwa Tennō (Shōwa Emperor)
- Son Goku
- Sugawara no Michizane
- Taira no Masakado
- Takasugi Shinsaku
- Takuan Sōhō
  Tanizaki Jun'ichirō
- Tokugawa Iemitsu
- Tokugawa Ieyasu
- Tokugawa Mitsukuni
- Tokugawa Yorinobu
- Tokugawa Yoshimune

- Tokugawa Yoshinobu
  Toyotomi Hideyoshi
- Tsukahara Bokuden
  Urashima Tarō
- Yagyū Jūbei Mitsuyoshi
  yakuza (gangster)
- Yamagata Aritomo
- Yamayoshi Morisuke
  yankī ("yankee," juvenile
    delinquent)
- yopparai (a drunk)
- Yoshida Shōin
- Yoshida Tōyō
- Yoshikawa Eiji

## Religion/Mythology/Belief

- Adachigahara
  Amaterasu Ōmikami
  Benten
  Bishamon
  Bon
  Bon Odori
  bonshō
  bosatsu (boddhisattva)
  Bukkyō
  butsudan (Buddhist altar)
  daikokuten
  daruma
  ebisu
  ema (votive tablet)
  ennichi (feast day)
  fudō-myōō
  fukurokuju
  gohei
- Gokuraku (Western Pure Land)
- Hachiman
  hakamairi
  hamaya
  hitodama (spirit lights)
  Hotei
  inari
  inori (prayer)
  inzō
  Jizō
  Joya no kane
  Jūni Jinshō
  junrei (pilgrimage)
  juzu (rosary)

- kagura
- kaihōgyō
  kaimyō
  kami
  kamidana (Shintō altar)
  kashiwade
- Katsuragawa Geango
  kei (bell)
- keisaku or kyōsaku (Zen stick)
  Kirisutokyō (Christianity)
  koma-inu
  kongōshō (vajra)
  kuji
- kumade (bamboo rake)
  meinichi (death anniversary)
- mikkyō (esoteric Buddhism)
  mikoshi (portable shrine)
  mikuji (fortune stick)
  misogi (purification)
  mizugori (waterfall purification)
  nenbutsu
  ofuda
  okiku
  omamori (amulet)
  Raijin (god of thunder)
- ryū (dragon)
  saifuku
  saisen (money offering)
- Sanemori-sama
- Sanzu no Kawa (River Styx)
  senja-fuda (shrine card)
  Shichifuku-jin (seven deities of
    good fortune)
  shimenawa (sacred rope)
  shinboku (sacred tree)
  shinkō shūkyō (new religion)
  shintai ("kami-body")
  Shintō
  shugendō
  sotoba
  Susanoo-no-mikoto
  tachimono (something abstained
    from)
  Takamagahara (plain of high
    heaven)
  temizuya
  tennyo (heavenly maiden,
    nymph, angel)
  teruteru bōzu (rain doll)

torii (shrine gate)
tsukimono otoshi (exorcism)
- ushi no koku mairi (nailing doll to tree)
- wara ningyō (straw doll)
yamabushi (mountain ascetic)
- yuki onna (snow woman)
Zashiki Warashi
- zazen (Zen meditation)
- zeichiku
- Zen (Buddhism)
- Zenki

## Sport/Activity

- aikidō
hanetsuki
jūdō
jūjutsu
kata (form or sequence)
kemari (Japanese football)
kendō ("way of the sword")
kōkō yakyū (high school baseball)
kyūdō (Japanese archery)

- ryū (martial arts style)
sukī (skiing)
sumō
tenisu (tennis)

## Weaponry/War

- ashigaru (foot soldiers)
- battō-jutsu
- Betty (aircraft)
bokken (wooden sword)
- bushi (warrior)
- bushidō (way of the warrior)
- Byakkotai (White Tiger Brigade)
Dannoura no Tatakai
- Emily (aircraft)
- Hokushin Ittō Ryū
Jieitai (Self Defense Forces; SDF)
- Jigen Ryū
jitte (truncheon)
- Kamikaze Tokubetsu Kōgekitai (Kamikaze Special Attack Force)
- kashira
- kenpō
- kenjutsu (swordsmanship)

- Kiheitai
- kusarifundo (weighted chain)
- kusarigama (chain and sickle)
- kusari-katabira (chail mail vest)
- Mugai Ryū
- musha shugyō (warrior pilgrimage)
naginata (halberd)
Nichiro Sensō (Russo-Japanese War)
nihontō (Japanese sword)
- Ōka
- saya (scabbard)
shinai (bamboo sword)
- shuriken (throwing stars)
- suntetsu
- taryū-jiai (duel)
- teppō (firearm)
- tonfa
- tsuba (sword guard)
- tsuka (sword hilt)
- Yamato (battleship)
- Zainichi Beigun (United States Armed Forces in Japan)
- Zerosen (Zero fighter)

# SIDEBARS

Following are titles of all the sidebar columns in Volume 1 and Volume 2 of *The Anime Companion*. Entries in this volume are marked by a bullet.

# SELECTED REFERENCES

Arai, Yūsei. *Shingon Esoteric Buddhism: A Handbook for Followers*. Fresno, Calif.: Shingon Buddhist International Institute, 1997.

Ashburne, John, and Abe Yoshi. *World Food Japan*. Victoria, Australia: Lonely Planet, 2002.

Averbuch, Irit. *The Gods Come Dancing*. Vol. 79 of *Cornell East Asia Series*. Ithaca, N.Y.: East Asia Program Cornell University, 1995.

Baten, Lea. *Identifying Japanese Dolls: Notes on Ningyo*. Leiden, Netherlands: Hotei Publishing, 2000.

Benjamin, Gail R. *Japanese Lessons*. New York: New York University Press, 1997.

Bestor, Theodore C. *Tsukiji*. Berkeley: University of California Press, 2004.

Bisignani, J. D. *Japan Handbook*. 2nd ed. Chico, Calif.: Moon Publications, 1993.

Bocking, Brian. *A Popular Dictionary of Shinto*. Richmond, Surry: Curzon Books, 1996.

Bornoff, Nicholas, and Michael Freeman. *Things Japanese*. Hong Kong: Periplus Editions, 2002.

Buckingham, Dorothea N. *Essential Guide to Sumo*. Honolulu: Bess Press, 1994.

Bush, Lewis. *Japanalia: A Concise Encyclopedia*. Tokyo: Tokyo News Service, 1965.

*Cambridge History of Japan*. Vol. 1. Cambridge: Cambridge University Press. 1993.

Campbell, Sid. *Exotic Weapons of the Ninja*. Secaucus, N.Y.: Citadel Press, 1999.

Chamberlain, Basil Hall. *Japanese Things*. Original published as *Things Japanese*. Rutland, Vt.: Charles E. Tuttle, 1971.

Cherry, Kittredge. *Womansword: What Japanese Words Say About Women*. Tokyo and New York: Kodansha International, 1987.

Clements, Jonathan, and Helen McCarthy. *The Anime Encyclopedia*. Berkeley: Stone Bridge Press, 2001.

Condon, Jack, and Camy Condon. *The Simple Pleasures of Japan*. Tokyo: Shufunotomo, 1975.

Constantine, Peter. *Japanese Street Slang*. New York: Tengu Books, 1992.

Craig, Albert M. *Chōshū in the Meiji Restoration*. Cambridge, Mass.: Harvard University Press, 1961.

Cunningham, Don. *Secret Weapons of Jujutsu*. Boston: Charles E. Tuttle, 2002.

———. *Taiho-Jutsu*. Rutland, Vt.: Charles E. Tuttle, 2004.

Cybriwsky, Roman. *Historical Dictionary of Tokyo*. Lanham, Md.: Scarecrow Press, 1997.

De Mente, Boye Lafayette. *Bache-*

*lor's Japan*. Rutland, Vt.: Charles E. Tuttle, 1991.

———. *Japan Encyclopedia*. Originally published as *Japan Almanac*. Lincolnwood, Il: Passport Books, 1995.

*Discover Japan*. Previously published as *A Hundred Things Japanese* and *A Hundred More Things Japanese*. Tokyo, Kodansha International, vol. 1, 1982; vol. 2, 1983.

Draeger, Donn F. *Classical Budo*. New York: Weatherhill, 1990.

———. *Classical Bujutsu*. New York, Weatherhill, 1990.

———. *Modern Bujutsu and Budo*. New York, Weatherhill, 1996.

Dunn, Charles J. *Everyday Life in Traditional Japan*. Rutland, Vt.: Charles E. Tuttle, 1969.

———. *Everyday Life in Traditional Japan*. Rutland, Vt.: Charles E. Tuttle, 1972.

Edogawa, Rampo. *Japanese Tales of Mystery and Imagination*. Rutland, Vt.: Charles E. Tuttle, 1956.

Enbutsu Sumiko. *Old Tokyo: Walks in the City of the Shogun*. Rutland, Vt.: Charles E. Tuttle, 1993.

*Exhibiting Animation:* Spirited Away Special *Exhibition at the Ghibli Museum, Mitaka*. Tokyo: Tokuma Shoten, 2002.

Farris, William Wayne. *Heavenly Warriors*. Cambridge, Mass.: Council on East Asian Studies, Harvard University Press, 1992.

Finn, Dallas. *Meiji Revisited*. New York: Weatherhill, 1995.

Frederic, Louis. *Daily Life in Japan at the Time of the Samurai,* *1185–1603*. Rutland, Vt.: Charles E. Tuttle, 1973.

———. *Dictionary of the Martial Arts* [Dictionnaire des arts martiaux]. Translated by Paul Crompton. Rutland, Vt.: Charles E. Tuttle, 1995.

———. *Japan Encyclopedia* [Le Japon Dictionnaire et Civilization]. Cambridge, Mass.: Harvard University Press, 2002.

Galbraith IV, Stuart. *Monsters are Attacking Tokyo*. Venice, Ca.: Feral House, 1998.

Gluck, Jay, Sumi Gluck, and Garet Gluck. *Japan Inside Out*. Ashiya: Personally Oriented, 1992.

Guttmann, Allen, and Lee Thompson. *Japanese Sports: A History*. Honolulu: University of Hawai'i Press, 2001.

Hillsborough, Romulus. *Ryoma: Life of a Renaissance Samurai*. San Francisco: Ridgeback Press, 1999.

———. *Samurai Sketches*. San Francisco: Ridgeback Press, 2001.

Hosking, Richard. *A Dictionary of Japanese Food: Ingredients and Culture*. Rutland, Vt.: Charles E. Tuttle, 1996.

Houchins, Chang-su. *Artifacts of Diplomacy*. Washington, D.C.: Smithsonian Institution Press, 1995.

Inaba, Kazuya, and Nakayama Shigenobu. *Japanese Homes and Lifestyles*. Tokyo and New York: Kodansha International, 2000.

Inagaki, Hisao. *A Dictionary of Japanese Buddhist Terms: Based on References in Japanese Literature* [Nichi-Ei Bukkyōgo jiten]. Kyoto: Nagata Bunshōdō, 1984.

Iwata, Masakazu. *Ōkubo Toshimichi*. Berkeley: University of California Press, 1964.

Jansen, Marius B. *Sakamoto Ryōma and the Meiji Restoration*. New York: Columbia University Press, 1994.

Japan Travel Bureau. *"Salaryman" in Japan*. Tokyo: Nihon Kōtsū Kōsha Shuppan Jigyōkyoku, 1991.

———. *A Look Into Japan*. Tokyo: Nihon Kōtsū Kōsha Shuppan Jigyōkyoku, 1986.

———. *A Look into Tokyo*. 6th ed. Tokyo: Nihon Kōtsū Kōsha Shuppan Jigyōkyoku, 1991.

———. *Eating in Japan*. Tokyo: Nihon Kōtsū Kōsha Shuppan Jigyōkyoku, 1995.

———. *Japanese Family and Culture*. Tokyo: Nihon Kōtsū Kōsha Shuppan Jigyōkyoku, 1995.

———. *Japanese Inn and Travel*. Tokyo: Nihon Kōtsū Kōsha Shuppan Jigyōkyoku, 1990.

———. *Living Japanese Style*. 13th ed. Tokyo: Nihon Kōtsū Kōsha Shuppan Jigyōkyoku, 1994.

———. *Martial Arts and Sports in Japan*. Tokyo: Nihon Kōtsū Kōsha Shuppan Jigyōkyoku, 1993.

———. *Must-See in Kyoto*. 7th ed. Tokyo: Nihon Kōtsū Kōsha Shuppan Jigyōkyoku, 1991.

———. *Must-See in Nikko*. 3rd ed. Tokyo: Nihon Kōtsū Kōsha Shuppan Jigyōkyoku, 1991.

———. *Outlook on Japan*. Tokyo: Nihon Kōtsū Kōsha Shuppan Jigyōkyoku, 1987.

———. *Today's Japan*. Tokyo: Nihon

Kōtsū Kōsha Shuppan Jigyōkyoku, 1991.

———. *Who's Who of Japan*. Tokyo: Nihon Kōtsū Kōsha Shuppan Jigyō-kyoku, 1991.

*Japan: An Illustrated Encyclopedia*. Tokyo and New York: Kodansha, 1993.

*Japan: At a Glance*. Tokyo: Kodansha International, 1997.

Joya, Mock. *Mock Joya's Things Japanese*. 3rd ed. Tokyo: Tokyo News Service, 1961.

*Kabuki Plays on Stage: Villainy and Vengeance, 1773–1799*. Vol. 2. Edited by James R. Brandon and Samuel L. Leiter. Honolulu: University of Hawai'i Press, 2002.

*Keiko Shokon: Classical Warrior Traditions of Japan*. Vol. 3. Edited by Diane Skoss. Berkeley Heights, N.J.: Koryu Books, 2002.

Klompmakers, Inge. *Of Brigands and Bravery: Kuniyoshi's Heros of the* Suikoden. Leiden, Netherlands: Hotei Publishing, 1998.

Kominz, Laurence R. *The Stars Who Created Kabuki*. Tokyo: Kodansha International, 1997.

*Koryu Bujutsu: Classical Warrior Traditions of Japan*. Edited by Diane Skoss. Berkeley Heights, N.J.: Koryu Books, 1997.

Krouse, Carolyn R. *A Guide to Food Buying in Japan*. Rutland, Vt.: Charles E. Tuttle, 1986.

Kurosawa, Akira. *Something Like an Autobiography*. New York: Vintage Books, 1983.

Kusano, Eisaburo. *Stories Behind Noh and Kabuki Plays*. Tokyo: Tokyo News Service, 1962. First edition

issued as *Wierd Tales of Old Japan* (1953).

*Kyōto-Ōsaka: A Bilingual Atlas*. Tokyo: Iris, 1992.

Leiter, Samuel. *New Kabuki Encyclopedia*. Westport, Conn.: Greenwood Press, 1997.

Levy, Ran. *Wild Flowers of Japan: A Field Guide*. Tokyo: Kodansha International, 1995.

Lock, Margaret M. *East Asian Medicine in Urban Japan*. Berkeley: University of California Press, 1980.

Malm, William P. *Traditional Japanese Music and Musical Instruments*. Rev. ed. Tokyo: Kodansha International, 2000.

McCarthy, Helen, and Jonathan Clements. *The Erotic Anime Movie Guide*. London: Titan Books, 1998.

McLelland, Mark J. *Male Homosexuality in Modern Japan*. Richmond, Surrey: Curzon, 2000.

Mikesh, Robert C. *Japanese Aircraft: Code Names and Designations*. Atglen, Pa.: Schiffer Publishing, 1993.

Milton, Giles. *Samurai William: The Englishman Who Opened the East*. New York: Penguin Group, 2003.

Miner, Earl, Hiroko Odagiri, and Robert Morrell. *The Princeton Companion to Classical Japanese Literature*. Princeton, N.J.: Princeton University Press, 1985.

Mol, Serge. *Classical Fighting Arts of Japan*. Tokyo: Kodansha International, 2001.

Morse, Edward S. *Japanese Homes and Their Surroundings*. New York: Dover Publications, 1961. Reprint of 1886 edition.

Nagasawa, Kimiko, and Camy Condon. *Eating Cheap in Japan*. Tokyo: Shufunotomo, 1972.

Naito, Akira. *Edo: The City that Became Tokyo*. Tokyo: Kodansha International, 2003.

Nelson, John K. *Enduring Identities*. Honolulu: University of Hawai'i Press, 2000.

Nishimura, Eshin. *Unsui: A Diary of Zen Monastic Life*. Honolulu: University Press of Hawai'i, 1973.

*Oracles and Divination*. Edited by Loewe, Michael, and Carmen Blacker. Boulder: Shambhala, 1981.

Ortolani, Benito. *The Japanese Theatre*. Princeton, N.J.: Princeton University Press, 1990.

Ozawa, Hiroyuki. *The Great Festivals of Japan*. Tokyo: Kodansha International, 1999.

*Package Design in Japan*. Vol. 8. Edited by the Japan Package Design Association and Rikuyo-sha. Tokyo: Rikuyo-sha Publishing, 1999.

Papinot, E. *Historical and Geographical Dictionary of Japan*. Tokyo and Rutland, Vt.: Charles E. Tuttle, 1972.

*Pictorial Encyclopedia of Japanese Life and Events*. Tokyo: Gakken, 1993.

Piggott, Juliet. *Japanese Mythology*. New York: Peter Bedrick Books, 1983.

Plutschow, Herbert E. *Japan's Name Culture*. Sandgate, Folkestone, Kent: Japan Library, 1995.

Pompian, Susan. *Tokyo for Free*. Tokyo: Kodansha International, 1998.

Ratti, Oscar, and Adele Westbrook. *Secrets of the Samurai: The Martial*

*Arts of Feudal Japan.* Edison, N.J.: Castle Books, 1999.

Readicker-Henderson, Ed. *Traveler's Guide to Japanese Pilgrimages.* New York and Tokyo: Weatherhill, 1995.

Richie, Donald. *The Image Factory.* London: Reaktion Books, 2003.

———. *The Inland Sea.* New York and Tokyo: Weatherhill, 1971.

*Road Atlas Japan.* Tokyo: Shobunsha, 1996.

Robertson, Jennifer. *Takarazuka: Sexual Politics and Popular Culture in Modern Japan.* Berkeley: University of California Press, 1998.

Rombauer, Irma S., and Marion Rombauer Becker. *Joy of Cooking.* New York: Penguin, 1973.

Rowthorn, Chris, and Mason Florence. *Kyoto.* Oakland, Calif.: Lonely Planet, 2001.

Sasaki, Atsuharu. *Japan in a Nutshell.* Vol. 1. Yokohama: Sasaki Atsuharu, 1949.

Schilling, Mark. *The Encyclopedia of Japanese Pop Culture.* New York and Tokyo: Weatherhill, 1997.

Schodt, Frederik. *Dreamland Japan.* Berkeley: Stone Bridge Press, 1996.

———. *Manga! Manga!* Tokyo: Kodansha International, 1986.

———. *Native American in the Land of the Shogun.* Berkeley: Stone Bridge Press, 2003.

Seidensticker, Edward. *Low City, High City.* Cambridge, Mass.: Harvard University Press, 1991.

———. *Tokyo Rising.* Cambridge, Mass.: Harvard University Press, 1991.

Shi Nai'an, and Luo Guanzhong. *Outlaws of the Marsh.* Translated by Sidney Shapiro. Beijing: Foreign Languages Press, 1988.

Shiba, Ryotaro. *The Last Shogun: The Life of Tokugawa Yoshinobu.* New York: Kodansha America, 1998.

*Shogakukan Progressive Japanese-English Dictionary.* Tokyo: Shogakukan, 1986.

Short, Kevin. *Nature in Tokyo.* Tokyo: Kodansha International, 2001.

Stevens, John. *The Marathon Monks of Mount Hiei.* Boston: Shambhala, 1988.

Stevens, Keith. *Chinese Gods: The Unseen World of Spirits and Demons.* London: Collins and Brown, 1997.

Suzuki, Daisetz Teitaro. *The Training of the Zen Buddhist Monk.* Berkeley: Wingbow Press, 1974.

Tajima, Noriyuki. *Tokyo: A Guide to Recent Architecture.* London: Ellipsis London, 1996.

*The Encyclopedia of Eastern Philosophy and Religion.* Boston: Shambhala, 1994.

*Tokyo City Atlas.* Tokyo: Kodansha, 1998.

*Tokyo Confidential.* Edited by Mark Schreiber, Tokyo: The East Publications, 2001.

*Tokyo Metropolitan Area Rail and Road Atlas.* Tokyo: Iris, 1993.

*Tokyo Metropolitan Atlas.* Tokyo: Shobunsha, 1991.

Turnbull, Stephen. *The Lone Samurai and the Martial Arts.* London: Arms and Armour, 1990.

———. *The Samurai Sourcebook.* London: Arms and Armour, 1998.

———. *Samurai Warfare.* London: Arms and Armour, 1996.

Turnbull, Stephen, and Howard Gerrard. *Ashigaru 1467–1649.* London: Osprey, 2001.

Turnbull, S. R., and Richard Hook. *Samurai Armies.* London: Osprey, 1979.

Tuttle, Charles E. *Incredible Japan.* Rutland, Vt.: Charles E. Tuttle, 1975.

Twigger, Robert. *Angry White Pajamas.* New York: Quill, 2000.

Vardaman, James M., and Michiko Sakaki Vardaman. *Japan From A to Z.* Tokyo: Yenbooks, 1995.

Waley, Paul. *Tokyo City of Stories.* New York and Tokyo: Weatherhill, 1991.

———. *Tokyo Now and Then: An Explorer's Guide.* New York and Tokyo: Weatherhill, 1984.

Warner, Gordon, and Donn F. Draeger. *Japanese Swordsmanship: Technique and Practice.* New York and Tokyo: Weatherhill, 1991.

Watts, A. J., and B. G. Gordon. *The Imperial Japanese Navy.* Garden City, N.Y.: Doubleday, 1971.

Weisser, Thomas, and Yuko Mihara Weisser. *Japanese Cinema Encyclopedia: The Sex Films.* Miami: Vital Books, 1998.

———. *Japanese Cinema: Essential Handbook.* Miami: Vital Books, 1996.

Wild Bird Society of Japan. *Field Guide to the Birds of Japan.* Tokyo: Wild Bird Society of Japan, 1982.

Yamakawa, Kikue. *Women of the Mito Domain: Recollections of Samurai Family Life.* Stanford, Calif.: Stanford University Press, 2001.

Yamasaki, Taikō. *Shingon.* Fresno, Calif.: Shingon Buddhist International Institute, 1996.

Yumoto, John M. *The Samurai Sword: A Handbook.* Rutland, Vt.: Charles E. Tuttle, 1958.

# VIEWING NOTES

# VIEWING NOTES

# VIEWING NOTES

# OTHER TITLES OF INTEREST FROM STONE BRIDGE PRESS

Obtain any of these books online or from your local bookseller.
sbp@stonebridge.com • www.stonebridge.com • 1-800-947-7271
P. O. Box 8208, Berkeley, California 94707 USA

## The Anime Companion

*What's Japanese in Japanese Animation?*

GILLES POITRAS

Get Volume 1! With more than 500 glossary-style entries, this book is a great cultural reference and a comprehensive guide to anime's distinctive visual style. Like *The Anime Companion 2*, it includes illustrations, film citations, and numerous references to the related art of manga. Excellent for the classroom and cultural exchange.

176 pp, 7 × 9", paper, 50 b/w illustrations, ISBN 1-880656-32-9, $16.95

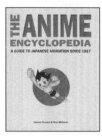

## The Anime Encyclopedia

*A Guide to Japanese Animation Since 1917*

BY JONATHAN CLEMENTS AND HELEN MCCARTHY

The absolute must-have book for every fan, collector, library, and video-store browser. Filled with information on over 2,000 anime. Fully indexed.

576 pp, 7 × 9", paper, 100+ b&w illustrations, ISBN 1-880656-64-7, $24.95

## The Dorama Encyclopedia

*A Guide to Japanese TV Drama Since 1953*

JONATHAN CLEMENTS AND MOTOKO TAMAMURO

Over 1,000 entries cover Japanese TV and examine the close connections among broadcast, anime, and print media.

480 pp, 7 × 9", paper, 100+ b&w illustrations, ISBN 1-880656-81-7, $24.95

## Anime Essentials

*Every Thing a Fan Needs to Know*

GILLES POITRAS

Answering just about every question a fan (or curious parent) has, *Anime Essentials* is an easy-to-read and fun-to-look-at overview of the pop culture phenomenon sweeping America.

128 pp, 7 × 9", paper, 50 b&w illustrations, ISBN 1-880656-53-1, $14.95

## Anime Explosion!

*The What? Why? & Wow! of Japanese Animation*

PATRICK DRAZEN

Anime is . . . exploding. But where did Japanese animation come from, and what does it all mean? Written for fans and culture watchers, this is an engaging tour of the anime megaverse.

320 pp, 6 × 9", paper, 100+ b&w illustrations, ISBN 1-880656-72-8, $18.95

## Hayao Miyazaki

*Master of Japanese Animation*

HELEN MCCARTHY

Mixing first-hand interviews and personal insights with critical evaluations of art, plot, production qualities, and literary themes, this book provides a film-by-film appraisal of the man often called "the Walt Disney of Japan."

240 pp, 7 × 9", paper, 60+ b&w illustrations, 8 pp in color, ISBN 1-880656-41-8, $18.95

## Watching Anime, Reading Manga

*25 Years of Essays and Reviews*

FRED PATTEN; FOREWORD BY CARL MACEK

Fred Patten helped establish anime as a serious art form in America back in the early days of fandom. This collection of his writings is an incisive history of how anime came to America.

360 pp, 5⅜ × 8⅜", paper, 40 b&w illustrations, ISBN 1-880656-92-2, $18.95